T3-BPE-233

RESOURCE ALLOCATION IN DIVISIONALIZED GROUPS

To the unsung administrators of investments

Resource Allocation in Divisionalized Groups

A study of investment manuals and corporate level means of control

ESBJÖRN SEGELOD
Department of Economics and Administrative Data Processing
Mälardalen University
and
Department of Business Studies
Uppsala University

Avebury

Aldershot • Brookfield USA • Hong Kong • Singapore • Sydney

© E. Segelod 1995

658.152
S45r

All rights reserved. No part of this publication may be reproduced, stored in a retrieval system, or transmitted in any form or by any means, electronic, mechanical, photocopying, recording or otherwise without the prior permission of the publisher.

Published by
Avebury
Ashgate Publishing Limited
Gower House
Croft Road
Aldershot
Hants GU11 3HR
England

Ashgate Publishing Company
Old Post Road
Brookfield
Vermont 05036
USA

British Library Cataloguing in Publication Data

Segelod Esbjörn
    Resource Allocation in Divisionalized
    Groups: Study of Investment Manuals and
    Corporate Level Means of Control
    I. Title
    658.152

Library of Congress Catalog Card Number: 95-83023

ISBN 1 85972 250 4

Printed and bound by Athenaeum Press, Ltd.,
Gateshead, Tyne & Wear.

Contents

University Libraries
Carnegie Mellon University
Pittsburgh PA 15213-3890

University Libraries
Carnegie Mellon University
Pittsburgh PA 15213-3890

Figures and tables

Acknowledgements

An empirical research project such as this cannot be accomplished without the assistance of helpful managers, colleagues and financiers. The author wishes to thank in particular the Swedish Council for Research in the Humanities and Social Sciences which has financed travels for the collection of data, the writing of this book and the correction of my English. The latter task was skillfully performed by Theodosia Tomkinson.

This study was preceded by two other studies of investment manuals; Olle Renck's study from 1964 and Bertil Tell's from 1977. The companies in their studies are anonymous but thanks to the efforts of Docent Bertil Tell it proved possible to identify those responsible for the results presented therein; this also enabled an investigation of how the investment manuals of some of the groups had changed during the twenty-six years covered by these three studies. This knowledge of the corporations in these earlier studies was also important for the design of the study. Similarly Professor Bertil Gandemo assisted in identifying the levels of authorization of the corporations in his study from the early 1980s.

A considerable number of the interviews were made by Roger Johansson, a lecturer at the Department of Business Studies, Uppsala University, and the following final year students: Yohannes Asrat, Joakim Bredbo, Gittan Carlsund, Peter Cedgard, Nils Ericson, Karin Folkeson, Helena Fredriksson, Arne Flemström, Per Högelin, Catharina Jönsson, Johan Linder, Catarina Neijmer, Pia-Sari Reponen, Carl Sandin, Johan Sjöquist, Vincent Terud, Olof Thörn, and Anna Wikström. As a preparation the students participated in a course on empirical studies of capital budgeting supervised by Professor Ingemund Hägg and the author. They later analysed the empirical data in their final year theses.

Finally I shall like to thank all those managers who have allowed us to analyse the investment manuals of their corporations and the forty-seven managers who allocated time for interviews. Without their participation this study could not have been made.

1 Introduction

The investment paradigm

The world economy is dominated by large divisionalized multinational groups. This book analyses their resource allocation systems. It seeks to illustrate the measures which corporate managers use to control and direct the investments of such groups, the content of their capital budgeting manuals, and how investment requests are to be designed. Furthermore, it also analyses industry differences, the important trade-off between long- and short-term investments and how the resource allocation system might develop in the future.

The examples are taken from Sweden, a country which in relation to its size, is the home of unusually many multinationals, some with more than one hundred companies and operations in a great number of countries. Comparisons are made with earlier studies of capital budgeting practice and management control of American, British and Swedish groups. The differences between Anglo-Saxon and Swedish groups are relatively small, perhaps because Swedish industry has been quick to adopt new management practice originating from the U.S.

To a company an investment is basically a sacrifice which will reduce profit in the present in order to make future profits possible. The concept of an investment is traditionally associated with investments in land, buildings, machinery and other kinds of production equipment which has to be allocated to the right periods and depreciated. In principle, however, all decisions which reduce present profit in order to render future profits possible can be regarded as investments. Using this wider definition the development of new technologies, markets, products, computer software, competencies, customer relations etc. must also be considered as investments.

Major groups make thousands of investments each year. To cope with this multitude of information and decisions most investment decisions are decentralized. Most investment ideas originate through contacts with customers and people in the production. To contribute to a positive development of the group they have to be coordinated. The management must feel certain that the investments can be expected to be profitable, can be financed in a suitable way, fit the business formula and strategies of the company, and can be implemented in a suitable manner. Investment decisions change the future composition of a company's resources, and thereby also its future competitiveness. Moreover, firm specific investments also involve commitments to long-term investments which have a limited opportunity value, as the value of such investments is dependent on the existence of other resources. Investment decisions are, therefore, relatively centralized also in major groups where most other kinds of decision have been decentralized. The management does not want to waive its right to control the direction of investment.

To be able to exert this control function when the evaluation of investment proposals has been decentralized, major groups have developed written accounting and financial routines stipulating how investments should be planned, evaluated, coordinated, approved, implemented and followed up. There is often a capital budgeting or an investment manual giving instructions on what kind of information is needed in an investment request, the formal decision process and who is responsible for what. Requests are ranked in connection with the annual budgetary control process, and limits of authorization help to bring the decision up to the right decision level. Pre-approval review improves the quality of the investment request and supplies feedback to project planners, while systems of classification help to focus attention and adjust the decision criteria to the character of the investment. An example from the Swedish multinational engineering industry could further clarify the elements of a resource allocation system and the issues treated in this book.

An example The multinational engineering groups which dominate Swedish industry are all divisionalized, and the divisions divided into business areas. The larger of these groups have production plants on all continents, except for Antarctica, and some of them a hundred different companies and still more business boards and a large number of profit centres. Investments in fixed assets (i.e. capital investments), research and development (R & D), and markets account for about a third each of the volume of investments of the industry.

Requests for investment expenditures originate from the business level and are ranked in the companies and divisions. Authorization limits decide how far up in the hierarchy a request must be referred for approval.

2

During its journey upwards in the hierarchy the investment request will be reviewed by several staff units with regard to its economy, market and technology. Pre-approval review allows investments to be coordinated in and between different businesses and divisions. However, the requester is often better informed about the details of the investment, than the reviewer. The accounting section must, therefore, scrutinize the reasonableness of the assumptions made in the request and demand supplementary information and calculations to be supplied. The burden of proof is on the requester.

Requests which need group level support are seldom rejected absolutely. They are more often referred back for supplementary information, additional pre-approval review and postponed, sometimes to become of no further interest.

The capital budget is fixed in connection with the annual budgetary control process. Usually there are more investment requests than can be accommodated within the investment budget approved by group managers, so that businesses and divisions have to rank their requests.

Two engineering groups have introduced an annual strategic process which precedes the budgetary control process. Strategies and important strategic investments are decided in the strategic process, all other investments in the budgetary control process. The idea is that a firm must have a business formula and a good strategy before deciding on investments. Other groups try to achieve the same goal by board representation and rules stipulating that investment programmes and major investments must be approved before requests for individual investments within such programmes can be processed.

All major engineering groups have an investment manual. This was introduced in the 50s or 60s. The manual contains a description of the formal decision process and division of authority, requirements for the design of an investment request, forms and instructions for their completion.

Many engineering groups have taken yet another step and issued directions that R & D, market and certain other type of costs that are expensed as incurred shall as far as possible be treated as fixed investments. We will term these intangible type of investments expense investments. Some groups have taken yet another step and developed separate manuals for investments in R & D and acquisitions.

The investment criterion for minor investments is the payback period; for major investments, and in some groups also for expansion investments, the payback period plus a discounted cash flow criterion. Some of the groups use different criteria for different types of investment and a few delegate the choice of criteria to lower levels.

Investments are to be followed up, but the responsibility for making ex post reviews is decentralized. Corporate staff concentrate on evaluating acquisitions and new corporate strategies.

Resource allocation systems under fire The bottom-up kind of resource allocation system just described has been strongly criticized during the last decade. When European and North American companies began to be surpassed by Japanese companies studies showed that the new competitors used very simple capital investment evaluation techniques. Little attention was paid to the discounted cash flow technique and other so-called sophisticated capital budgeting techniques which have seen increasing use in Western firms in recent decades. More emphasis was instead placed on challenging the assumptions behind the investment and creating consensus regarding the investment decision among managers on different levels and with different functions.

These observations led many researchers to question the bottom-up type of resource allocation system found in most divisionalized groups in the U.K., U.S. and Sweden. The critics maintained that these bottom-up systems give group managers too little influence over strategic investment decisions. The content of the investment budget is determined months in advance far down in the organization, so that group consent to the investment budget and individual investments only sets the seal of approval.

Others have encouraged the critics by pointing out that technological and strategical changes often proceed in small steps, so that they tend to come to the attention of group management only after that they have occurred. Furthermore that horizontal communication between the functions of the firm also needs to be improved. These problem can only partly be remedied by introducing a top-down strategic process or directions that strategy must precede investment.

The critics remarked that the traditional resource allocation system found in Western firms is biased against long-term investments, technical renewal and the growth options which such investments create. This has caused Western firms to lose market shares and led investments away from growth markets. It is alleged that the resource allocation systems found in Western groups do not allow for strategic control. The important intangible investments in building up new competencies and strengthening old ones tend to be overlooked by top management when the resource allocation system focuses attention on financial criteria and individual investment requests.

However, it should also be observed that we have only limited knowledge of how corporate managers in Western groups try to influence the direction of investment of the companies of their groups and the investment manual. There have been a great many postal surveys, especially in the U.K. and U.S., and earlier also some interview studies. However, the vast majority of these studies focused on capital budgeting evaluation techniques. In general their purpose seems to have been to measure the extent to which companies apply the techniques which business schools teach. Our knowledge of the resource allocation system of divisionalized groups is therefore still poor, and the criticism and recommendations rest on uncertain grounds. This

4

study will give us a better knowledge of the resource allocation systems of divisionalized groups and a better base for criticism and recommendations.

The design of the study

Two points of departure The most common approach to study resource allocation procedures consisted, as previously stated, of postal surveys. Other methods included interviews with company managers, especially in the late 50s and 60s, and case studies of capital investments. The analysis of capital budgeting manuals is another approach which has produced valuable information about capital budgeting procedures but has only sporadically been used.

Most large corporations with a large number of capital investments have a capital budgeting manual which contains information about the formal decision process and design of capital appropriation requests, i.e. the information which postal surveys normally request. Strangely enough there are very few studies of these written routines, especially as already Istvan (1959/61a) showed that they could yield valuable information about capital budgeting procedures in large companies. In fact, Istvan's study still stands out as one of the best in the field of capital budgeting, although it describes conditions more than thirty-five years ago when many large corporations still had a functional structure.

Turning to the Swedish language area there are two major studies of capital budgeting manuals of major Swedish corporations. The first one was carried out by Renck (1966), who in 1964 collected manuals from twenty-eight large Swedish companies. In 1977 this study was replicated by Tell (1978) who collected manuals from thirty large companies of which twenty had been included in Renck's initial study.

Another fact which seems to have been disregarded by many researchers is that corporate managers do not direct the investments of the group by choosing and ranking individual investment requests, but by influencing the rules of the game, as described by Bower's (1970/72) case studies already twenty-five years ago. Although Bower's study has become a classic it seems to have had little impact on all the later empirical studies, being limited to the evaluation and appropriation routines of individual investments. In fact most studies still disregard the fact that investments are controlled and directed also by several other administrative routines, including, the annual budgetary control process, strategic planning processes, investment committees, profitability requirements such as e.g. ROI, influence through company and business board representation, executive meetings, staff units and travels within the group by group executives and staff managers.

Some groups and groups in some industries emphasize one measure of control more, than do other groups. Some use a capital budgeting manual

5

and some do not. Some treat major investments in a planning process separately from the annual budgetary control process. In some groups group management takes strategic initiatives and engage in major investments, in others, they merely react to strategic initiatives developed on the business level. To map these procedures it is necessary to interview the managers responsible for their design.

With these facts in mind it was decided that the study ought to combine these two points of departure. First, to build on Istvan's (1961a), Renck's (1966) and Tell's (1978) earlier studies of capital budgeting manuals. Secondly, to interview managers responsible for the capital budgeting procedures in a sample of major groups with their head office in Sweden. The interviews focus on the instruments, whereof the manual is one, which corporate management uses to control and direct the investments of the group; moreover it was considered necessary to include both groups which do and groups which do not use a manual.

Groups studied With some knowledge of which companies could be expected to use a capital budgeting manual, a request for a copy was sent to all fifty-four corporations assigned by the Swedish business magazine *Veckans Affärer* to the engineering industry (including the electro-engineering and metal industries), the chemical industry (including the pharmaceutical industry), the forest industry and the category remaining companies (conglomerates and other groups not classified as belonging to the building and real estate, trading and retailing, shipping, investment, or banking industry). The sample excluded small groups in these lines of business which appear on the over-the-counter (otc) list.

Each letter was addressed to the chief financial executive of the group, and in accordance with practice developed by Renck (1966) and Tell (1978) participating companies were promised anonymity.

Thirty-four of the fifty-four groups used a group manual, although three were under development and still not approved. Another five had abandoned the group manual and allowed the divisions to develop their own manuals. Three of these groups supplied the manuals of their core business. Altogether, twenty-nine manuals were received.

This means that the study is based on 74 per cent of those groups which used a manual; 81 per cent if we only take into consideration those groups that had an approved manual at the time of the request. The principal reason why some groups refused to participate in the study seems to have been that the financial executive of the group did not want to supply an outsider with this internal document. Despite the restructuring of Swedish industry the manuals have a division into lines of business similar to that in the earlier studies.

The analysis of manuals was followed up by interviews in nineteen of the fifty-four groups, fourteen of which used a manual. These groups were selected at random from a list of the fifty-four groups stratified with regard to the market value of the groups. The interviews were conducted with the chief financial executive of the group, the corporate controller, or another manager responsible for the capital budgeting routines of the group. In 1993 short interviews were held with the same managers who had been interviewed earlier to investigate the development during the recession 1990-93.

In order to place the manual in a wider context additional interviews were conducted at corporate level with financial executives of fifteen groups in lines of business where capital budgeting manuals are not normally used, e.g. eight banking, shipping, trading and retailing, building and real estate groups, and five small computer software, consulting and engineering groups listed on the otc list. All interviews were taped, transcribed, and sent to the interviewees for comments. For a more detailed account of the design of the study see Appendix A.

The generality of the study A study of this kind may be criticised on the ground that the results are only valid for Swedish groups of companies. However, such is not the case. Sweden has comparatively many multinationals. The group language is English and the same manual is valid for all companies in the group. It sets the rules of the game and provides the group with a common language with regard to investment issues. This also means that a multinational cannot deviate too much from standard practice in Europe, the U.S. and other parts of the world. Those using the manual must be able to understand it regardless of cultural background. Those responsible for compiling the manuals have therefore studied manuals from other European and American groups, and claim that by and large these have similar manuals, although tailored to their needs.

A great many articles have been published in English on the capital budgeting practice of British and U.S. companies and also some on Australian, Canadian and New Zealand practice, but few on non-Anglo-Saxon companies. Relatively little is known about how the competitors of U.K. and U.S. companies control and direct their investments, but judging from some recent studies of German and Japanese practice, and from the opinions of some of the managers interviewed, most major Swedish groups seem to have more in common with U.K. and U.S. practice than with German or Japanese, perhaps, as was earlier stated, because Swedish industry has been quick to adopt new management techniques from the U.S. However, there are also differences which will be mentioned in the text, evidenced by U.S. studies of capital budgeting manuals, case studies, interview studies, and the many postal surveys of major U.K. and U.S. groups.

One advantage of studying major Swedish groups was that two earlier studies of capital budgeting manuals (Renck, 1966; Tell, 1978) already existed, and no similar material on Anglo-Saxon groups could be found. These older studies made it possible to trace the development of the capital budgeting manual between 1964 and 1993. Most Swedish financial executives seem to have read one of these earlier studies and it was probably

7

partly due to this fact that unusually few companies refused to have their written routines analysed, and only two of them declined an interview with the corporate manager responsible for the capital budgeting procedures of the group.

The outline of the book

The book moves from the general to the specific and back to the general. The first two chapters give an account of the structure and investments of the groups studied, and present an overview of their resource allocation systems. The next four chapters describe and analyse their investment manual, and the situation therein regarding the determination of cash flow, investment criteria, taxes, inflation, risk and ex post review. Then, in the last four chapters, we return to the general issues, analyse differences in the resource allocation system of groups in different industries, the requirements for and the trade-off between long- and short-term investments, and describe the development of investment procedures in recent decades and possible future lines of development.

Chapter 2: The firm and its investments During the post war years the composition of the investments of the firm has gradually changed, from buildings and machinery to investments in R & D, markets, computer software, employee training and the development of new competencies. Today Swedish industry invests about one third each in markets, R & D, and fixed investments.

However, the composition of the volume of investment differs from one line of business to another. Forest groups like SCA and STORA might one year invest 10 per cent of sales in machinery and less than 1 per cent in R & D. Pharmaceutical corporations like Astra, and telecommunication groups like Ericsson less than 10 per cent in production equipment and 15 to 20 per cent in R & D. This chapter describes these changes and the structure of multidivisional groups.

Chapter 3: Administrative routines This chapter gives an overview of how capital appropriation or investment requests are handled in large divisionalized groups. Together with Chapter 2 it sets the scene and introduces the issues analysed in greater detail in the following chapters.

Building on interviews and the literature Chapter 3 discusses the role of the head office in the capital budgeting process, and the means used by the corporate level to influence the volume and direction of the investments of the group. It also shows on which level different types of investments are initiated, who makes the appraisal and formulates the capital appropriation request, who decides the input, and who reviews the request.

In this chapter, as well as in the rest of the book, we relate the findings of the study directly to the literature when a specific issue is treated. Thus, we do not discuss differences between Swedish or Anglo-Saxon groups, between theory and practice, or between earlier studies and this study in separate chapters.

Chapter 4: The investment manual This chapter deals with the structure and role of the investment or capital budgeting manual. It answers such questions as which companies use a capital budgeting manual and the purpose and role thereof, its structure and content, and the types of investment treated, why systems of classification are used and why some manuals are more detailed than others. Most groups have different routines for different types of investment. The limits of authorization, pre-approval review procedures, project evaluation techniques, forms and requirements for the investment request may differ with the size and type of investment. No two groups have identical manuals, but there are similarities and dissimilarities and this chapter describes and analyses these patterns.

The chapter is based on the manuals, supplemented by analysis of interviews. Comparisons are made with earlier studies of these issues and especially Renck's (1966) and Tell's (1978) studies of capital budgeting manuals. As in other parts of the book references to other studies are made issue by issue.

Chapter 5: Cash flow determination practice Studies have shown that managers perceive the correct estimation of the cash flow of an investment, as both the most important, and the most difficult part of the capital budgeting process; hardly surprising as only a small change in the assumptions will often make a profitable investment look unprofitable, and vice versa. The discounted cash flow technique presupposes the ability to make good cash flow projections, but amazingly little is still known of how companies arrive at their estimates and the assumptions that they make.

This chapter reports how major Swedish groups, now and earlier, define and estimate the cash flows of their investments; how they define and determine payments and receipts, initial outlay, salvage value and the period of calculation, changes in working capital and inventories. Furthermore, it describes the role of tangible and intangible factors in the investment request, how they determine their discount or cut-off rate, and differences in practice for different types of investments.

Chapter 6: Investment criteria Project evaluation techniques or investment criteria is by far the best researched issue treated in the book. There are numerous postal surveys of project evaluation techniques, but very few analyses of the requirements stipulated in capital budgeting manuals and capital appropriation request forms.

This chapter describes the investment criteria of the groups studied, the way they are used and how they have developed over time. Comparisons are made with the many postal surveys done within the Anglo-Saxon area, and between results from studies of manuals and postal surveys. Furthermore, it describes the use of multiple criteria and discusses the meaning of a primary criterion.

Chapter 7: A few issues in capital budgeting This chapter shows how the groups studied treat inflation, taxes, risk and uncertainty in the capital appropriation request and capital budgeting system. It shows when and why they adjust appraisals for inflation and taxes, use formal risk analysis and evaluate the flexibility of major investments and companies.

Another issue treated in this chapter is ex post control. It analyses different types of ex post review of individual investments, why, and when and by whom such follow-ups are done. Finally it also analyses the role and engagement of corporate staff in the review of individual investments.

Chapter 8: Resource allocation and organizational structure The study builds on analyses of capital budgeting manuals and interviews with managers responsible for investment procedures in a large number of groups and industries, both with and without written routines. In this chapter we analyse differences between groups in different industries.

In some groups and industries group management takes strategic initiatives and actively engages in the strategic direction of individual group companies and major investments, while others are far more passive, rely on financial control and react only to requests sent to them. Groups in different lines of business tend to emphasize different measures of control. For some the capital budgeting manual is important, others handle investments in an annual strategic planning process separately from the annual budgetary control process. Still others place great emphasis on ROI types of measure, influence through board and business board representation, review by staff units, executive meetings or travel-around-management.

There are no two groups whose resource allocation systems are identical, so that the use of and emphasis on different measures of control may be adjudged accidental and chaotic. However, a comparison of groups in similar lines of industry reveals distinct similarities. The parts of a resource allocation system are obviously related to each other, and if these industry archetypes are unravelled patterns emerge and a logic behind the system can be glimpsed. This chapter gives an account of these differences between groups in different lines of industry, first describing the resource allocation system of the multinational machine engineering groups which dominate Swedish industry and the material on which this study is based, and then comparing their system with those of the other industries studied.

These industry differences can be explained, on the one hand, by the volume and composition of the investments of the industry and, on the other hand, by the need to coordinate investments of different types and in different part of the group. High-tech groups on competitive markets with large investments in new products and markets, for instance, have a greater need to coordinate investments, than trading and retailing groups, and therefore a more centralized system of resource allocation. The engineering and forest groups dominating Swedish industry will be found somewhere in between these extremes.

Chapter 9: Requirements and trade-offs between investments U.K., U.S. and Swedish industry have been losing market shares especially on high-tech growth markets. This has directed researchers' and policy-makers' interest towards the cost of capital, the function of the capital market and how companies allocate resources. Comparative studies have shown that German and especially Japanese industries invest more in capital-intensive industries and make more long-term investments than U.S. industry. High hurdle rates and the bottom-up type of resource allocation systems found in U.K., U.S., and in fact also in Swedish groups, have been blamed for causing this aging of U.K. and U.S. industries.

This chapter will analyse how hurdle rates and payback requirements have changed over time in Swedish and U.S. industry. To be able to carry this analysis further and explain how these criteria are used in different decision situations we shall first describe the characteristics of investments which create and exploit business opportunities. Then we shall turn our attention to specific decision situations like basic and contingent investments, design and reinvestment decisions, the profitability of R & D and ventures in new areas, investments rich and poor in options. This overview of whence the profit comes in different types of investment puts us in a better situation to discuss how management makes the trade-off between short- and long-term investments, how the design of the resource allocation system influences this trade-off, and the pros and cons of using unitary investment criteria or criteria differentiated according to the type of investment.

Chapter 10: Resource allocation systems in change On the basis of the results of this study and observations of past trends, we shall close by discussing the direction in which the resource allocation system of groups in a few lines of industry may develop in the future.

Appendix A: Research methodology This appendix gives an account of how data were collected through analyses of investment manuals and interviews with financial managers on the corporate level, and which groups were contacted for manuals and interviews.

Appendix B: An investment manual This appendix contains a fictitious investment manual constructed by the author. It must not be seen as a prototype or ideal. It is intended to enable the reader without access to investment manuals to visualise the content of an hypothetical manual in an multinational machine engineering group.

2 The firm and its investments

The multidivisional corporation

When Renck (1966) carried out his study of capital budgeting manuals many Swedish companies still had a functional organization. Today the pharmaceutical group Astra is probably the only major Swedish company which still has such a structure, which per se is by no means unique for a company with very heavy R & D expenditures. Most European pharmaceutical companies, as well as some Japanese and U.S. high tech companies still, for some reason, have a functional, or a semi-functional structure.

The functional structure made it possible to achieve economies of scale within the different functions of the company. However, when the companies grew and entered more and more markets with more and more products, it became increasingly difficult to form an accurate picture of the situation and of how the different parts of the company developed; so larger and larger staff units were needed to coordinate and administer the company. The problem was solved by splitting the operation into divisions with regard to products, markets, geographical areas, technology or a combination thereof. This transition from a functional to a multidivisional structure appeared first in the U.S. (Chandler, 1962; Scott, 1973), but eventually also pervaded European (Scott, 1973; Franko, 1974), Japanese (Pascale and Athos, 1982) and Swedish industry (Edgren, Rhenman and Skärvad, 1983).

It should be observed that divisionalization is not a change which appears overnight, but a process of decentralization which often takes decades (Chandler, 1962; Edgren, Rhenman and Skärvad, 1983); so although most of the groups studied had a divisionalized structure already in the 70s, the process of decentralization continued during the 80s. Earlier corporate staff

13

units have been decentralized to business areas or divisions, been turned into staff companies with the right to market their services to external customers, or simply sold off or wound up. At the same time, decision processes, the division of responsibility and top management means of control have changed.

Today almost all major Swedish companies have a divisionalized structure. Many units have been given a business board or even been turned into independent companies in a juridical sense. Companies marketing similar products, serving similar markets, or in a certain part of the world, have been brought together into divisions and, in the larger groups, the divisions into business areas. To exemplify it can be mentioned that the white goods group Electrolux had about 640 legal entities in 1994, and the relatively small multinational engineering group Atlas Copco about 300 company and business boards. Three years earlier, in 1991, ABB had 1,200 companies and 4,500 profit centres. The divisions of Atlas Copco are divided into three business areas, Electrolux into four, and ABB into fifty business areas grouped into eight business segments.

It may be of interest to note that the largest business area of Atlas Copco, compressor technique, has its head office in Antwerp. The head office of the group is located in Stockholm, but many of the divisions have their head office outside Sweden. Atlas Copco is one of the multinational groups which in the face of the integration of the European and world economy has followed in the footsteps of ABB (Forsgren, 1989; Taylor, 1991; Rapoport, 1992; Vandermerwe, 1993) and developed toward "a federation of national companies" without a distinct national place of abode.

> We are a federation of national companies with a global coordination centre. We are not homeless. We have many homes. (Percy Barnevik, President and CEO of ABB cited in Taylor, 1991)

Atlas Copco has fifteen production units in Europe. The largest are situated in Antwerp, Cologne, London, Stuttgart, and in Sweden Kalmar, Tierp and Örebro. Formerly there was one central for each national market. These warehouses have now been replaced by three central warehouses in Belgium and Holland, one for each of the three business areas. The warehouses are in on-line contact with the sale companies. The product ordered should reach the customers within 24 to 72 hours. This concentration and just-in-time thinking has made it possible to reduce tied up capital and increase delivery safety. The many national European markets have been transformed into three European regions. In a longer perspective we can foresee for some groups a development toward production in three different parts of the world; in the Far East, in Europe and in North America. Such global strategies and above all the European integration is and has been an important driving force behind the high volume of foreign investment by Swedish industry.

The administrative routines for decisions on capital expenditures vary depending on the organizational structure of the group, whether the firm has a functional or a divisional structure and how far the process of decentralization has been driven. Moreover, it should be noticed that some groups also have different routines in certain divisions and companies. We shall term this a diverse or heterogeneous business structure. It will be seen that the use of heterogeneous administrative routines affects the role and wealth of details of such routines. Furthermore that corporate managers in some groups rely more on lower levels to handle investments, and that others devote more effort to directing investments toward strategic priorities, and that these differences can partly be explained by the character and composition of investments of the group in question.

The composition of the volume of investment

The investment decision concerns how much to consume in the present and how much to invest to render future consumption and investments possible. To optimize investment decisions is to maximize the expected utility derived from consumption over the planning horizon of the investor, decision-maker or they whose consumption one wants to maximize.

An investment is also an asset and a firm can therefore be seen as a bundle of assets built up through investment projects. The value of these investments is determined by how these assets are put to use and coordinated and the profit of one investment is dependent on its interaction with other assets.

Investments in the production of services and products are often irreversible in that they have a limited opportunity value. They involve commitments delimiting the freedom to choose investments in the future, and past investments are therefore important determinants for the future direction of investments. It is not surprising that investment decisions have traditionally been perceived as one of the principal types of decision whereby top management can influence the future composition of the assets and thereby the strategic direction of their organization.

The concept of an investment has traditionally been associated with the accumulation of fixed or tangible assets such as land and buildings, stocks, machines and other types of production equipment. Such assets are capitalized and depreciated according to a plan, but for practical reasons are only investments of a certain size with, for instance, an expected life of above three years and initial outlay of SEK 5,000, considered as investments. However, as production has become more and more knowledge-intensive fixed investments have come to include a smaller and smaller part of all long-term commitments which firms have to make to create growth and profit. This has provoked a discussion of whether not also long-term investments in intangible investments such as investments in R & D, markets, training, etc. should be allocated to the period of consumption and depreciated. There is no formal obstacle thereto (Hägg, 1992), but only some firms do so and then in general only for goodwill and patents. The great majority of intangible investments are rarely budgeted as investments and corporate managers often have vague ideas about their size.

Fixed or capital investments in Swedish industry manifested a steady growth of four per cent between the end of the war and the mid 70s when they reached a peak (Örtengren, 1992). The growth rate was stable in the long run at the same time as the volume and composition changed due to the business cycle, decisions regarding European integration and other important events.

Investments have traditionally been seen as a source of economic growth and employment. Thus it is not surprising that many economists were concerned when the volume of fixed investment stagnated in the mid 70s. Studies were initiated to find the causes and soon revealed that the drop in fixed investment could partly be explained by a shift in the composition of investments; from fixed investments in machinery and buildings towards more knowledge-intensive investments like investments in R & D, markets, employee training and the development of new competencies.

Starting in 1985 Statistics Sweden (1986; 1987; 1988; 1989; 1990; 1991; 1992; 1993; 1994; 1995) tried to map investments in both fixed investments, and intangible investments, and since 1987 the surveys have comprised all manufacturing companies with over 500 employees, or about fifty companies (see Table 2.1). Market investments are in this context defined as "special long-range decisions about marketing, the purpose of which is to keep old and find new markets" (Statistics Sweden, 1993). Current sales costs are excluded. The measures relate to investments in Sweden only, i.e. investments of foreign subsidiaries are not included. This should mean that investments in R & D are over-estimated, and investments in markets under-estimated, as R & D tend to be allocated to companies geographically close to the head office, and market investments close to the customers (Bergholm and Jagrén, 1986).

Property and buildings, which accounted for about 50 per cent of fixed investments in the 40s, then experienced a steady decline to 20 to 30 per cent in the 80s and 17 to 20 per cent in the early 90s. One cause of this development was the introduction of more flexible manufacturing systems, and later on, just-in-time thinking, which made it possible to increase production without erecting new buildings to store additional machine capacity and inventory. The use of computerized machines and equipment, so called advanced manufacturing techniques, has increased. Calculations by Statistics Sweden showed an increase from 23 per cent of investments in machinery in 1986 to 31 per cent in 1993, in the engineering industry from 29 per cent to 43 per cent.

Table 2.1 shows that fixed investments, R & D and market investments account for about one third each of the total volume of investments. Investments in R & D and markets, i.e. investments which are written off immediately, today accounts for about 60 per cent of the total volume of investments. Observe that while fixed investments decreased during the recession which began in 1990, intangible investments increased also in real terms. In Germany, where intangible investments have been measured since 1979, the hypothesis has been proposed that intangible and tangible investments tend to co-operate through the business cycle inasmuch as capital investments harvest the benefits of R & D and market investments made in a recession, and vice versa (Scholz, 1990). If we widen the concept of an investment in this manner to comprise both tangible and intangible components the volume of investment tends to smooth out over the business cycle.

Table 2.1
The composition of the volume of investment

	1985	1986	1987	1988	1989	1990	1991	1992	1993	1994
Percentage of investment in										
Fixed assets	48	44	47	47	48	47	39	36	39	40
R & D	26	28	27	28	29	30	34	35	36	37
Markets	27	29	26	25	24	24	27	30	25	23
Percentage of investment in machinery allocated to computerized										
machinery	12	23	26	27	25	23	22	26	31	30

Notes: Investments in Sweden divided between fixed or capital (machinery and buildings), R & D, and market investments in percentage, and percentage of investments in machinery allocated to computerized machinery.

Source: Statistics Sweden (1986) to (1995).

Statistics Sweden also tried to estimate investments in employee training and arrived at an average of 2.7 days per employee in 1986. This figure had increased to 4.9 days in 1990; moreover the service industry invests most in its employees. Thus the interview study comprised one consultancy group which had as a policy to invest five per cent of its turnover in its employees' training and development of new knowledge and skills, partly by accepting assignments demanding the development of new competencies and therefore unprofitable. This was supplemented by knowledge and skills developed during work on ordinary assignments paid for by customers. Service groups sell services with a high content of knowledge, so that the development of new knowledge and skills can be compared with the product development projects of the manufacturing industry. However, nor can the traditional engineering industry refrain from improving the competence of its employees. The personnel director of ABB Sweden has estimated that some Swedish companies in the ABB group invest as much as four per cent of their sales in competence development (*Affärsvärlden*, 1992 (49), p. 25). If these investments in employees are treated as traditional investments the volume of investment must be adjusted upwards a further few percent.

As with investments in employees, investments in fixed and intangible investments vary widely between different lines of industry (see Table 2.2). Fixed investments dominate in the capital-intensive basic industries - the forest, steel and metal industries - and the volume of R & D is small. The food industry has large market investments, relatively large fixed investments and very small expenditures on R & D. Industries with large R & D expenditures are the transport and electro industries.

Table 2.2
Investment and line of industry

Type of investment	Fixed	R & D	Market
The forest industry	82.1 %	10.2 %	7.7 %
The steel industry	65.2	13.8	21.0
The food industry	51.9	4.5	43.6
The transport industry	41.4	46.4	12.1
The chemical industry	39.6	28.4	32.0
The electro industry	17.1	44.8	38.1
Other engineering industries	37.2	24.0	38.8
All industry	47.8	28.6	24.3

Source: Statistics Sweden (1988).

Turning to individual groups we find that the composition of the volume of investment differs considerably from one group to another. Table 2.3 is based on annual reports and shows the volume of investment in 1990 and 1994 in percentage of sales for twenty Swedish corporations and multinationals participating in this study. The engineering groups have a very complex structure of investments as they have large investments in machinery, product development and markets, and also both many small investments and some large investments, but there are also differences. The ball-bearing producer SKF invests only a few percent in R & D while investments in R & D by the telecommunications group Ericsson are only equalled by the pharmaceutical corporation Astra. The forest industry, on the other hand, has very large fixed investments with regard to both the total volume of investments and individual investments; a new paper mill or paper machine represents an investment of a thousand million SEK.

The composition of the volume of investment is changing. We are moving from traditional fixed investments in machinery and buildings towards more investments in markets, product development, employee development and also more software in the machines, at the same time as the land and building share of fixed investments has decreased below the 20

Table 2.3
Investments in some Swedish corporations 1990/1994

	Total sales in billion SEK	Foreign sales in % of total sales	Foreign employees % of total employees	Invest- ments in % of total sales	R & D in % of total sales
Engineering groups					
ABB[1]	189/210	88/-	-/-	4/3	7/8
Atlas Copco	16/21	93/95	80/83	4/3	3/3
Avesta[2]	8/17	84/91	24/52	6/2	-/-
Electrolux	82/108	85/92	82/87	5/4	-/1.3
Ericsson[3]	46/83	88/90	56/51	8/6	11/16
Nobel[4]	26/-	70/-	44/-	9/7	6/5
Sandvik	18/25	93/93	60/66	6/5	5/4
SKF	28/33	96/94	90/84	6/4	2/2
Volvo	83/156	86/83	31/41	7/4	9/3
Chemical and pharmaceutical groups					
Aga	12/13	84/88	90/88	9/14	2/-
Astra[5]	9/28	84/91	57/63	9/3	17/14
Perstorp	7/10	79/88	55/66	10/6	3/3
Forest groups					
ASSI	16/17	84/73	53/41	18/8	-/0.5
MoDo	18/20	82/86	23/30	9/5	-/-
SCA	31/34	80/84	66/67	15/9	1/-
STORA	66/49	83/82	40/48	9/7	1/-
Groups in other industries					
Esselte[6]	17/12	67/94	77/96	4/2	-/-
Euroc	12/14	56/72	57/66	14/3	0.5/0.5
Gambro	4/10	98/98	85/90	7/7	5/5
Procordia[7]	37/-	47/-	35/-	8/-	5/-
Pharmacia[7]	-/26	-/92	-/92	-/7	-/14

Notes: The table shows some of the corporations in the study. ABB, Avesta, and Nobel are today transnationals, and Pharmacia will probably become that. 1. ABB was a transnational with its head office in Switzerland when the study started. Total sales amonted to 27/30 billion US$, or 189/210 billion SEK at 1US$ = 7SEK; 2. During the period covered Avesta and British Steel formed Avesta Sheffield. Figures for 1994 relates to the new group Avesta Sheffield; 3. Total investments in R & D including market adjustments are 17/20 per cent of sales; 4. During the period covered Nobel

Industrier AB merged with Akzo N.V. to form Akzo Nobel N.V.. Figures for 1994 relate to the new group Akzo Nobel; 5. In addition to the figures shown, market investments amounted to 6/33 per cent of sales; 6. The Esselte group was restructured during the period of study; 7. In 1990 the pharmaceutical company Pharmacia was part of the Procordia group, later on it was broken out and it is now suggested that it shall merge with Upjohn to create still another transnational group.

Sources: Annual Reports.

per cent line due to new manufacturing techniques needing less space and inventory. Investments in machinery and buildings, markets and R & D account for about one third each. Moreover investments in the development of employees' knowledge and skills are considerable and increasing. However, it should also be noticed that the composition of investments varies considerably from one line of industry to another, and from company to company. Traditional investments still predominate in the capital-intensive processing industry although the processes are controlled by computers and investments in control equipment are substantial. The pharmaceutical, engineering and service groups have much larger intangible investments in product development, markets and employees.

3 Administrative routines

Resource allocation in divisionalized groups

The resource allocation process of divisionalized groups has been described by Bower (1970/72). He followed four major investment projects in a large U.S. divisionalized group. Bower's model is summarized in Figure 3.1. It consists of three hierarchical levels, two processes and context, and applies also to Swedish divisionalized groups.

Level	Phase	Process		
		Definition	Impetus	Context
Corporate	Corporate	Aggregate targets product/market mix	Yes or No	Design of corporate context
Division	Integration	Financial aggregate ↑ ↓ Product Market	Company wants ↑ ↓ Business wants	Corporate needs ↑ ↓ Sub-unit needs
Business	Initiation	Product market	We've got a great idea	Product/market not served by structure

Figure 3.1 Bower's model of the resource allocation process

Source: Adapted and printed by permission of Harvard Business School Press from Managing the Resource Allocation Process by Joseph L. Bower (1972, pp. 80-1). Copyright © 1970, 1986 by the President and Fellows of Harvard College.

21

The process of definition stands for the process whereby the investment idea is developed into a feasible investment project, and technical solutions and economic characteristics are chosen. Another term for this process could be the project planning process. The process of impetus stands for the process whereby the investment and investment request travels upwards in the hierarchy towards approval and funding. Approval presupposes that middle managers, and if necessary also higher levels, can be made committed to sponsor the request.

The group management can influence these processes by changing the context of the processes. One subset of the context is corporate structure, i.e. the formal organization, and systems of information, control, performance measurement, and incentives. According to Bower, this structural context is particularly important as it enables top management in hierarchic organizations to influence investment behaviour many levels below. By changing the structural context corporate managers can influence the generation, evaluation and direction of the investments of the group.

According to Bower's model an investment project has to pass through three phases; an initiating, an integrating and a corporate phase. The initiating phase is triggered on the business level by a discrepancy defined in product-market terms. In the integrating phase middle managers integrate business level 'wants' with the intentions of higher levels, and in the corporate phase requests are either approved or rejected. This means that the phase of initiation is most important to the process of definition, the integrating phase to the process of impetus, and the corporate phase to the determination of the structural context.

In short, it can be said that top management decides the rules of the capital budgeting game, i.e. the context. Investment ideas are generated and developed into investment requests by engineers at the business level. Middle managers choose investment requests which conform to corporate management intentions, and refer such requests for appropriation.

The makers of the investment request

According to Bower (1972) new investment projects are initiated when a production manager, plant manager, process engineer, etc. experience "a discrepancy between 'what the company wants of me' and the state of existing investment in facilities". Signals from the control system indicate a misfit between what could be achieved with present production equipment and the demand imposed on it, there being three different versions of this event: "costs are too high", "quality is inadequate", and "sales" or "sales forecast" "cxcccds capacity".

Bower's description finds good support in other empirical process studies (e.g. King, 1975; Burgelman, 1983a; 1984b), and from the respondents, although one can make a strong argument for the position that these discrepancies often come to the attention of the company through market contacts. In divisionalized companies most investment ideas originate from the business level and people in contact with production. Apart from suggestion boxes little is done to stimulate the generation of new investment ideas. There is, for instance, no formal brain-storming committee for new investment ideas (Istvan, 1961a; Mao, 1970; Petty, Scott and Bird, 1975).

Most investments are small and medium-sized reinvestments, often combined with capacity, product or productivity improving measures. Requests for major investments, expansion investments or ventures in new areas, were (Lundberg, 1961; Istvan, 1961a) and are still much rarer. The motives for investing are often mixed (Gutenberg, 1959; 1992; Lundberg, 1961; Gandemo, 1983; Segelod, 1986) insofar as an expansion investment also involves the replacement of worn out or unproductive parts of the plant and the application of a more productive and flexible manufacturing technique.

In general it is an engineer at the business level who makes the investment appraisal, often together with the plant controller and with the help of the company's investment manual; in some companies the company management or a staff unit. The investment proposal is handed over to the factory manager, who no doubt has been informally notified about the plans which the engineer and the controller have been investigating.

The plant manager becomes the first review unit. However, if the initial cash outlay is above his or her level of authorisation the manager must submit a request for approval and funding. Therefore, if the plant manager considers the investment necessary and the chances of having the expenditures approved good, he or she can choose to sign the investment request and refer it upwards in the hierarchy. By signing the request the manager shows a commitment to the economic assumptions and descriptions made in the request.

This description fits most of the groups in which interviews were made, but with a few exceptions. Thus in four of the multinational groups many of the investment requests seemed to be made by, or in cooperation with, staff units on the divisional level. Furthermore, in the smaller groups listed on the otc list the appraisal was often made by a staff unit or otherwise more centralized.

However, corporate staff in major groups nowadays seldom engage in making investment appraisals. They no longer have the resources to do so. The only kind of investments which they might appraise are acquisitions, the location of new plants, divestures of companies, relocation of production within the group, and new kinds of investment common to many companies of the group in which evaluation needs standardization:

> If it is a matter of an investment such as a new kind of machine which will be used in many of our plants then it can start here with us. We have for instance today a project in the packing line which will cost 7 to 8 million per plant. There we have started. We have all the informa-

tion needed to build up an appraisal and the plant director does not have that. We develop an appraisal and discuss it with the plant director and the local management and present it to the board.

In this case group staff developed a standardized appraisal, which could later be used for similar investments in other plants. The standardization procedure by group staff became a part of the corporate managers' initiative to renew the packing lines in the plants and also to standardize the production equipment of the group.

Similar standardization work has been done in some of the groups in recent years in the information technology (IT), flexible manufacturing system (FMS), and in-house training areas. As lower levels have found it difficult to show that such investments can be expected to be profitable at the same time as common sense has told managers that they are of great strategic importance, the issue has been referred upwards. In some cases this has had the result that corporate staff have reviewed prior investments in IT and FMS investments, and developed standardized procedures or guidelines for the evaluation of such investments, whereby it once more has been possible to decentralize the evaluation.

The makers of the assumptions

Another question which can be asked is whether the group has a unit to decide which volumes, prices, costs, inflation etc. the appraiser must use in the calculations, or if the appraiser is wholly free to choose assumptions. This is of course a vital issue as often a minor change in the assumptions can make a profitable investment unprofitable, and vice versa.

In this respect the interviews showed a distinct difference between groups with a capital budgeting manual, and those that lacked such written routines. Respondents in groups which had written routines usually said that they required the directions of the manual to be followed strictly, at least with regard to requests which needed group level approval.

Those groups that lacked a manual lacked directions not only on which profitability criteria were to be imposed - the internal rate of return, net present value, payback period, etc - but also on how investment expenditures, costs of operation and maintenance, and sales revenues, were to be estimated, and which rate of interest and inflation should be used in the calculations. Consequently, it was more up to the appraiser to choose assumptions and design the investment request in the groups which lacked written routines. Although some interviewees in groups without written routines said that a certain practice with regard to investment requests had developed through requesters imitating older requests, the main hypothesis must still be that investment requests vary more in groups lacking written routines. On the other hand, all groups with substantial investments in machinery and production equipment use a capital budgeting manual.

Capital investments play a less significant role for those groups which lack a manual. Thus the manual is a very important measure of control to achieve unitary assumptions and investment requests.

Pre-approval review of investment request

The process of pre-approval review of capital appropriation or investment requests starts already when the controller or economist of the plant is consulted and later when the factory manager assess, approves and signs the request. Depending on the type of investment and how far up in the hierarchy the request must travel, the request will pass through several review stations, staff units, boards, and managers who are responsible for different interests and aspects of the investment, so also in U.K. (Scapens and Sale, 1981; Pike, 1982) and U.S. (Istvan, 1961a; Mukherjee, 1987) groups. Particularly the multinational engineering groups in the present study have a very well developed system of pre-approval review of investment requests.

> Major investments pass through us and certain other departments plus our technical director, product line director. Each request is reviewed by many. We do the groundwork many times. If the material is insufficient, then we comment on it, ask for more information. It is a little like a cake. Everyone sees different things in an appraisal; sees different inaccuracies.

Most corporate staff only review requests which need approval from the board of directors.

> All investment issues that are to be approved by the group board shall be reviewed by the group staff and presented to the CEO before submission to the group board.

There may also be directions that the finance function be contacted before entering into a lease agreement or deciding how to finance major projects, and that technical staff units be contacted early when preparing major projects and certain other types of investment, and it is of course not forbidden to contact a staff unit also for other types of investment if lower levels find this necessary.

Istvan (1961a) and also some later studies (e.g. Scapens and Sale, 1981) tell us that in some corporations major projects can go directly to top management without passing through any form of pre-approval review. With one exception, this does not seem to be the case in the Swedish groups in this study. In fact, the interviewees in two of the largest multinationals stated that they had tightened the manual, the pre-approval review procedures and decision process considerably during the last few years, and a few more groups expressed a need to do so, partly to counteract an earlier wave of decentralization. Decentralization of the right to make certain investment

25

decisions seems to some extent be counteracted by stronger central control of the division of responsibilities in the investment process, pre-approval review and assumptions made in the request. A comparison of present practice with that described by studies from the 50s and 60s (Istvan, 1961a; Renck, 1966) indicates that one of the marked changes is the more general decentralization combined with more sophisticated pre-approval review found in the major groups of today.

By letting the request pass through several review stations, for scrutiny by specialists and managers in different areas and on different levels, all major inaccuracies and inconsistencies will, hopefully, be discovered and a high quality in the investment requests guaranteed. During this process investments will be coordinated in time and space, and the joint competencies of the group utilized. If, for instance, another company in the group has executed a similar investment, what experience did it gain? Does the company need to acquire new competence to implement the investment? Is the time right for investment considering financial conditions, economic conditions, technological development, management resources and other investments, etc? However,

> it is often difficult for us [corporate staff] to argue for another opinion than the business area or division controller. They are better informed about the investment.

In most cases corporate staff can only criticize and give feedback to investment planning: review the soundness of the reasoning, see whether the calculations are correct, and the assumptions not mutually contradictory, and ask questions. However, the burden of proof rests on the requester:

> The division knows how much a machine cost. It is the same type of machine all over the world. They are tough in the control. We cannot question their estimates. The control we make is more to see whether their calculations are consistent, that they have considered changes in working capital. If they have not, then I send it back and say 'you can't increase sales by 20 per cent without increasing your working capital'. It's not realistic or, if it is, then you have to prove it. ... We [corporate staff] cannot judge whether they can increase their volume from 200,000 crowns to 300,000. We cannot see whether that is reasonable. That is something they on the market side and production side have to say - that it is realistic. It is their commitment.

If a doubt is discovered, additional information is demanded. Only in exceptional cases do corporate staff try to produce the information needed themselves. However, even if most groups, and especially the multinational engineering groups, devote great effort to pre-approval review, there are also examples of the opposite, most clearly represented by one of the large forest groups:

26

Nobody makes a critical review of the investment request before it is presented to the board [company, divisional and group board]. It is assumed that the principal who goes to the board is so serious that he can be trusted. We have no control at all.

There are probably two reasons why this group has no pre-approval review apart from that performed by company, divisional and group boards, and possibly also group staff. The first is connected with the character of planning and investments in the forest industry, and the second, with the fact that this group is highly decentralized and relies heavily on board representation to control the group.

Forest companies have high in-house knowledge of their technology, and several consultancy companies sell the knowledge which they may lack, costing and evaluating new investments and giving feedback on investments. Individual investments are often rather large. They are evaluated and implemented through project management, a management technique of which forest groups have long experience; the review process is therefore to a great extent carried out within the framework of a project organization. Additional review and feedback is supplied by the boards of the group.

The selling of the investment request

In the impetus process the requester acts as seller of the request. He or she must be able to convince his or her superiors of the necessity for the investment project so that they will promote its approval. Building on earlier research by Lindblom (1959) and Aharoni (1966) Bower (1970) talks about the need to get superior committed to the request. Such a process inevitably promotes a strong trait of game-playing. Consequently, many studies show (Bower, 1972; Burgelman, 1983a; 1984b; Lumijärvi, 1991a; 1991b) how lower management succeeded in pushing through investments which higher levels were initially hesitant to approve, and all the game-playing situations which can arise in such situations. Requesters use an array of tricks to get their superiors committed and enforce their will; they do not always tell the whole truth or reveal their real motives.

The requester can be seen as a seller of investment proposals, and the appropriator as a buyer of proposals. The requester must be able to obtain the backing of his superiors by convincing the buyer that the description of the issue is correct and that this is exactly the right investment. One problem in this selling process is that the seller has a deeper knowledge of the proposed investment than the buyer, another that the buyer has interests to protect. How then can the buyer know that the proposal made by the seller is consistent with the interests for which the buyer is responsible?

Questions of this kind are treated within the fast growing body of research into agency theory (see e.g. Fama and Jensen, 1983; 1985; Eisenhardt, 1989; Thakor, 1989; 1990; 1993; Hirshleifer, 1993). The seller is an agent for the

27

buyer and, since the agent is better informed about the proposal, there is a state of information asymmetry. Being less well informed about the details of the investment the buyer finds it difficult to argue for a another view than the one marketed by the seller. Using these theoretical assumptions researchers have analysed how asymmetric information can be expected to affect the design of the resource allocation system and distort project choice by affecting the trade-off between short- and long-term investments, the propensity to take risks and herd behaviour (e.g. Scharfstein and Stein, 1990; Banerjee, 1992), i.e. the propensity of firms in an industry to choose to invest in similar projects and cause waves of investments. Agency theory offers explanations thereof and many other empirical observations on how organizations makes investment decisions based on the assumption on rational economic behavior.

The asymmetry problem is aggravated when the manager and the company lack experience of similar earlier projects. Comparisons of the impetus process for major expansion investments and major ventures in new areas (Segelod, 1995) show that managers acting as buyers in the latter case tend to attach more weight to assessing the requester and the company of the requester in accordance with the maxim; when you cannot assess the request, assess the requester instead. There are several studies (Mao, 1970; Carter, 1971; Dugdale and Jones, 1994; Jones and Dugdale, 1994) showing that the track record of the proposer affects the credibility or trust attributed to a proposal also for the funding of other types of investment; but the importance attached to the track record of the requester tends to increase when something new is suggested, which is not irrational as it is then more likely that the existing investment procedures might not be able to guarantee the necessary feedback for the request to be properly evaluated.

This game playing and sometimes also the simple fact that the idea of an investment always precedes the appraisal, and not the other way round, has prompted many observers to wonder what functions the appraisal and investment request really perform. Langley (1988; 1989; 1990, 1991), for instance, discerned four different types of purposes for formal analysis, namely information, communication, direction and control, and symbolic purposes. She studied twenty-seven strategic decisions in three organizations representing three different types of organizational structure. In all 183 "written documents reporting the results of some systematic study of a specific issue" (1991, p. 80) were identified and classified as having an information, communication, direction and control, or symbolic purpose.

- Fifty-three per cent of the cases were made to receive better information and understanding of the decision situation: in some of the cases to reduce uncertainty around the decision, in others to verify others' ideas.
- Fifty-seven per cent of the studies were made for a communicative purpose. The study sought to communicate a certain image of the investment, often to superiors, and less often to subordinates. Investment procedures can also serve as a means of communicating informa-

tion about an investment. A similar study of investment appraisals by Jansson (1989; 1992a; b) confirms the importance of both the communicative and the informative purpose.

- Twenty-five per cent of the studies were initiated by management, not from a desire to inform or convince, but because they thought an issue needed further clarification. If subordinates failed to respond to this demand, members of staff were often assigned to make another study as a further measure of control.
- In 19 per cent of the cases the initiation of the study was in the main a symbolic action. The initiation of a formal analysis was thought to convey a message of rationality, concern or willingness to act, when in reality the true purpose was to postpone the decision, create jobs, if anything.

It is not difficult to find other plausible purposes than the four just mentioned. There are several studies in the areas of capital investments (Cooper, 1975; Hopwood, 1976; Hägg, 1977; Segelod, 1986; Jansson, 1989; 1992a; b), accounting (Burchell et al, 1980; Morgan, 1988; Northcott, 1991), planning (Wildavsky, 1973; Sager, 1992) and strategic planning (Mintzberg and Waters, 1985; Mintzberg, 1987) which suggest also other purposes. Formal analysis and investment requests can serve several purposes, and also meet different needs for employees in different positions and parts of the organization, also symbolic aims, as shown by Hägg (1977) and Feldman and March (1981). The principal purpose is not always to reduce uncertainty and provide better information about the future, as normative theories of capital budgeting assume and simple textbooks teach.

Perhaps as a reaction some behavioural scientists (Gimpl and Dakin, 1984) have suggested that the entire capital budgeting process should be seen as not more than a ritual to justify decisions based on other considerations. One piece of evidence which has been adduced consist of the fact that few investment requests are definitely turned down when they reach corporate level in major corporations (Bower, 1972; Gitman and Forrester, 1977; Oblak and Helm, 1980; Scapens and Sale, 1981; Mills and Herbert, 1987). However, this last observation pertains to the function of the head office in major groups. The interviews showed that corporate managers were more actively involved in the ranking of requests in the smaller groups on the otc list, an observation supported by a postal survey of similar U.K. groups by Diacogiannis and Lai (1989).

Lower levels have an information and a cognitive advantage and the possibility to adjust information so as to promote their interests and conceptions. They avoid referring requests which they do not think will receive approval. That would mean losing prestige. For the same reason, managers on higher levels find it difficult to turn down a request. That would be to put the competence of the requester in question. Therefore, when a request has started to move upwards and more and more managers and members of staff become committed to the investment it often gathers its own momentum so that the final decision is in the nature of "a blessing than a rational approval decision", to use the words of Clancy, Collins and Chatfield (1982, p. 30).

Head office requirements for investments

The interviews with managers responsible for their group's investment or capital budgeting procedures indicated four different criteria or requirements which all investments had to satisfy to be approved. They had to comply with certain requirements regarding

- profitability
- finance
- strategy
- coordination

Profitability It should be observed that these four types of requirement have different weight at different levels of a group. The profitability calculation is in major groups normally made at business level. The important design decisions are often made by engineers on the business level, technical staff units, or consultants and suppliers engaged in the project. The investment options and investment requests are ranked on the business and divisional levels, partly before the request is submitted, through the continuous communication about investment plans within the group. In accordance with this decentralization only a few manuals stipulate that the investment request present more than one investment option. For some reason this is contrary to what has been reported for major U.S. groups. Klammer and Walker (1984) found that 76 per cent of their corporations in 1980 required a written analysis of the options, and Mukherjee (1988) found in his study of U.S. manuals that

> almost all project justifications require information on alternative proposals (other than the one being justified and why they were rejected. Manuals make it very clear that 'do nothing' option should always be considered as one of the alternatives. (Mukherjee, 1988, p. 30-1)

It is difficult to say why American and Swedish manuals differ in this respect. Perhaps it has to do with the fact that writers on capital budgeting in accordance with the theory of investments have often emphasized that decision-makers should always be faced with a real choice between options, and top management are the ultimate decision-makers. However, it is difficult to see how top management can arrive at a better or a different decision inasmuch as business and divisional managers have the best knowledge about the market, technology and the status of their own company.

Finance Corporate level is more involved in the finance issue e.g. by approving the volume of investment, debt-equity ratios, profitability requirements, hurdle rates, leasing and the raising of funds by companies in the group. Head office has not delegated the finance decision. It decides how the group shall be financed or how individual companies may raise capital. Moreover, many groups have rules which stipulate that corporate level financial staff must be contacted before a company enter into a lease agreement or decides how to finance a major investment. It can also be noticed that requests for a major investments must be accompanied by a cash flow estimate, and in some groups also by an evaluation of how the company's balance sheet and statement of income will be affected by the investment.

Strategy The most important issue for corporate managers is strategy. Many of the interviewees pointed out that the internal rate of return or the payback period promised by an investment request is not always particularly important. If the investment is considered as necessary for continued competitiveness or for some other strategic reason the investment is made notwithstanding: "We don't invest in plant and equipment; we invest in strategies" (Leighton and Thain, 1990, p. 5) is a quotation which sums up what many of the interviewees have explained, in one way or another, and is also a remark often made by practitioners writing about capital budgeting (see e.g. Bofors årsredovisning, 1978; Gallinger, 1980; Marshuetz, 1985; Leighton and Thain, 1990).

You must have a plan before you can invest, a plan that can constitute a point of departure against which the individual investment can be assessed. The vision always comes first, and the formal approval of individual investment requests therefor often becomes a control of how already approved strategies are implemented and progressing. This of course makes the timing of investment an important issue; When should new capacity be acquired and new technology introduced considering the present and possible future situation of the firm, the market for the product and the technology, to achieve balanced growth.

Corporate managers want to make sure that the investment is in agreement with previously approved strategies, and if it is not, to consider it in more detail. This may explain why the corporate level in most groups seldom turns down a request definitively or is asked to make decisions on alternative investments, and not as the textbooks inculcate that decision makers shall be presented with a real choice between investment options.

Coordination and implementation According to Bower (1972) business level defines the investments, and corporate level influences the investments generated and chosen by manipulating the structural context. Divisional managers act as linking pins between these levels, managing the part-whole relationship between lower level investment needs and higher level plans for the group as a whole.

Bower gives corporate managers a passive role, which does not coincide with the image conveyed by most of the corporate managers interviewed. Without questioning the notion of middle managers' key role in coordinating investments, one must therefore add that also corporate managers responsible for investments at corporate level in many Swedish groups devote much time to coordinating investments and to realizing the synergies that the group structure offers. They help to controll how production is allocated to different countries and plants, ensure that the managerial resources to implement and make the investment successful exist, that similar technology is used, that experiences are transferred from one project to another, and design and control the process of pre-approval review. If, for instance, the Italian company has already carried through an investment similar to the one planned by the American company they try to ensure that this experience is transferred to the American company. Do they have the managerial competence to implement the investment or must it be strengthened, and can the group supply this competence.

The description given by Bower (1972) of middle managers as coordinaters of the investments of the group, and top managers as controlling through manipulating the context is far too simplistic, even if divisional managers play a key role in the coordination of investments. Investments in Swedish groups are coordinated on all levels and through many different channels for horizontal and vertical communication, and in many groups also corporate managers devote much time to coordinating investments in different parts of the group.

Corporate level means of control

Bower's (1972) most important contribution can be claimed to be that he showed that corporate executives in divisionalized groups do not decide the direction of investments by choosing among individual investment requests, but through designing a structural context which will favour investment requests which are in line with the desired strategic direction; he defines structural context as

> the formal organization (with associated definitions of managers' jobs), the system of information and control used to measure performance of the business, and the systems used to measure and reward performance of managers. (Bower, 1972, p. 71)

Corporate managers do not have the time to acquaint themselves with all investment issues, and therefore, the structural context offers a system of decentralizing investment issues without losing all the control. To survey which parts of the structural context the interviewees on corporate level

32

perceived as most important for their control of the direction of investment they were asked open-ended questions like: "How does your group control the direction of your volume of investment? Which means and possibilities do the group management and accounting and finance function have to influence the composition of the volume of investments and the direction of individual investments?" These questions and discussions led the respondents to identify the means of control listed in Table 3.1 as particularly important.

Table 3.1
Head office means of investment control

Precepts for individual investments concerning
- the formal decision process
- the division of responsibility
- the implementation of investment projects
- the investment request

Planning processes
- the budgetary control process
- the investment or strategic planning process

Profit centre performance measures

Other means of control and coordination, e.g.
- investment committees
- board representation
- staff units
- executive meetings
- management travel within the group

Notes: The Table is based on open-ended interviews with managers on the corporate level responsible for the investment procedures of their groups who were asked how they try to direct the investments of the group.

There are relatively many empirical studies of the structural context, or more precisely head office means or measures of strategic control in multinational groups (see e.g. Chandler, 1962; 1991; Doz and Prahalad, 1981; 1984; Spångberg, 1982; Bartlett and Ghoshal, 1987; 1989; Goold and Campbell, 1987a; 1987b; 1988; Goold and Quinn, 1990a; 1990b). These studies have identified a great number of administrative mechanisms used to exert control, such as e.g. information and measurement systems, planning processes, management selection, development and career policies, and reward systems. In this book we shall only map and analyse a small part of this system, namely those measures or means of control which managers on corporate level responsible for the investment procedures of the groups studied experienced as most important and spontaneously mentioned. Thus,

33

if the interviewees had been confronted with a longer list of means they would probably have come to think of a greater number of means. It should also be remembered that none of the interviewees referred to all the measures listed in Table 3.1, and that the emphasis placed on the measures differed from group to group. Some groups seemed to rely heavily on some of the means, others on another constellation of means, although there were doubtless similarities between groups within an industry no two groups seemed to be run exactly the same way.

Precepts for individual investments Most groups with large amounts invested in machinery and other kinds of depreciable investments have developed a capital budgeting or investment manual. This manual gives the requester instructions on how to work out an investment request. In addition, many manuals also supply a description of the formal investment process and who is responsible for what in this process, as well as instructions regarding how investment projects are to be appraised, implemented, and reviewed, both ex ante and ex post. The content of the investment manuals of the groups studied, and the role of this instrument of control will be analysed in detail in Chapter 4. Chapters 5-7 will survey what the same manuals stipulate regarding the investment appraisal and request concerning the determination of cash flow, project evaluation criteria, taxes, inflation, risk analysis and ex post review.

Planning processes - the annual budgetary control process Investment requests are incorporated into a capital budget as a part of the annual budgetary control process, and all but the two most profitable and liquid groups considered themselves to have more good requests than they could finance. The ranking of these requests occurred in general at business and divisional levels (Istvan, 1961a; Bower, 1970; Petty, Scott, and Bird, 1975; Oblak and Helm, 1980; Mukherjee, 1988), and in some of the groups was performed by an investment committee at divisional level.

The American capital budgeting manuals which Mukherjee (1988) analysed contained detailed information about this process. This is rarely not the case in the manuals of Swedish groups. In major Swedish groups of today the capital budgeting manual is a part of the accounting, financial, or the finance and administration manual of the group. Information about planning processes is found in that part of the financial manual which deals with the budgetary control process and the comments here about planning processes are therefore mainly based on interviews.

All groups in which interviews were carried out had an annual budgetary control process and a capital expenditure budget. Thirteen of the nineteen groups and almost all multinational groups in the engineering industry only had a one-year capital expenditure budget at corporate level, three a three years capital spending plan and three a five years plan. The capital-intensive forest and metal industries usually have a longer capital budget than the engineering groups. Whether some of these groups have a longer capital budget on division or business levels has not been surveyed, but the interviews showed that such could be the case.

The shape of the annual budgetary control process varies from group to group. One of the groups within the metal industry which uses a three year capital expenditure plan describes its planning process as follows.

> All operating companies within the group must draw up a three year rolling investment plan. The plan must consist of two parts, a one year capital expenditure budget, and proposals for the additional two years.
>
> The one year budget is a detailed budget divided among individual projects which comprise appropriations budgeted, budgeted expenditures for already approved projects, and budgeted new projects which are expected to cause expenditures during the budget year. The one year budget must be an integral part of the total budget of each company. The effects of the investments on personnel requirements, expenses, revenues, assets, debts and payments must be fully recognized.
>
> The budget also contains a lump sum for sundries. This amount is released by the board on a quarterly or half-yearly basis.
>
> The two year plan added to the one year budget is preliminary and only specifes planned appropriations. However, these must be allotted to projects as far as possible.
>
> The work on the capital expenditure budget starts early every autumn. A well thought-out capital budget must be available when the limits for the other sub-budgets are decided. The final capital expenditure budget is approved in connection with the total budget of the company.

British studies show that 62 per cent (Scapens and Sale, 1981), 78 per cent (Mills and Herbert, 1986) and 64 per cent (Pike and Wolfe, 1988) supplement their short-term capital budget with a long-term capital budget. Similar surveys of U.S. industry show even higher figures, or 75 per cent (Klammer and Walker, 1984), 77 per cent (Scapens and Sale, 1981), and 82 per cent (Hendricks, 1983). According to the last mentioned study of major U.S. corporations in 1981 17 per cent of these 82 per cent had a 2 to 3 year capital budget and 70 per cent a 4 to 5 years budget. U.K. and U.S. industries have seen a gradual increase in long-term capital budgets, from 19 per cent according to Istvan (1961a) and 43 per cent in 1960 according to Klammer (1972) towards these very high figures compared with the 32 per cent we have observed for major Swedish groups in 1990-93.

The capital budget is followed up three to twelve times a year by the corporate level; indeed the reviews have become more frequent in many of the groups during the last few years of recession. In fact, many groups do this today on a monthly basis. Swedish groups tend to use shorter capital budgets than their U.K. and U.S. counterparts, at least on corporate level, and the trend is toward more frequent reviews. It is true that some of these groups used long-term planning in the mid 70's, but this fact does not suffice to explain the whole difference. Differences in the composition of the industries, the degree of decentralization, the emphasis laid by top management on different means of control, and cultural factors, may be more valid explanations.

Planning processes - the investment or strategic planning process Three of nineteen groups, and at least one in which no interviews were carried out, have in the last decade introduced some kind of annual strategic or investment process. The strategic process runs during the spring and precedes the budgetary control process which takes place during the autumn. Decisions on new products, markets and major investments are made in the strategic process; other investments are decided in the budgetary control process. All these four groups have large R & D expenses. The strategic process has been introduced to improve strategic control and coordination of resources. For a more detailed description of a strategic process see Vancil and Lorange in Lorange (1993).

The traditional bottom-up kind of resource allocation system has been criticized (Goold and Boyland, 1975; Hayes and Abernathy, 1980; Hayes and Garvin, 1982; Pinches, 1982; Hayes, Wheelwright, and Clark, 1988; Baldwin, 1991; Baldwin and Clark, 1992; Porter, 1992a; 1992b) for focusing interest on individual investments and hard data, instead of soft data and the contribution of the investment to the strategy of the company and group. The critics maintain that the system with authorization levels, systems of classification and instructions for the evaluations and requests of individual investments will contribute to fragmentation. Referring to the more centralized German (Carr, Tomkins, and Bayliss, 1991; Currie, 1993) and especially Japanese (Currie, 1991a; 1991b; 1993; Jones, Currie, and Dugdale, 1993) groups some writers have recommended increased central-ization of investment decisions (Baldwin and Clark, 1992; 1994; Porter, 1992a; 1992b), e.g. through the introduction of an annual strategic process or a centrally controlled investment committee to improve horizontal and vertical communication, and the focus on strategic implications of the investment.

The introduction of an annual strategic process in research intensive groups is one way of solving this problem and confers better strategic control. A less ambitious routine which works towards the same end has been adopted by six multinationals, mainly engineering groups. Large investment projects usually consist of a number of independent steps, or can be structured along these lines. Therefore, these groups have issued directions stating that the requester may not apply for grants for a project which will be followed by consequential new investments. First a request for the major project or investment programme must be approved at the right level. Then requests can be submitted for sub-investments within the

36

programme when these investments come to the fore. Still other groups rely on board representation to focus attention on strategic decisions.

Profit centre performance measures Return on investment (ROI) and other performance measures are perhaps viewed usually as an ex post criterion; if the unit makes the wrong investments then this will sooner or later be discerned in its ROI. However, it can also be seen as an ex ante criterion.

As ROI is estimated on accounting measures of capital, the return can be increased by reducing the capital invested. Thus, it may for instance seem more profitable to choose reinvestments, than expansion investments. U.K. and U.S. (e.g. Dearden, 1962; 1969, Hayes and Garvin, 1982) industry have been criticized for demanding an excessive ROI and thereby to favour short-term investments to compensate for short-term ROI reduction. The managers interviewed seem well aware of this risk and some of them remarked that they sometimes have to curtail the volume of reinvestments suggested by lower levels.

In many multinationals the requirements vary considerably for operations in different countries, and markets. In general corporate managers estimate, and make proposals on requirements. However, most interviewees also pointed out that the performance measures used are target rates fixed in a process of negotiation, and that the agreed rate is primarily seen as a commitment by the unit in question.

Other means - investment committees Many groups have investment committees especially on divisional level, and in some groups different committees for different types of investment. There may be one committee for machine investments, one for in-house training, and one for investments in information technology, etc. The total extent of these committees has not been surveyed as the interviewees on corporate level rarely referred to these committees as one of their, and the corporate level's, most important means of control.

The exception is one group with very large fixed investments. The investment committees on divisional level are in this group headed by the person responsible for investments on corporate level, formerly the vice-president for finance and accounting of the group, and are regarded as an important means of control to corporate level. Through this representation corporate level has a direct say in the ranking of investment requests, the shaping of the yearly capital expenditure budgets and the coordinaton of investments. In this capital-intensive group these investment committees seems to serve a purpose somewhat similar to that of the annual strategic processes in the groups previously mentioned. In the other groups the influence on most committees seem to have been less direct through, for instance, executive meetings.

Other means - board representation A large number of interviewees emphasized the importance of influence through board representation. All groups have many companies which are controlled by a board, or a business board, if the company is not legally an independent unit. In principle, group managers are represented on the boards of the divisions, and divisional managers on the boards of the companies. Through this system corporate executives receive information on the major investments, strategic options and other changes under consideration by lower levels before these plans result in a request for expenditures; this gives them an opportunity to influence the direction of investments. Board representation thus offers an alternative to strategic processes and directions stipulating that major investments and investment programmes must be assessed and approved before the plans agreed on generate sub-requests for capital expenditures.

Other means - staff units Staff units can be seen as agents for executive managers, and are of course an important means of information and control. However corporate staff units have been reduced in recent decades to the extent that many groups today only retain juridical, accountant and finance functions at corporate level. Technical staffs have been decentralized to lower levels, turned into staff companies or simply abolished. A staff company is a group company and profit centre selling its services to other group companies, and also often on the open market. Staff units are of course a very important means of control, but it is today difficult to know how large they are as the majority of the staff units of major groups are found on levels below corporate level.

Other means - executive meetings Several of the interviewees, especially in the service and multinational engineering industries, emphasized the importance of executive meetings. Many groups regularly gather executives and representatives of group companies at seminars, over for instance a weekend. These meetings are not primarily intended to direct investments but it happens that the investment policy, investment priorities, and other investment issues are discussed. Such executive meetings and other fora for face-to-face communication can constitute an important means of creating a common way of thinking on investment issues, and of influencing e.g. the ranking by the investment committees.

Other means - management travel within the group A minority of interviewees saw travelling-around-management as an important means to disseminate group executive thinking on investment issues, pushing strategic initiatives and certain kinds of investment, coordinating investments and the joint competence-base of the group. In some of these groups only corporate executives travel, in others, also representatives of staffs and staff companies selling technical know-how.

As stated by way of introduction none of the respondents pointed out all the means of control mentioned as important. Some of them stressed some of the means and others others. The importance attached to the means varied between groups and industries, and we shall return to these differences in Chapter 9.

A note on the volume of investment

The volume of investment is determined in the budgetary control process, the shape of which differs. However, capital-intensive groups seem to begin by estimating how much the group as a whole can invest during the coming year to show what is considered as an acceptable balance sheet and income statement. Starting from an estimation of a preliminary volume of capital investment for the group, the volume is later broken down and distributed among lower units. Groups with a small capital budget, e.g. many service groups, may instead start from the bottom by adding up the investment requests when determining the volume of the capital budget.

Representatives of all but two of the groups studied regarded themselves as having more good investment proposals than they could finance and implement. The two groups which experienced a lack of good investment proposals are those with the highest liquidity. As a result of successful investment in the past both of them are today in a harvest period. This means that almost all groups practice some form of capital rationing; they must rank their investment requests, and reject or at least postpone some requests. This ranking is done in the companies and divisions. Postal surveys of major U.S. corporations show that 70 to 80 per cent of these groups claim to practice capital rationing (Istvan, 1961a; Fremgen, 1973; Brigham, 1975; Gitman and Forrester, 1977). However, this of course changes depending on the economic conditions.

Penrose (1959) argued that the growth rate and thus the volume of investment of a firm is limited by its managerial capacity. First, the availability of managerial capacity limits the amount of expansion which a firm can undertake at any one time. Secondly, the expansion is limited by the amount of new managerial capacity which a firm can absorb. Several researchers later expressed similar ideas (Barna, 1962; Richardson, 1964; Wright, 1964; Bromiley, 1986). Wright, for instance, has argued that it is not the number of managers which is critical but

> the ability of a few individuals in key positions to accept additional responsibility. (Wright, 1964, p. 183)

The interviews partly support these ideas. The shortage of skilled engineers had restrained six out of the nineteen groups from investing, and eleven of them had refrained from investing because they lacked key individuals deemed necessary to make the investment successful, e.g. experienced project managers and managing directors. It is obvious that investments are sometimes turned down because of a lack of key individuals, and not always because of a lack of financial resources, or bleak market expectations.

There is also another aspect of this, namely managers' inability to comprehend and work on too many different issues at once; "You can't keep too many balls in the air at one time", as one of the respondents expressed it.

This recalls an analogy from cognitive studies of decision-making which demonstrated that the quality of a decision depends on the amount of information to be processed (Hoffman and Blanchard, 1961; Hogarth, 1981). The quality of decisions improves with the amount of information, to reach a maximum and then decrease when information becomes too extensive and unwieldy. Keeping too many balls in the air at one time prevents reduction of uncertainty and the achievement of a decision. The number of options must be reduced to make the decision situation manageable and to focus learning.

Investments not initiated on the business level

We commenced by referring to Bower's (1972) model and description of how investments were initiated. A manager on the production side experienced "a discrepancy between 'what the company wants of me' and the status of existing investment in facilities". This description befits the great majority of investments, but there are types of investment which may be initiated at higher levels of management. Among the more important are acquisitions, investments in new areas due to a strategic reorientation, or due to the restructuring of a group, investments due to strategic initiatives, sometimes also major investment projects and investments in groups where market or R & D investments are large and centralized.

Acquisitions All groups seem to have rules stipulating that all acquisitions need group level approval, at least all acquisitions above a certain expenditure level. This holds true also for U.S. groups (Jemison and Sitkin, 1986; Mukherjee, 1988), and may often be a consequence of corporate bylaws stating that such approval is needed, according to Jemision and Sitkin (1986).

Who and which level has taken the initiative for the acquisition differs from case to case. The interviews gave examples of acquisitions which had been initiated at all levels; from corporate board members down to a salesman on the business level.

Several of the groups appointed a manager on the corporate level as responsible for acquisitions. Among the groups which have made many acquisitions some have evaluated all acquisitions on the corporate level, others have decentralized the evaluation and developed manuals and instructions for these evaluations.

A good example of decentralized growth by acquisition was given by one group which through a large number of acquisitions has been transformed from a home-based industrial group to a multinational within the office equipment industry. The acquisitions have been initiated from business level, which had the market contacts, and evaluated in cooperation with divisional managers. In fact, when the new group management made two "strategic" acquisitions these acquisitions caused many problems. Another industrial group which has been transformed in a similar way evaluated all acquisitions at corporate level. Why these groups chose different ways to handle their acquisitions is unclear.

Reorientations The strategic development of a company used to be characterized by strategically relatively calm periods, interrupted by periods of crises and strategic change (Chandler, 1962; Hedberg and Jönsson, 1977; Whittington, 1989; 1991; Segelod, 1995). As long all goes well few companies would question the present business formula and develop new formulas and strategies (Burgelman, 1983b; Detrie and Ramanantsoa, 1986). Instead success tends to strengthen the belief in the present formula of success. The doubts and reorientation ensue when all no longer goes well, when management anticipates or experiences a permanent decline in demand; such insight often comes in connection with one of those recessions that the economy seems to encounter with some regularity (Whittington, 1989; 1991).

However, a decision to reorient the resources of a company into more attractive areas has to be approved and sponsored by top management. The idea of a new formula may originate on the business level, but it is not difficult to find examples of reorientations where top management was directly involved in the development of a new strategy or even took the initiative for ventures in new areas through acquisitions or sponsored internal development (Normann, 1971; 1975/77; Miles, 1982; Allaire and Firsirotu, 1985; Segelod, 1995). Well-known examples are General Electric's shift from traditional electric products to computer services and factory automation, Sears, Roebbuck and American Express's entry into the financial service markets, and Philip Morris's entry into the beer and soft drinks industries.

Restructuring and coordinations Some Swedish groups on mature markets have taken on the role of restructuring an industry. They have acquired competitors and coordinated production. This has meant divestment of products, product lines and companies, reallocation of production and also investments to enable such reallocations and divestments; as these reallocations are planned above business level also the investments can be said to be initiated at higher levels.

Empirical studies of restructuring and divestment decisions have shown that such decisions are reached in an iterative process of impetus. The most influential actors proved to be the coordinators one level above the divested unit, who however, did not inform the divested unit of their conclusions and plans before the decision process was completed (Nees and Danielle, 1978-79; Gertman, 1988). These conclusions were on the whole confirmed by the interviewees.

A similar need for coordination to optimize a production system exists in infrastructure systems like roads, railroads, electricity and telecommunication systems. It is then not feasible to rely only on investment requests coming from below. It is also necessary to have a plan for the whole production system, which means that investments might be prompted by e.g. the analyses made by a central staff unit.

A parallel at plant level is the restructuring of a production plant intended to give an old plant a better lay-out. If a company for half a century adds on new systems and improvements to a plant there will often come a time when the opportunities for additional profitable contingent investments are exhausted. A new, more rational plant lay-out is then needed to provide better logistics and thereby create opportunities for future profitable additional investments.

Other types of investment There are several other types of investment which may be initiated at the corporate or divisional levels. Market investments and major investments projects such as a new plant or product line may be initiated and handled by managers and staff units on divisional level. A higher level may be pushing strategic initiatives to reduce tied up capital, delivery times, investments in a certain market etc, initiatives which may generate investments on lower levels. It should also be observed that some types of investment are normally more centralized. Funds for R & D are in some groups allocated from corporate level, and market investments handled on divisional level. Moreover customer contacts in, e.g. companies selling infrastructure investments to governments, are partly handled by top management, making them more involved in decisions initiating investments.

Misfit between the organization and its environment It is possible to consider this question of the level of which investments are initiated as a question of which type of misfit prompted the investment. Bower (1970) held that investments are initiated by a discrepancy between the demand imposed on production and the status of existing production equipment, i.e. a misfit between the business formula and the means of production. This ought also be the case for the large group of reinvestments, quality and productivity improving investments which are forced through from within the company by production managers. However, it does not apply to all investments, and we have indicated particularly domain- and structure-changing investments such as acquisitions and the reorientation and restructuring of groups and companies. Such investments can often be said

42

to have been initiated by corporate or divisional managers who perceived a misfit, not between the business formula and the means of production, but between actually experienced or anticipated demands imposed on the company or group, and its structure, business formula and means of production. And even if such domain-changing investments are initiated at the business level they must always be sanctioned by top management and the board. Furthermore we also have the situation when customer contacts are handled on levels above business level and when investments can be said to be initiated as a consequence of these market contacts.

4 The investment manual

Many companies and groups have put down their investment procedures in writing. The most commonly used term for this document is perhaps "the capital budgeting manual", although both American (Mukherjee, 1988) and Swedish groups use many different terms for this as well as for other issues treated therein. The confusion of languages is great. Even the term capital can be somewhat misleading as many companies use the manual also for intangible and expense type of investments. In these cases investment manual would be a more appropriate term.

Postal surveys by Klammer (1972) and Klammer and Walker (1984) show that almost all major U.S. companies use standard forms for invest-ment requests. The figure was 97 per cent already in 1970, and is slightly higher for investments approved by middle managers than for those ap-proved by top management. Pike (Pike, 1982; Pike and Wolfe, 1988) in two postal surveys asked major U.K. companies if they had "an up-to-date capital budgeting manual". The answers revealed an increasing use of such documents within British industry, from 65 per cent in 1975, to 76 per cent in 1981 and 84 per cent in 1986. Mills (1988c) and Mills and Herbert (1988) could in another British study combining a postal questionnaire and inter-views conclude that

> [f]urthermore, these interviews revealed that the techniques required to be used and the importance assigned to them were usually specified within the capital budgeting *manual*. (Mills and Herbert, 1988, p. 77)

Still, there are very few studies of capital budgeting manuals. The author could only identify four such studies, two American and the two Swedish. The first seems to have been made by Istvan (1959; 1961a; b) more than

44

thirty years ago. He interviewed financial executives and studied capital budgeting manuals in forty-eight large American companies.

A more recent American study was undertaken by Mukherjee (1988). He sent a request to Fortune 500 companies "to send documents pertaining to their capital investment policies and procedures", but only received sixty complete manuals. Provided that all 500 companies had a manual this means a response rate of 12 per cent.

Turning to the Swedish language area there are, as stated in Chapter 1, two major studies of capital budgeting manuals of Swedish companies. The first was carried out by Renck (1966), who in 1964 collected manuals from twenty-eight large Swedish companies. In 1977 this study was replicated by Tell (1978) who collected manuals from thirty large companies of which twenty had been included in Renck's initial study.

Besides these four studies Weaver (1974) presented the capital budgeting manual of ICI United States and Istvan (1961a), Renck (1966), Bower (1972), Tell (1978), Claesson and Hiller (1982), Mukherjee (1988) and Wilson (1988) examples of project evaluation forms, and Marshuetz (1985) the administrative routines of American Can for allocating capital. Marshuetz' description accords fairly well with many of the groups investigated in this study, while Weaver's manual belongs to a company with large staff units, a *rara avis* in Swedish groups of today.

As there are so few studies of investment manuals there is reason to ask oneself whether the manuals used by non-Swedish groups are different, but according to the respondents such is not the case. The reason is that multinationals cannot diverge too much from international practice. Employees from different business cultures must be able to use the manual and understand the rules of the game.

The purpose of the investment manual

Capital budgeting and the discounted cashflow technique were hailed in the 50s as one of the major advances in management techniques. It was probably also then that the first companies introduced such techniques and an investment manual. Renck (1966) assumed that his companies had introduced their manual in the late 50s or later, and we know that some of today's users introduced theirs in the 60s.

Renck's respondents told him that the requester formerly designed their requests for appropriation and presented the data which they themselves adjudged suitable. This situation was perceived as unsatisfactory. Therefore, written instructions and forms were developed to ensure that the investment request always contained those data which the decision makers considered relevant. This standardization of assumptions, calculations and presentation also had the positive effect of rendering the requests more reliable and easier to rank. These experiences led Renck's respondents to point out the

45

following three purposes with their manuals: (1) unitary appraisals, (2) the assessment of the advantages of individual investment projects, and (3) the ranking of investment requests based on their advantages. When Tell (1978) analysed manuals thirteen years later he could conclude that only about half the companies defined the purpose of the manual, and that the purposes stated were still the same as the three which Renck (1966) had described.

Today a partly new picture has emerged. No less than 22 of the 29 groups begin their manuals by explaining why the manual exists and should be followed. Thirteen of these state the three traditional reasons, four that unitary rules are necessary to follow investments up and two say that they need to estimate the value of the assets of the company (see Table 4.1). In addition, an array of new purposes has appeared. The classification thereof indicates that six manuals in one way or another emphasize that it is necessary to follow the instructions given in the manual because it is thereby easier to estimate, monitor and plan the future capital requirements of the group.

Table 4.1
Purposes of the investment manual

Unitary principles for evaluating and ranking investments whereof		13
unitary appraisals	6	
evaluating investments	9	
ranking investments	2	
Asset determination and follow-up whereof		4
asset determination	2	
follow-up	4	
Financial planning		6
Strategic planning and control whereof		11
strategic planning	8	
investment coordination	6	
Create a uniform group language		3

Notes: Based on 22 manuals. A manual can state more than one purpose.

A second additional purpose comprises strategic planning and control. Eight of the manuals state that the rules should be followed to facilitate testing of the investment request against the business formula and strategies, and six mention coordination of fixed investments with investments in markets, R & D and other fixed investments within the group. Finally, we have three which emphasize the role of the manual in creating a common way of describing and thinking about investments and thereby a platform for discussing investment issues.

It would be wrong to say that one group of companies stresses one of the purposes mentioned, and another group another. However, in general it is the small groups which do not give a reason, and the multinational groups which have introduced the three new purposes financial planning, strategic planning and control, and creation of a uniform group language.

What is at the bottom of these shifts in meaning? First of all it should perhaps be remembered that the manual serves different purposes for different employees and levels of a group. To evaluate, rank, and follow up investments is usually incumbent on the divisions. Unitary principles are needed to compare investments, communicate and discuss investment issues, and thus a prerequisite for the coordination of investments which occurs on divisional and higher levels. Finance is centralized. Companies are not allowed to raise their own external finance without the approval of the group's financial manager. Financial planning and control is a purpose of interest to the corporate level, as is of course also strategic planning and control. The old purposes had to do with the evaluation and ranking of investment requests, the new with coordinations and assessments which partly are done above divisional level.

The recorded shift in meaning reflects the structural changes which Swedish industry has undergone during the last four decades; from relatively small companies with a functional structure and organic growth, towards divisionalized multinational groups with far greater growth by acquisitions. It seems probable that the assessment of investment requests was more centralized in the early 60's and that it was decentralized to the divisions when many Swedish corporations developed a multidivisional structure during the 60s and 70s. This change separated the functions of different levels of the group, and, *inter alia*, gave middle managers an important role in coordinating investments.

These changes became still more prominent when the interviewees were asked about the purpose of the manual. They emphasized the role of the manual for financial planning, strategic control and the development of uniform rules and a common language within the group, which is hardly surprising as the interviews were held at the corporate level. In particular representatives of those multinational groups which had evolved through international acquisitions emphasized the importance of the investment manual and other written routines in creating uniform rules of the game and a group language whereby all concerned could easily communicate and discuss investment issues. A few quotations serve to illustrate these points.

> The advantage of having written routines is that you have something to put in the hands of new employees when you buy a company.

> The purpose is to have people to think along the same lines.

The purpose of the investment manual is that everybody should know the rules of the game, and learn how to make investment requests.

It is an instrument of control. We have to speak the same language, to refer decisions to the right level. It is very important to be in control of expenditures. We are such a large group that we could not take in the whole situation without these instructions.

First of all, investments are the most important instrument by which the board can direct and control the strategic direction, and another important purpose [of the manual] is to have a similar treatment of all investments so that all know where they stand. As the board is made up of representatives of the executive part of management. It is essential that it look the same in all companies. There are so many companies involved that there must be certain formal guidelines and instructions. A minimum requirement on how appraisals are made, presentations, follow-ups. An investment request is also in principle a commitment from the manager signing it; I believe in this; This is the way it will turn out. Then, it is up to the person to prove it.

Which groups have an investment manual

Pike and Wolfe's (1988) study of U.K. groups showed that the user frequency for investment manuals varied according to line of industry between 78 and 94 per cent. Moreover that groups with a large capital budget more often had a manual and that "nearly all of the largest firms" had a manual (Pike och Wolfe, 1988, p. 44). The size of the capital budget and group is obviously important.

Then, what about Swedish industry? The interviews showed very clearly that investment appraisals and requests are made in all companies; however not all groups have put these procedures on paper. Still, with some knowledge of the business areas of groups listed on the Stockholm Stock Exchange, it is not difficult to guess which groups use a manual. All major groups within the engineering, pharmaceutical, power and forest industries do so, and also some conglomerates and major firms in other industries. These are groups which have many, and a large volume of, fixed investments. However, there are exceptions to this general rule which seem to pertain to

- the investment manual as an instrument of decentralization
- the homogeneity of the group
- the relative importance of fixed investment
- the initiative to introduce an investment manual

The investment manual as an instrument of decentralization If investment decisions, or a specific type or aspect of investment decisions, are not decentralized then there is no reason to commit the practice to writing. The manual makes it possible to decentralize investment decisions and still retain a certain degree of control. The two shipping groups are good examples of this. They both have very large fixed investments, but as all investments are evaluated and decided by top management and their staff, there is no need to put the practice which might have evolved onto paper.

Another example was given by a small divisionalized engineering group on the otc-list. This group had a dominant owner and active chairman of the board. There was no investment manual. It was not needed as the owner decided on all investment issues, as the financial executive of the group explained. One can see this group as an example of a corporation where the owner and management functions had not yet been separated.

It can be of interest to notice that the board of directors in six of Istvan's (1961a) forty-eight major U.S. corporations finally approved or rejected all investment requests. Eliasson (1976) and Scapens and Sale (1981) also observed large individual corporations which did not delegate decisions on investments. However, the shipping groups and the owner controlled engineering group were exceptions, and as major companies have grown and been decentralized it is reasonable to assume that this practice is far less common today than when Istvan did his study.

A third example was given by a divisionalized textile group with relatively large fixed investments of which it was said that

> the chain of command is so short and informal that it works without an investment manual. I suppose that nobody has found it worth while to draw up a manual, but there must be an appraisal before we can decide on an investment. ... Our company is rather informal and oral with regard to this issue.

This group can be classified as homogeneous. Its growth has been organic. All its production units are in Sweden. Employee turnover has been low and communication is informal. Investment appraisals and requests are made. The maker of the request turns to old investment requests for guidance, and if he or she feels uncertain, then they phone the head office.

The homogeneity of the group The opposite situation is found in those multinational groups which have grown through international acquisitions and thereby taken over employees from many different company cultures. In these heterogeneous groups the investment manual is adjudged indispensable to control investments and create a common approach and group language by which investment issues can be communicated and discussed.

However, there is a limit to how heterogeneous are the business areas a certain manual can serve. Thirty-nine of the fifty four groups had an investment manual, but five of them had abolished the group manual and allowed business areas and divisions to develop their own. Two of these five groups had replaced the manual by a short investment policy document.

Other rather heterogeneous groups have couched the group manual in general terms and allowed lower units to develop specific instructions if they find this necessary. Already Renck (1966) mentions that supplementary manuals may exist on lower levels, but neither he nor Tell (1978) reports any examples thereof, so that we may assume that this practice has become more common. The reasons given for choosing a diverse or heterogeneous business structure have either been that the group has acquired other companies and refrained from integrating their investment procedures, or that the preconditions for the business areas have been so different that it was considered unwise to use a common manual.

At least ten of the major groups have supplemented their manuals with a shorter document with many names which will be termed "a templet for board decision". This templet is a one to three pages long document stipulating how investment requests presented to the group board - in a few of the groups all requests presented to a board - should be drawn up; which questions should be treated and in which order. For a fictitious example see Appendix B.

Some of the groups emphasize that the principles stated in the manual also apply to the templet, others have developed supplementary instructions for investment requests presented according to the templet. Soft data are more heavily emphasized, as is the importance of placing the investment in its context; the requester is thereby given more freedom to design and adjust the appraisal to the decision situation. Istvan (1961a) talks about free forms and fixed forms. The templet resembles the free form in that it offers the developer of the request this greater freedom. Renck (1966) and Tell (1978) give no examples of such forms, and perhaps some of them have been introduced during the last decade. The dividing-line between a detailed templet, an investment policy document, and a traditional investment manual is today vague, if it exists at all.

The relative importance of fixed investment The third point could be illustrated by a large multinational group. This group has considerably larger investments in development projects and markets, than in production equipment. There is a manual for investments in machinery and other types of production equipment but as these investments ensue more and more from decisions to develop new products and invest in certain markets the manual has lost some of its significance. This might explain why the Swedish service industry does not have investment manuals; fixed investments are enforced by intangible investments.

The initiative to introduce an investment manual An investment manual is always somebody's baby. There must be somebody who finds it worthwhile to make the effort necessary to develop a manual, as well as to change a manual in use. This could explain why some of the smaller groups on the otc-list had a manual and some did not, and also why the previously mentioned textile group did not have a manual; nobody had taken the initiative to develop one.

Pike and Wolfe (1988) found that more and more British companies between 1975 to 1986 considered themselves to have "an up-to-date capital budgeting manual". No such increase has been observed in Sweden. Most of the major companies with substantial fixed investments had developed a manual already in 1964 (Renck, 1966), and those which had not would soon do so. Then the market became saturated, and this seems to have been the case also in the U.S. Already in 1960 84 per cent of the Fortune 500 companies used "standard forms", a figure which in 1970 had increased to 97 per cent (Klammer, 1972; Klammer and Walker, 1984). Few corporations have introduced an investment manual during the last few decades; probably more which have abolished the group manual. The steep increase reported from the U.K. goes against the trend, or should it just be interpreted as a measure of the fact that companies have come to update their manuals with greater regularity.

Investments treated according to the manual

As reported in Chapter 2, fixed investments are today in many groups smaller than investments in markets and R & D. This development towards more intangible investments, which has been highly perceptible in the engineering groups, causes problems as the manual was originally devised for investments in machines and production equipment. Some users have therefore

- abandoned the accounting based definition of an investment,
- decided that the manual also covers certain types of intangible investments,
- developed special manuals for certain types of intangible investments.

From an accounting point of view, an investment is an expenditure which can be included among the assets and depreciated according to a plan; this seems also to have been the dominant definition in the 60s (Istvan, 1961a; Renck, 1966). Today, however, Swedish groups seem to have abandoned this definition to include in the initial outlay also certain kinds of expenditure associated with the implementation of the investment project; expenses which are not capitalized but included in an expense budget. Twenty-three of the manuals are clear on this point.

An investment has earlier been defined as expenditures which can be capitalized. However, the definition has been somewhat vague and varied within the group.

The new rules state that the decision-making and review process refer to both capitalizable expenditures and expenses associated with the investment project and larger non-recurrent expenses. Both types of

51

expenses shall in the statement of income be referred to extraordinary expenses.

One consequence of the definition is that capital budgets must be extended with expense budgets.

Another change is that certain groups, particularly the multinational engineering groups, today state that also certain kinds of intangible investments shall be handled as if they were capital investments and according to the manual (see Table 4.2). This change can also help explain why todays manuals are couched in more general terms, or are more flexible and applicable to different types of investment, if we prefer to consider them from another angle.

The routine is not intended to cover everything. It must be possible to sidestep it. After all, it is not intended to stop investments. It is intended to be a help so that we know what is going on, and to help the units to think the proposal through a little better. The routine must not be totally inflexible; to say that this investment is not in the investment manual so you cannot make such an investment. That is not the way we work.

Table 4.2
Types of investment covered by the investment manual

Machinery, land and property		29
Certain kinds of intangible investments whereof		14
product development	8	
market investments	7	
expense investments, unspecified	3	
in-service training	1	
Leasing		17
Acquisitions		2
Separate manual for		
R & D	3	
acquisitions	2	
FMS investments	1	

Notes: Based on 29 manuals. The number of separate manuals might be higher as such manuals were not specifically requested.

Yet further groups with large investments in acquisitions and R & D have developed written routines for such investments. The total number of such "manuals" is probably under-estimated in Table 4.2, as such manuals were not requested for. However, it may be of interest to note that, in accordance with what was said earlier about the manual as an instrument of decentralization, the two groups which have developed manuals for the evaluation of acquisition candidates have both decentralized this work. Some of the groups which have made a great many acquisitions do not have such a manual, the reason being that acquisitions are handled centrally.

Manuals or written instructions can of course also be developed for other types of intangible investments. Wallén and Sjöblom (1990) describe the system of employee competence development used by the Ericsson group, a major type of investment for many companies; moreover one of the bank groups in the study was developing a manual to help them decide on and rank investment requests for employee education and training. The development seems to have gone from manuals for machine investments, to more general manuals for investments in machinery and expenses, perhaps we are now witnessing a new step in this process when procedures and manuals are developed for those kinds of intangible investments which are most important to the firm in question.

The content of the investment manual

One way of achieving an overview of the content of the manuals is to count pages. Most manuals contain rules for the decision-making process for investments, the limits of authorization, chains of reporting, system of pre-approval review, division of responsibility, one or several forms and instructions for their filling in and the requirements for investment requests. Some of the manuals also contain educational material, advising users on how to discount and calculate different investment criteria, examples of filled in forms and investment requests, check-lists, and instructions for the review of current and implemented investments. The size of the manuals varies between three and 64 pages, with a median of 18 pages, as shown in Table 4.3, the number of forms ranging between one and nine, with a median of three. The variance is great. Some manuals are detailed in some areas, and others in other areas.

One of the changes which Tell (1978) noticed was that educational material was less common in 1977 than in 1964. This development has continued. Today only two of manuals still have the character of textbooks, and these two are those with the earliest dating. Thus, it is generally assumed that the requester knows how to discount a cash flow, estimate the payback period, net present value, and internal rate of return.

> This is about one year old. It is after all a development of the old routine which we had earlier. I have tried to keep it rather thin also, not to include too much. Those who really want to learn more can turn to the books.

The quotation also illustrates the development in another respect. Twenty-five of the manuals are dated. Wholly ten are dated 1990, viz. the year in which they were collected, and the median for all manuals is one year or

53

1989. The median age for Tell's (1978) manuals was four years, which in fact was a higher age than Renck (1966) recorded in 1964. However, companies seldom introduce completely new evaluation techniques or manuals. Only seven of the twenty companies which remained in Tell's (1978) follow-up study had altered their procedures, and only five had made any significant changes. Companies seldom develop completely new routines. Instead they up-date existing routines, mostly by adjusting limits of authorizations and the division of responsibility, more and more often in preparation for the annual budgetary control process; this is probably the reason why today's manuals are of so late a date.

Table 4.3
The content of the investment manual

	Number of manuals	Number of pages Median	Min-Max
Definitions and descriptions of the decision-making process	28	3	1-37
Instructions for the filling in of forms	27	6	1-19
Forms	25	3	1- 9
Educational material	17	3	1-34
The size of the manual	29	18	3-64
The size of the manual excluding educational material	29	16	3-42

Notes: The content of 29 manuals has been classified into four categories. One manual consist of three to 64 pages with a median of 18 pages. The median becomes 16, if the educational material found in 17 of the manuals is excluded.

Systems of classification

Early observers of industrial practice (Dean, 1951a; b; Istvan, 1961a; Lundberg, 1961; Barna, 1962; Cannon, 1966) noticed that firms do not rank all investments against each other. Instead they classify investments, allocate capital to classes of investments, and allow the assessment of the investment to be influenced by the class to which the investment has been assigned. Remarkably little has been written about this practice from a theoretical point of view, at least considering its widespread use and unwavering popularity (e.g. Fremgen, 1975; Rosenblatt, 1980; Gitman and

Mercurio, 1982; Klammer and Walker, 1984; Pike and Wolfe, 1988). Nor does there seem to be any agreement on the basis for such classification systems, or why they are used.

Disregarding size as a basis for classification Tell (1978) informs us that the average manual classified investments into four classes. Today twenty-four of the manuals classify investments and there are on average eight classes per manual; median six. Why the number of classes has doubled is unclear, but one reason why four of the groups have very many classes is that they classify investments in two steps.

As an example, one of these companies starts by classifying the invest-ment request as "new investment", "reinvestment", or "environmental control investment". Then the same investment is classified as either "machines and equipment", "office equipment", "land and buildings, real estate", "company-owned moulds", "cost projects", or "other" ("administra-tion, including accounting, employee relations, finance, communications etc, research and development, technical - customer - support, sales, produc-tion, and service").

It is difficult to generalise about classification systems as no group uses exactly the same system. However, there seem to be two or three different bases for classification.

First, we have the distinction between, on the one hand, replacement or upkeep investments, and on the other, investments in new capacity, products or markets. Already Dean (1951a; b) noticed this division and Istvan (1961a) and Barna (1962) found that most companies used it. All classifica-tion systems express this distinction in one way or another, between what could be termed operative and strategic decisions.

Secondly, we have systems which divide investments with regard to functions, e.g. computers, land and property, machinery, education, etc.

The third and last base for classification is clearest in one of the most multinational groups of the sample. This group has introduced a classifica-tion scheme which reads: "mandatory", "environment", "capacity for maintaining the market share", "new generation product", "flexibility and reduction of setting and leadtime", "market share increase - capacity", "market share increase - marketing & sales", "new business - new customers or applications".

This system of classification is partly built on organizational capabilities, a term usually used to denote specific organizational combinations of production equipment, human competence, and administrative procedures, routines and information systems etc. which are essential to the company's ability to make good on the markets where it is competing. The ability to generate new generation products, maintain a high market share, win new customers and increase flexiblity in the production system can been claimed to be important for the success of this group.

It often happens that an investment has more than one purpose. Do not make a split-up in such cases. Attribute the investment to the predomi-

55

nant purpose which as a matter of fact prompted the investment. The other purposes are by-products and should be indicated as other benefits.

It has already been pointed out that investments often have more than one purpose (Lundberg, 1961; Gandemo, 1983; Segelod, 1986). An old machine is often replaced by a more modern version capable of producing more, more high quality products and a greater variety of products. However, in general an investment can only have one purpose according to the classification scheme of the request. Eight of the manuals make this very clear, as does e.g. that quoted above. Two state that one or several of the purposes listed on the form may be crossed out. The rest are vaguer on this point but most of them seem to prefer only one purpose.

While the practice of classifying investment requests is no doubt very popular, it is nevertheless unclear why companies use it. Piper (1980), who seems to have performed the most thorough survey of systems of classification, found thirteen different bases for the various systems proposed in the literature, and concluded that all systems of classification in some way or another expressed the riskiness of an investment. This indicates that firms may have been applying the risk-return principle of the capital asset pricing model long before it was invented, by demanding higher return from investments belonging to riskier classes of investments.

> The opportunity cost of capital varies from project to project, depending on risk. In principle, each project has its own cost of capital. In practice, firms simplify by grouping similar projects in risk classes, and use the same cost of capital for all projects in a class. (Myers, 1984, p. 127)

It is a widespread assumption in Anglo-Saxon literature that companies classify investments and use risk-adjusted hurdle rates to evaluate different classes of investments; however, the empirical evidence for this assumption is not equally convincing. Only two of the Swedish groups have issued class dependent hurdle rates. The results from surveys of Anglo-Saxon practice are very mixed - 15 to 90 per cent adjust their hurdle rate for risk according to Scott and Petty (1984) - but indicate that one third, or probably more, of the major U.S. groups do not adjust their cost of capital for differences in risk between different projects and that individual measures of risk are more common than risk classes (e.g. Gitman and Mercurio, 1982; Kim, Crick and Farragher, 1984; Scott and Petty, 1984; Ross, 1986); furthermore, that this practice is still less common in the U.K. (Pike and Wolfe, 1988), Australia (Freeman and Hobbes, 1991) and New Zealand (Patterson, 1989). The explanation is perhaps that the hurdle rate or payback is often adjusted at the assessment stage and then not always for all projects.

Turning our attention to the manuals only one of them gives any reason at all why requests should be classified; this says that the system will "provide Group Management and the Board of Directors with a uniform basis for

56

decisions" and "also provide possibilities of assessing risk and uncertainty and a better basis for ranking of priorities". The interviewees were often vague on the reason for classifying investments, although the most frequent answer was that the system makes it easier to rank and curtail the requested volume of investment to the volume approved for the group as a whole, as illustrated by these two quotations from two of the largest multinational groups.

> There are more requests than funds, which implies capital rationing. That is mostly done by payback, but by classifying investments it becomes easier to see what one can cut down on. You cannot cut down on certain commitments, others are more marginal.

> This division [the system of classification] is the criterion for analysis and decisions on the capital budget, because if reductions are necessary the company must know the consequences of cutting down on a customer commitment or quality improvement.

The classification system helps to structure the decision process (Piper, 1980) and communicate information about investments (Weaver, 1974). Classifying hundreds and thousands of minor requests summarized on one piece of paper makes it easier to handle this mass of information and create an overview of the situation. Management knows the categories of the form and this helps them to reach an opinion about the strategic direction and significance of these investments, and thereby exert financial and strategic control. Requests for really large investments, on the other hand, are in many groups presented on a templet without such a system of classification. The classification system carries information which helps managers to focus attention on important strategic projects and assign priorities when capital rationing is necessary.

One obvious problem with systems of classification is that managers cannot be certain that all investment requests have been allocated to the right category. Weaver (1974) suggested that this may explain why there is no agreement between companies on how investments should be classified. As Gandemo (1983) also remarked this can also explain why many groups do not know how much they have allocated to different classes. Investment classes are an unreliable basis for capital budgeting and the subsequent interviews revealed that in most major groups the corporate level does not collect information on how much the group invests in each class as a whole.

Division of authority

The practice of delegating capital budgeting decisions for investment outlays below a certain sum is older than the manual itself. Already Heller (1951) informs us of such fixed limits of authorization. Limits of authorization are used to specify both the right of executives and units to make investment decisions, and when an investment request has to be reviewed by a staff unit or a staff unit informed or contacted. The limit can be the same for all types of investments and companies, or can be differentiated, or the group might rely on other procedures to refer the investment request to the right level for review and decision. We shall find all these three options represented in our sample of major Swedish groups, and we also give examples of another common practice; that of defining who is responsible for what in the investment process and transferring responsibility by requiring lower levels and stations of review to sign the request.

Fixed limits of authorization At least 24 of the 29 groups, or 83 per cent, used fixed limits of authorization, which is in line with studies of U.K. and U.S. groups. Thus, studies of U.K. groups have shown user frequencies of 85 per cent (Scapens and Sale, 1981) and 77 per cent (Mills and Herbert, 1987), and of U.S. groups 75 per cent (Istvan, 1961a) and 89 per cent (Scapens and Sale, 1981). Twenty-one of these groups also state one or more of the actual limits. An example reads:

Investment amount	Approval
< 1 MSEK	Subsidiary President ...
1- 5 MSEK	Business Area President ...
5-10 MSEK	Chief Executive Officer
> 10 MSEK	[X] Board of Directors

The example given is unusually detailed. A more common practice is to state that the group board has delegated investment outlays below 10 MSEK to the CEO, and to add that "[l]imits for Business Area Managers are set by the CEO", or that "[t]he limits of authorization are set by the boards of the [X] group". In other words, it is customary not to give a complete list of limits of authorization, only the limit for group board or corporate level decision and the rules for fixing limits of authorization. The very detailed instructions on authorization levels found in U.S. groups, according to Mukherjee (1988), do not occur in Swedish groups.

The directions can also be supplemented by rules giving managers the right to use a certain amount of the investment budget for urgent investments etc. without prior approval of the request. Some of the manuals also stipulate that, for instance, a business area or division executive may embark on an urgent investment without waiting for a formal decision, if the manager had had an oral approval to do so from his/her superior or the board. Fixed limits are rarely inviolable.

If because of shortage of time it is not possible to await group board decision, investment outlays exceeding 50 MSEK can in exceptional cases be decided by a business board provided that the managing director of the business area has previously obtained approval from the CEO and chairman of the group board.

The larger the capital expenditures requested the higher the request needs to be referred. Twenty-one of the groups stated the limit for group board decision or, when such a limit was lacking, for decisions by corporate level. The limit varied between 1 and 50 MSEK (10 MSEK is approximately £1 million), and for the multinationals in the sample from SEK 4 to 50 million. One group had a considerably higher limit of probably more than SEK 100 million, as it expressed the limit as a percentage of the volume of investment.

When Gandemo (1983) surveyed the limits in fourteen major Swedish groups with large capital expenditures the limit for divisional level was on average 0.5 MSEK and for corporate level SEK 3 million. A little less than ten years later these limits were SEK 5 and 16 million respectively, disregarding the just mentioned group with a very high limit and the fact that Gandemo's sample is biased towards capital intensive groups. The groups in the two studies are not identical but limits were no doubt steeply increased during the economic boom of the 80s, especially for divisional levels. The follow-up interviews during 1993 showed that this wave of decentralisation had ceased during the recession of 1990-93. Still, these limits seem in line with, or possibly higher than, the few measures which exist of U.K. and U.S. groups (Scapens and Sale, 1981; Goold and Campbell, 1987a) at least considering the smaller average size of these Swedish groups. Scapens and Sale (1981), for instance, recorded an average limit for divisional level approval in 1980 for major U.K. corporations of £104,000 and for U.S. $136,000, or about 1 MSEK, however, also the limits varied widely and apparently more than for a similar sample of Swedish industry.

Differentiated limits of authorization Most groups require all acquisitions to be decided by the group board; some so rule for all acquisitions above a certain expenditure limit, and this seems to be the practice also in U.S. groups (Jemison and Sitkin, 1986; Mukherjee, 1988). The reason is that the group board is reluctant to delegate all decisions on the strategic direction of the companies of the group and of their business formula; They want to exercise strategic control. Furthermore, board approval might also be stipulated by company bylaws.

A less common but perhaps more interesting practice is that four groups state that also acquisitions below a fixed limit, and development projects which might alter the strategic direction of a company of the group regardless of size, need board level approval. Yet other groups have directions stipulating that product development "leading to considerable changes of product range should be reported to the Board of [group X]". A similar practice seems to exist among U.S. groups

An exception [to fixed limits] includes 'New Business' capital projects which may require the approval of the Board *regardless* of dollar magnitude. (Mukherjee, 1988, p. 33)

59

Differentiated expenditure limits otherwise seem to be less common in U.K. and U.S. groups than in Swedish. Studying major U.K. and U.S. groups Sale and Scapens (1982, p. 26) could conclude that '[o]n the whole, although ceilings increase with corporate size, they do not vary with the nature of the project or the size or focus of the division', a conclusion which has to be modified as Mills and Herbert (1987) later on found that 16 per cent of major U.K. groups had such differentiated limits. Still this is few compared with Swedish industry as a whole, as 13 of the 24 groups using fixed limits have such differentiated limits, or 54 per cent, and we then exclude decision rules for acquisitions. In addition, as most larger groups only state the limit for decisions on the group level, and allow lower units to develop supplementary administrative routines the real number can be expected to be even higher.

Differentiated expenditure limits are particularly common within the multinational engineering groups. Many of these groups have a lower limit for investments in telecommunication equipment and computer hard- and software, or what is called information technology, meaning that also small investments in information technology must be referred upwards for review and decision. The reason given is that they want to develop a compatible communication system and perhaps also that they regard investments in information technology as strategic investments.

> There is a strong need for coordination within the Group regarding investments in computer and communication equipment. The goal is to reduce the total costs, which can only be done if the Group's long and short-term communication strategy is followed by *all* companies. Sooner or later, special solutions for individual companies will create extra costs for the Group.

Other types of investments for which certain individual, especially major engineering, groups have differentiated expenditure limits are investments in land and property, intangible investments including R & D, market development and training, product development, certain types of machine equipment, leasing, and investments made by different divisions etc. Expenditure limits can also exist for the projection of major projects and cost overruns; if the final project cost is expected to exceed the budget by say ten per cent a new request must be approved. In addition, many groups have directions stipulating that the financial function on the corporate level must be contacted before a company enters into a lease agreement or chooses how to finance a major investment project.

There are several reasons why groups have varying limits of authorization. The corporate level wants to decentralize investment decisions without losing control over the strategic development of the companies or their choice of finance. Therefore the raising of funds and the choice of finance is centralized. Differentiated limits make it possible to decentralize decisions without losing control over the strategic decisions of acquisitions, ventures in new areas, information technology, etc.

Land and property have different expenditure limits in some groups because all their land and property is owned by a separate company. The users of space then pay a rent to this company. Similarly some groups have a leasing company in charge of all lease businesses. Finally, a third reason is probably that some types of investments need to be coordinated, so that a staff unit must review the request and sometimes also be consulted early in the process of drafting the request. The use by the multinational engineering groups of differentiated limits could then be explained by their greater need to coordinate certain types of investments at the same time as their process of decentralization is far advanced.

Non-fixed limits of authorization Not all groups have fixed limits of authorization. Studies of planning procedures (Istvan, 1961a; Eliasson, 1976; Scapens and Sale, 1981; Gandemo, 1983; Mills and Herbert, 1987) present examples of companies which manage to refer the right decision upwards without using expenditure limits, and the interviews revealed two such large multinational groups.

One of these groups is a multinational engineering group. Investment requests are ranked in investment committees on the divisional level. The investment committee decides whether the request is of such 'strategic importance' that it needs to be referred upwards for approval. Instead of expenditure limits group executives rely on executive meetings with those working on the committees to create a common investment policy and approach to, e.g., which investments should be promoted or referred upwards for decision.

The other group is a major forest group which previously had expenditure limits. Since then it has been decided that these limits are unnecessary as the boards of the group are in a better position to decide which decisions need to be referred upward. Corporate level is represented on the boards of the divisions, the divisions are represented on the boards of the companies, and the companies are few and relatively large. In this group it has been decided that a capital investment decision need not be referred upwards as long as the investment does not violate the business formula and agreed strategies, and the company can finance the investment itself. Therefore, a major investment need not necessarily be decided by corporate board even if it is an investment of a thousand million SEK. On the other hand, requests even for very small investments in new areas, a new market or product, might have to be sent to the group board for scrutiny and decision.

Sign in token of commitment The form and appraisals submitted in the request must usually be signed by its originator, the manager making the request, managers and staff units which have to review it:

As a token of commitment the templet shall be signed by all responsible.

To ensure that all parts concerned feel personally responsible for the investment project the templet for board decision and each investment appraisal shall always be signed by the project manager, the product line manager, and, in the case of major projects, also the CEO of the company.

Twenty-one of the manuals emphasize that the request must be signed by one or several managers, which is only one group more than those specifying when a request needs to be reviewed by a staff unit. The manuals also contain information about who is responsible for what in the definition, impetus and implementation processes. Four of the manuals are very detailed on this point, devoting several pages to division of responsibility and job descriptions, while there seems to be a connection between decentralization and the stress on individual responsibility.

Decision routines

All groups have several different decision routines with regard to investments, i.e. the requirement imposed on the appraisal, the forms used for the investment request, the channel of the request and its pre-approval review vary depending on the size and type of investment. It is difficult to determine precisely how many separate routines there are since this figure depends on how the concept of an investment routine is defined and whether business areas and divisions have developed separate routines.

The size of the initial outlay All groups impose higher demands on a capital budgeting request for a major, than for a minor investment. The manuals contain 53 routines with regard to size, 68 if it is assumed that some of them delegate investments procedures below a certain limit, as is probable. This implies 1.8 or 2.3 routines per group with regard to size, or that companies seem to have one routine for small investments and one for large investments, and sometimes also one for medium-sized investments.

For a small investment it is enough to calculate the payback period. The capital budgeting manual can normally be said to be designed primarily for small and medium-sized investments. It is for this category of investments that the manual is the most detailed. The number of forms differs from one to nine with a median of three, and many groups demand two forms in an investment request; one project request form which summarizes the appraisal and one profitability calculation form. Requests for major investments are in at least ten groups presented according to a templet. This templet gives more room for qualitative data, than the traditional forms used for minor and medium-sized investments.

Investment programmes Six of the groups have introduced a special routine for investment programmes and major investments. Such investments may not be divided up into sub-projects before a decision has been reached on the investment programme as a whole; strategic decisions shall precede operational decisions. The procedure is very similar in these six groups and well explained in the following quotations compiled from two of the manuals.

> Larger investment projects usually consist of a number of independent steps. The aim should always be to structure big projects in this way. Investment grants should be requested, and follow-ups made, accordingly.
> For investments, exceeding SEK 10,000,000, which can be split into independent subprojects, the request *should* be made in two steps:
>
> 1. *Initiative* - Presentation of the whole investment. Each subproject should be specified.
> 2. *Subproject request* - Approval of each subproject. Specific quotations from contractors should be enclosed.
>
> This means that the investment Request forms are used twice - first for the whole investment and again for the specified subprojects.
> During the implementation of larger projects, the underlying assumptions may change considerably. The information should always be as updated as possible, and new profitability calculations should be made also for the total project. Comments explaining the change in the assumptions should be given.

The initial outlay determines when this kind of routine for investment programmes is to be followed, and also when the so-called templet is to be used. This expenditure limit varies between 2 MSEK and over 100 MSEK, for the seven groups which supply such information. For some reason, these limits are often higher than the limits stipulating when board level approval is needed, although an example of the opposite also exists.

Types of investment Another basis of division is type of investment. Five groups have special forms for reinvestments, a few special forms for development projects, acquisitions, land and property, and the buy or make decision. The forms specially designed for reinvestments assume that only the costs of the options must be compared. An even more widespread practice is to have differentiated limits of authorization and pre-approval review for different types of investments, a practice which was described in detail in the previous section.

An attempt to estimate the total number of routines with regard to the rules for the investment request and pre-approval review which are described in the twenty-nine manuals arrived at a figure of approximately 200 routines, or almost seven per manual and group. Still, this is probably an under-estimation as it appears that lower levels are frequently allowed to develop their own supplementary routines if they find this suitable.

5 Cash flow determination practice

The discounted cash flow technique

When Gitman and Forrester (1977) asked managers in major U.S. groups what they considered to be the most difficult and critical stages in the capital budgeting process their answers were unambiguous. The most difficult and the most important phase was the definition and estimation of cash flow (see Table 5.1). The financial analysis and ranking of investment proposals, the implementation of decided projects and ex the post review were experienced as far less difficult.

Table 5.1
Cash flow determination is difficult

Stage	Most difficult	Most critical
Project definition and cash flow estimation	64 %	52 %
Financial analysis and project selection	15	33
Project implementation	7	9
Project ex post review	14	6

Notes: Adapted from Gitman and Forrester (1977, p. 68)

Gitman and Forrester's (1977) results were confirmed by similar survey studies by Fremgen (1973) and Patterson (1989). Notwithstanding, students of capital budgeting practice have repeatedly discovered that "[t]he details

65

of cash-flow computation are not known" (Mukherjee and Henderson, 1987, p. 81). There is a great amount of research on capital budgeting practice but most of it has been directed toward the evaluation and selection phase, and especially the cash flow definition and selection stage has remained uncharted (Ang, Chua, and Sellers, 1979; Pinches, 1982; Mukherjee, 1987; Mukherjee and Henderson, 1987; Pohlman, Santiago, and Markel, 1988). The best descriptions are still to be found in the earlier studies of capital budgeting manuals (Istvan, 1961a; Renck, 1966; Tell, 1978).

Almost all Swedish groups using an investment manual also employ a discounted cash-flow technique to evaluate investments, viz., future payments associated with the investment are discounted to a certain date to enable comparision of the cash flow of different investments. The estimates express expectations about the future. They are ex ante estimates, which is something wholly different from post-completion reviews or follow-ups which are based on ex post estimates. Cost overruns and other deviations between plan and outcome are thus differences between ex ante and ex post estimates.

The discounted cash flow technique as such is simple, but often difficult to apply as it presupposes an ability to transform expectations about the future into a reasonably accurate cash flow projection. The method requires the appraiser to

- make a reasonable good projection of the future cash flow associated with the investment.
- separate the cash flow caused by the investment from those caused by other investments; the problem of interdependences.
- estimate the opportunity cost of funds and discount the cash flow using this discount rate.

The appraiser's ability to satisfy these requirements varies depending on the type of investment and the appraiser's knowledge. It is generally easier to make the projection when the appraiser and his/her company have previous experience of the type of investment under consideration. Reinvestments are therefore easier to assess than expansion investments, as the payments can be estimated by analysing past costs and revenues. Cash flow estimates of investments in new areas and intangible investments are particularly difficult and uncertain, and this is of course a reason why companies classify investments.

The payments caused by the investment are usually divided into initial outlays, yearly payments and receipts, working capital, and salvage value. The capital investment, for instance a machine or plant, causes payments in the beginning of the period of calculation while the machine is paid for, installed and run in. Later on supplementary investments are normally needed for repair and maintenance.

The yearly payments are, on the one hand, the payments which the firm can expect from sales of products, on the other those needed to operate the machine. An investment in a machine will tie up capital in accounts receivable, accounts payable, and inventory depending on how payments are handled. These changes in working capital can be allocated either to the capital investment and salvage value, or to the yearly payments.

An appraisal has a period of calculation. This period might be shorter than the economic life of the investment, and in such case a salvage value should be estimated. This salvage value might be either positive or negative. A good example of the latter is nuclear power stations which must be decommissioned when wound up and nuclear fuel which has to be stored and reprocessed.

The concept of payments and receipts

Readers of investment manuals are confronted with a mixture of terms, like payments and receipts, incomes and expenditures, costs and revenues. The concept of payments and receipts is associated with the time of payment, income to the date when an invoice for a product is sent and expenditures to the time when an invoice is received. Costs and revenues, on the other hand, are associated with performances achieved and resources used up, i.e. they are not tied to a specific occasion but to a continuous process.

Investment theory makes it very clear that the proper measurement to use when calculating a cash flow is payments and receipts. However, it is difficult to collect information about all payments. Companies therefore turn to their accounting system and use costs and revenues, or with regard to the basic investment, expenditures. This solution is chosen partly to make it easier to collect data, partly to integrate investment requests and follow-ups with the company's accounting system, or as one of the groups explains:

> An investment shall in principle be described using expected payments. ... However, in the appraisal costs and revenues are used. In this way, agreement with accounting system and budget is achieved, which makes it easier both to appraise and to review investments.

Although this and other interview studies (Honko, 1966; Renck, 1966) have demonstrated that companies do not use payments, many groups do mix the terms in their manuals, as shown by Table 5.2. Eleven of the groups use the terms costs and revenues consistently throughout the manual, two incomes and expenditures, and five payments. Yet another two use payments when writing about discounted cash flow techniques, but costs and revenues when advocating payback calculations. The remaining nine manuals either mix the terms inconsistently, or are couched in such general terms that it is difficult to know which concepts they actually direct appraisers to use. The figures for 1977 are similar.

67

Table 5.2
Concepts used in defining the cash flow

	1990-91	1977
Payments	7	6
Income and expenditures	2	1
Costs and revenues	11	15
Miscellaneous	9	8
Sum	29	30

Notes: The figure is based on 29 manuals and Renck (1978).

The initial outlay or capital expenditures

Capital expenditures as a concept When Istvan (1961a) and Renck (1966) did their studies most of the companies defined an investment as expenditures which can be depreciated. Today all manuals also include certain expenses in the initial outlay. An example of such a definition is:

> The capital investment includes all payments made until the investment is in operation. This comprises all payments due to the procurement of equipment, installation and testing.

After the decision to invest is made, it can take several years to implement an investment. Fifteen of the groups have forms which allow the requester to distribute the capital expenditures over several years. In 1977 the figure was fourteen, and it is not surprising to find that this procedure is common in the forest industry and other groups which often carry out major investments. The forms which require the capital expenditures to be allocated to one specific year are either intended for minor investments, or must be supplemented with a more detailed cash flow diagram if the implementation of the investment stretches over more than one year.

The determination of the project budget To avoid unpleasant surprises and cost escalation it is essential not to omit any items from the project budget. This is a major problem when trying to estimate the correct investment expenditures. Most manuals therefore try to help their investment appraisers to identify all the relevant budget items. They do this by supplying forms with lists of budget items which may belong to the initial outlay of the type of investments that the group has, separate check-lists, and instructions to think the project through carefully so that no expenditures are forgotten. To exemplify, one of these investment calculation forms reads:

- Buying costs incl. freight, customs duty etc. or Accumulated Leasing/Rental fees

- New tools, methods & preparatory work
- Installation and transfer costs
- Costs for test runs
- Training costs
- Additional investments in present equipment/system
- Miscellaneous

Although it is important not to forget any items, only eighteen of the manuals can be said to give the appraiser very detailed instructions and help in identifying all relevant budget items. Four are totally unspecified and six are to be found in between these extremes. A plausible explanation of these differences, earlier pointed out by Renck (1966), seems to be that the more complete a list of items is, the more important it becomes that the list really is complete. The items of an investment differ from industry to industry, and it can be dangerous to rely on a detailed list if it does not fit the investment which is evaluated. It is therefore not surprising to find that many of the groups which are less detailed with regard to the capital investment, are also the groups which have more diverse business areas. One would expect at least some of these groups to have more detailed instructions developed by and within these different business areas.

A number of things can make it difficult to estimate the correct capital expenditures. We shall end this section on the determination of capital expenditures by analysing how the manuals treat the issues listed in Table 5.3.

Table 5.3
Issues in determining the capital expenditures

	1990-91	1977
Sunk cost	0	?
Testing and running in	13	25
Additional investments	8	-
Subsidies	2	>>2
Contingencies	2	9
Salvage value of replaced investment	15	22
Investment programmes	6	-

Notes: The figure is based on 29 manuals from 1990-91 and Tell's (1978) 30 manuals from 1977.

Sunk cost It is not without cost to project an investment undertaking and develop an investment request on which a decision can be based. These pre-decision activities can account for perhaps 2 to 3 per cent, sometimes even more, of the total investment expenditures of a major investment. This may be a large sum of money, but managers want to make sure that the investment decision is right. However, these costs should not be included in the capital expenditures. Only cost incurred due to the decision should be included. Investment theory is forward looking. Renck (1966) and Tell (1978) doubted whether one or two companies actually excluded these costs. Today, there is no evidence that any of the groups do so, provided that also the requester and pre-approval reviewer are clear on this distinction.

Testing and running in New plants, machines and alterations to existing production equipment, need a time of testing and running in before they can be taken into normal operation. This means extra costs for rejects, test runs, production losses and disturbances, abnormal usage of raw materials and labour, and training of labour. Thirteen of the manuals exhort their users to consider these extra costs in the initial outlay. The number was higher in 1977. Then, twenty manuals incorporated these costs in the investment amount, three in the yearly payments, and two in either of these. An earlier study of British practice (Rockley, 1973) showed that 42 per cent of the companies considered such costs. The growing decentralization and particularly of staff capacity, probably provided the main impetus for this development toward less detailed instructions.

Additional investments Plants which have been developed through several decades may eventually assume a highly complex structure with subsystems acquired at different times and used in different functions. The addition of a new machine or sub-system will affect the degree of utilization and the profitability of already existing investments. Thus when we assess the cash flow implications of the investment in question we must also estimate the changes in the cash flow of other investments consequent upon the first investment. The cash flow implications of these so-called interdependencies are in practice very difficult to determine; How do we separate one investment from another? For a survey of interdependencies in capital budgeting see Amey (1972).

Eight manuals point out that also future possible additional investments must be considered in the appraisal, whereof six discuss these interdependencies in greater detail. Three of the manuals especially stress the importance of investigating whether other machines and parts of the production equipment will have to be rebuilt and adjusted due to the investment and instruct the appraiser to include these expenditures in the initial outlay. One of them, a forest group, describes in great detail how idle capacity and bottle-necks should be valued in different decision situations.

Subsidies The authorities have tried to stimulate investments through various subsidies, cheap finance, low charges for electricity and water, subsidised transports for companies in depopulated areas, etc. All West European states have systems for stimulating investments in particularly under developed areas, the fundamental principle of this planning philosophy being of course that the companies making investments consider these subsidiaries in their investment appraisals. Although Sweden has had such subsidies for a long time the results are depressing. Only two manuals mention such subsidies, which is far less than in 1977. One of them states that such grants should be included in the investment amount, the other that they must not be. The latter group does not see subsidies as an asset which should be allowed to affect the expected profitability of an investment, as they pertain to finance. This is in line with Gandemo (1983) who came to the conclusion that government subsidies in general are of minor importance for the decision to invest.

Contingencies If project planners knew exactly what was needed for the implementation of an investment, they would probably also be able to make a very good estimate of the investment expenditures. However, the production of so detailed an estimate would in many instances be far too costly to be economically reasonable. Planners therefore tend to concentrate on the major items of the project budget together with those which are vital if the investment is to function and yield normal production as fast as possible. Many less important items are therefore costed using rules of thumb. Consequently there will be additional problems and costs which must be attended to en route. Project management allows for these additional costs, either through a budget item called contingencies, or through adding on a safety margin in the other items, or both. In 1977 nine manuals had an item called contingencies, today only two.

One explanation why fewer manuals today include such an item may be that many decision makers are reluctant to allocate money to purposes which are unspecified; it is an accountant's duty to think that it promotes wastefulness to allocate funds to project managers who do not know exactly how they will use the money. What they forget, however, is that also other items can contain contingencies. Segelod (1986) has through postal surveys and interviews with project managers endeavoured to estimate the combined size of these contingencies in budgets for major investment projects. Project managers in the public sector stated that they had included contingencies of totally 1 to 20 per cent in the project budget, and managers in the private sector 5 to 15 per cent, or on average 9 per cent.

The salvage value of replaced investment The salvage value of the old machine should not normally be subtracted from the initial outlay. The new investment does not become more profitable because it is replacing a machine which can be sold at a profit, but it becomes easier to finance. If we want to subtract the profit made on the sale of the old machine, then we must also include the yearly payments and receipts associated with that machine. What we then obtain is a so-called differential calculus. The choice stands between the net present value of the new machine, and the net present value of the old machine assuming that it could be bought for the

71

value for which it would otherwise be sold. In this situation the salvage value becomes an incremental cost.

Fifteen manuals state that the salvage value of the replaced investment should be subtracted, however, only three that this should be done only when evaluating replacement investment. The other manuals do not mention this restriction but as all these fifteen groups have many machine investments we may suppose that replacement investments are assumed. Earlier studies too (Renck, 1966; Rockley, 1973; Tell, 1978) have shown that many companies are vague on this point, and that some companies subtract the salvage value when it should not have been subtracted.

Investment programmes Six of the groups had introduced special routines for major investments and investment programmes. Their manuals state that an investment must not be divided up into investment requests for smaller investment, unless the larger investment is first approved. As for the ten groups which also supplied a templet for board decision some apply the same principles of calculation for these major investments, while others have issued supplementary instructions. For a more detailed account of this type of routine see the previous chapter. The investment programme routine is relatively new in those groups where interviews were held, and as no mention is made of such routines in previous studies, this is presumably the case also for most other groups.

Yearly payments and receipts

The determination of yearly payments and receipts The initial outlay is for most types of investments much smaller than the discounted costs during the life of an investment. A relatively correct estimation of yearly payments and receipts is therefore crucial. Unfortunately, this is also the area in which the manuals are most vague and varying. Not the least problematic is the confusion of terms.

Table 5.4 summarizes the directions given in the manuals and forms regarding the determination of yearly payments and receipts. The Table shows that 25 of the 29 manuals state that the investment request should contain a cash flow projection for the investment, and five that all requests for major investments should be accompanied by a projection of the company's statement of income and balance sheet during the first years of the investment, a practice which according to interviews is far more common for major investments than these manuals indicate but not decentralized by means of written routines. Thirteen of these manuals and forms state that this cash flow should show both costs and revenues, ten that it suffices to show only revenues minus costs, and three that it is enough to include only average revenues minus costs, viz., to calculate with constant net revenues during the period of calculation. As constant payments are more often used for small investments, the use of simplified cash flows could be expected to be more common in groups where such investments dominate and the manual is primarily intended for small investments.

Table 5.4
Determination of yearly payments and receipts

	Total
A cash flow projection is compulsory	25
The cash flow estimate should show	
both costs and revenues	10
only revenues minus costs	10
only average revenues minus costs	3
Major projects require an analysis of	
the balance sheet and income statement	5
All assumptions made in the cash flow	
estimate should be clearly stated	12

Notes: The Table summarizes what 29 manuals state concerning the determination of cash flow in investment requests.

Many manuals distinguish between the determination of cash flows for replacement and expansion investments. Replacement decisions are often based on differential calculus showing how the cost side differs for the new and the old investment. Two groups also have different forms for these two kinds of investment. However, when the investment includes expansion then also the revenue side has to be considered, which implies estimates of changes in prices and sales volume.

Five of the manuals can be said to give the requester detailed assistance in identifying all the items of the cash flow by supplying check-lists of cost items which might affect the investment, and eight others to give some form of guidance although less detailed. One of the shorter lists reads as follows:

- Pay
    - Direct labor
    - Indirect labor
    - Additional pay
- Direct materials
- Consumable supplies
- The handling of materials: freight, duty, inspection
- Tools and fixtures
- Maintenance and repair
- Rejects and waste
- Adjusting and setting-up

73

- Rents
- Power, water, ventilation
- Insurances
- Costs of marketing

Some manuals also give some assistance in identifying the revenue items; nevertheless, the number of cost items listed on the forms and in the manuals is always much larger than the number of revenue items. The explanation given is that it is more difficult to estimate revenues than costs, as these are more affected by forces outside the control of the company, and it has been suggested that this imbalance might favour reinvestments and investments in known technologies.

Thirteen of the manuals supplied some kind of check-list to assist appraisers in identifying the relevant elements of the cash flow. In the rest of the cases, i.e. fifteen manuals, it is incumbent on to the requester to define the items of the cash flow projection. The latter group includes all forest and chemical groups, i.e. lines of industry which require high competence in their technology, sometimes technical staff companies and long experience of project management. Thus it is reasonable to assume that they have excluded such lists because project management and the companies can supply this knowledge themselves. Moreover the instructions seem to be less detailed in groups where the manual is intended to cover several different types of investments.

It is also interesting to notice that twelve manuals clearly instruct the requester to state the preconditions for the investment and the assumptions made in the appraisal. The requirements vary from manual to manual, but the assumptions most often requested are those which concern the market, volume of production, sales volume, prices and the projection of future prices, the need for personnel, raw material, transports and inventory, capacity utilization and set-up time.

Joint assets An investment uses many resources which are common to many activities, e.g. administration and other common services, costs which are treated as common or overhead costs in calculations according to the absorption costing concept. However, according to investment theory only incremental costs should be considered in the appraisal, as long as joint cost is not affected by the investment, or as it is expressed in one of the manual

> [i]t is only when the company can divest a resource that a cost reduction may be credited to the investment, and it is only when it is necessary to add on a resource that it should be considered as a cost.

Twelve of the manuals mention joint costs, but only seven clearly state, as the example above, that incremental costs alone should be included in the appraisal. The fact that at least one of these groups uses full costing technique to estimate the cash flow, indicates that some companies might include joint costs in the investment appraisal. Then there is one group which adds on joint costs as a percentage on incremental costs, when the common resources are not affected by the investment. It is somewhat unclear whether joint costs are always included when they should be or whether this is corrected for in the ranking stage, but the author has seen examples of appraisals where it is not.

Profitability versus financial appraisals A distinction can be made between investment appraisals evaluating the profitability of the investment, and financial appraisals showing how an investment could or should be financed. In the former case the cost of capital is considered via the hurdle rate and restrictions on the volume of investment; in the latter by including loans, interest payments and other financial payments in the cash flow evaluation. Four manuals explicitly instruct the appraiser to disregard financial payments and another sixteen seem to exclude such payments. Some manuals are difficult to classify, and three clearly instruct users to include financial payments. One of these manuals belongs to a fast growing high-tech company and the other two to companies which for many years have had a weak economic development. It appears that shortage of cash may be the reason why they focus on the financial aspects of the investment.

Changes in capital tied-up

Investments tie up capital in inventories, accounts payable and receivable. Expansion investments, for instance, usually increase inventories and working capital, while replacement investment often have the opposite effect. One of the positive effects of the much debated investments in flexible manufacturing systems is, for instance, shorter lead and set-up times, and thereby smaller inventories.

Twenty-two of the 29 manuals instruct users to consider changes in tied-up capital when evaluating investments. Three machine groups, however, consider such changes only in connection with cash flow evaluation techniques, and not when using the payback period. Changes in tied-up capital were not systematically evaluated in 1964 (Renck, 1966). This was one factor which companies had to learn to consider between 1964 and 1977, due to the high inflation during the 70s. Six manuals did not consider changes in capital requirements. However, in later interviews in five of these groups all managers interviewed claimed to have considered such changes in connection with certain investments.

Working capital can in principle be considered in two different ways: as a payment brought either as an investment or yearly payment, or a rent. The first alternative totally predominates, as Table 5.5 shows. Which payment-oriented method is preferred should not matter provided it is used with consistency. It is important to be consistent when using ratio type criteria, e.g. the payback period or profitability index, to ensure that the requests are comparable. Fifteen of the groups use some form of ratio criteria, but there is no indication of a correlation between the use of such criteria and the method employed to consider changes in working capital.

Table 5.5
Working capital in investment requests

	1990/91	1977
Payment-oriented: Working capital is brought to the capital investment	13	15
brought to yearly payments	7	4
Cost-oriented: Working capital is treated as a rent added on yearly payments	2	4

Notes: The Table is based on 29 manuals from 1990/91 and 30 manuals from 1977 (Tell, 1978).

Another point to be remembered when adding changes in working capital to the capital investment is that the capital should be dissolved and allotted a salvage value at the end of the period of calculation. Capital which is tied up will be freed at the end of the period. However, only four of the 13 manuals clearly state that such a salvage value must be included. It may be of interest to note that eight of these groups are in the machine industry and that only the smallest mentions this salvage value. Omission of this salvage value will cause the profitability of investments which reduce working capital to be over-estimated. Case studies (Welam, 1992) indicate that this is a common error.

Two groups treated changes in tied-up capital as a rent. Their methods differ, but both use a rate distinctly higher than their hurdle rate to calculate an interest payment which is later added onto the yearly payments. The explanation which they give in their manuals indicates that the rate and practice used may be experience based.

When the investment results in a reduction of the capital tied-up in the material flow and inventory a secondary effect will be a reduction of obsolescence, storing facilities, transportation, insurance etc. For these reasons a special interest rate has to be set, normally at 25 per cent.

The period of calculation issue

The period of calculation can be determined as the economic life of an investment, as a planning horizon, or treated as a variable. The problem of determining the period of calculation is discussed, or in one way or another touched upon, in all but three of the manuals. However, although most manuals mention the problem less than half can be said to give clear guidelines on what to do, which is in line with earlier studies (Renck, 1966; Tell, 1978).

Economic life The economic life of an investment is always shorter than its technical life. Investment frequently become obsolete before they are worn out, and their technical life can often be extended through good maintenance and major repair. Twenty-three of the manuals introduce the term economic life, and five of them give a precise definition of this concept.

A problem arises when two investments of unequal life have to be compared. Then an assumption must be made regarding what the cash flow of the differential investment - viz. the cash flow pattern of one of the investments minus the cash flow pattern of the other investment - can be expected to yield. There are several models for solving this problem, but none of them can provide an answer without making an assumption about this yield when determining the optimal time of replacement. Most manuals seem informed about theory. Nevertheless, none of the three studies of capital budgeting manuals could identify a company using any of these models, apart from the groups which apply the MAPI model; a formula developed by Terborgh (1949) and Machinery and the Allied Products Institute in Washington (1950) for replacement investments and later (Terborgh, 1958) also for other types of investments. The MAPI formula compares the total manufacturing cost for the old and the new machine during the next year, and is based on experiences of how machines age.

However, calculations of economic life are complicated. Therefore, after explaining the concept most companies rely on guidelines for economic life based on earlier experiences of similar investments, guidelines which often equal the time of depreciation used for the type of investment in question. Conformity is thereby achieved between investment planning and the accounting system.

Planning horizon Another way of solving the problem is to fix a planning horizon. Investments in use after the end of the horizon must then be assigned a salvage value at the end of the planning period. Eight of the manuals recommend this method, at least for some of their investment, and eleven mention the concept of the salvage value of an investment, but only three of these instruct their appraiser always to try to estimate a salvage value. The reasons given for not including a salvage value are, first, that the salvage value is difficult to estimate realistically and therefore uncertain, secondly, the principle of conservatism in accounting, leading to exhortations to omit uncertain payments, and thirdly, that the salvage value will have very little impact on the net present value provided that the planning horizon is long enough. In consequence of the last argument, two of the groups using a planning horizon instruct the appraiser to use economic life if this is estimated to be shorter than ten years, otherwise a planning horizon of ten years. As both Renck (1966) and Tell (1978) recorded such a mixture this does not seem to be a totally unusual practice.

The period of calculation as a variable A third way of solving the problem is to treat the period of calculation as a variable and to evaluate the impact on the net present value etc of reducing or extending the planning horizon or economic life of the investment. Two manuals recommend this kind of approach, compared with three in 1977.

Disregarding salvage value A fourth way used by some of the groups is simply to disregard anything that happens after say 10 to 15 years. Provided that the hurdle rate is high enough any payments past that time limit will have very little impact on the net present value of the investment. Almost all the interviewees raised this pragmatical argument, and as said above, this seems to be a common practice especially when calculating with a time horizon extending beyond 10 to 15 years. This would mean that guidelines for calculating economic life predominate as a way of determining the period of calculation, and that the salvage value is often disregarded in long-term cash flow evaluations.

The determination of the hurdle rate

> Some manuals provide hurdle rate for computing NPVs or for comparing with IRRs. When a single hurdle rate is given, it ranges from 10 per cent to 25 per cent. Whether this rate is the firm's cost of capital or it is derived in an ad hoc manner is not clear from these manuals. Only one firm is specific: (Mukherjee, 1988, p. 31)

Our Swedish manuals are more detailed on this point. Thirteen of the manuals specify how the hurdle rate, cost of capital or cut-off rate, should be calculated. None of them uses exactly the same formula, although the formulas reveal one distinct difference, namely that between more and less multinational groups. Less multinational here denotes groups which have most of their investments in Sweden or perhaps some plants in western Europe, and more multinational those which have their production units and investments more spread out and also outside Europe. Today, at least eight of the twenty-eight groups in our study use a centrally fixed group rate, and at least eleven a differentiated rate (see Table 5.6).

Theory advocates that firms use the weighted average cost of capital (WACC) based on market values (Copeland and Weston, 1979). All the less multinational groups, using a unitary rate for the whole group, followed the recommendations and calculated a weighted average cost of capital. However, none of them uses market values. They all use accounting-based data, and, none of them apply exactly the same formula for estimating the hurdle rate.

Table 5.6
Principles for the determination of hurdle rates

	Unitary group rate	Differentiated group rate	Total
WACC	8	0	8
CBLC	0	7	7
Decentralized	0	4	4
Principle unknown	?	?	10

Notes: WACC = weighted average cost of capital; CBLC = cost of borrowing in local currency.

Studies of major U.S. groups have shown that the weighted average cost of capital is the most common measure also among U.S. groups, used by approximately 50 per cent of major U.S. groups (e.g. Brigham, 1975; Oblak and Helm, 1980; Hendricks, 1983; Gitman and Mercurio, 1982; Kim, Crick and Farragher, 1984) and also by, for instance, 62 per cent in Australia (Freeman and Hobbes, 1991). Furthermore, that only about 30 per cent (Gitman and Mercurio, 1982) of the large U.S. groups use market values, and that the ways in which the weighted average cost of capital is calculated are very numerous also in the U.S. (Gitman and Mercurio, 1982). The major difference seems to be that some U.S. groups use market values while others prefer hurdle rates adjusted to the risk of the individual project (e.g. Gitman and Mercurio, 1982; Scott and Petty, 1984). The latter practice has good theoretical support. However, it has also been criticized both on theoretical grounds (Robichek and Myer, 1965; 1966) and during the last decade for causing U.K. and U.S. firms to invest in too few risky projects. Good or bad, only two Swedish groups formally differentiate their hurdle rate with regard to project risk. They both use two investment classes and the risk premia are three and five percent. Nor do any of the groups in the study use the capital asset pricing model advocated by textbooks for twenty years, although almost all managers interviewed are familiar with that model and the theory.

A multinational company should according to theory differentiate its hurdle rate with regard to country (Shapiro, 1988). Looking at the seven more multinational groups we can also verify that they all apply different rates of interest for companies in different countries. However, they all use an interest rate determined by the cost of borrowing in local currency (CBLC) and four of the companies add a risk premium. Two have taken yet another step by letting the risk premium be determined by the debt-equity ratio of the company or the market value of the local firm; two indirect ways of calculating a weighted average cost of capital.

Looking back we can establish that in 1977 only one of eight groups used different rates for different companies (Tell, 1978). Comparing with U.S. studies we can validate that about 50 per cent of the U.S. multinationals use differentiated rates, although only about 15 per cent make borrowing in local currency their point of departure (Oblak and Helm 1980; Hendricks 1983; Kim, Crick and Farragher, 1984). Instead, most of them estimate a weighted average cost of capital for the country in question.

The interviews revealed three more groups, all truly multinational groups, which had abandoned the unitary group rate. Two of these groups do estimate their cost of capital but have refrained from communicating this rate to the subsidiaries. The reason why these three groups do not fix a rate was claimed to be that preconditions changed so rapidly and were so different for different companies, that group management did not want to fix the rate for requests which needed group level decision. How the hurdle rate used for investments which did not need group level approval should be calculated, and which rate should be used was in these three groups left to lower levels to decide. In other words, they had decentralized the choice of hurdle rate and its determination. Perhaps we could interpret the omission of details on how hurdle rates are determined in Mukherjee's (1988) U.S. manuals as an indication that the fixing of the hurdle rate less often is decentralized in major U.S. groups.

Finally, still another group should be mentioned. This always estimates the profitability of its investments using three different fixed rates to see the effect thereon of the hurdle rate.

Qualitative factors in the investment request

An investment can influence the return of a company in many different ways, giving rise to effects which can be measured in both monetary terms and such that are very difficult to assess. One of the purposes of the project planning and the capital budgeting process is to identify these effects and possibly also to evaluate and assess them. Only those which are identified can be considered in the investment appraisal and request, and only those which can be costed will be considered in the economic calculation determining the payback period or internal rate of return, as illustrated in Figure 5.1.

Factors which are difficult to price are called intangibles or qualitative factors, and eight of the manuals give a clear definition thereof. Qualitative factors are no doubt an important part of the appraisal, at least for types of investments which break new ground. Thus, divestments, for instance, can usually be assessed using accounting data while their opposite, investments in new areas, also presuppose the estimation of future sales and prices in an area where the company lacks previous experience (Häckner, 1988). The same situation prevails between reinvestments and expansion investments, although the return of reinvestments is not always quantified as they are so obviously profitable, necessary due to safety regulations, quality require-ments, delivery commitments or more or less guaranteed sale. Similarly, quantitative or hard data tend to play a greater role in decisions on reinvestments and divestments, than on those pertaining to expansion investments and especially new ventures (see Table 5.7). For the same reason soft data may be expected to become more important for decisions on strategic than non-strategic investments, long-term than short term investments, basic than contingent investments, capital than financial investments, and intangible than tangible investments.

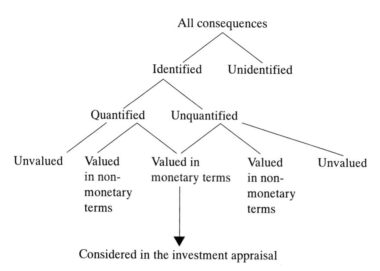

Figure 5.1   Factors considered in the investment request

Source:　　Adopted from Hägg (1979, p. 15).

Table 5.7
The emphasis on hard versus soft data

Emphasis on hard data	*Emphasis on soft data*
Reinvestments	Expansion investments
Divestments	Investments in new areas
Tangible investments	Intangible investments
Financial investments	Capital investments
Contingent investments	Basic investments
Operative investments	Strategic investments

There is no question that our groups consider the qualitative factors to be an important part of the investment appraisal, especially with respect to major and strategic investments. The investment decision is not based merely on quantitative data. All the forms have space for the requester to

81

describe the reason for the investment and place it in its context. In fact, all manuals mention the necessity of placing the investment in its context and nine of them can be said to be very detailed on this point, supplying check-lists or page-long descriptions of qualitative factors which the requester should try to identify and consider. One of the multinational engineering groups which devotes a separate chapter in its manual to intangibles writes, for instance, that

> The economic calculus only reflects the economic consequences of quantifiable or measurable factors. It is incumbent on the appraiser also to identify the unquantifiable factors and to ensure that the decision-maker is informed about these factors.

Renck (1966) and Tell (1978) also mentioned that the forms provided space for both quantitative and qualitative factors, that they used check-lists and that the qualitative factors were sometimes considered as the most important. In fact, they also describe one corporation which had a system for balancing the pros and cons of the qualitative factors into an index. Qualitative factors have no doubt always been very important for many investment decisions, even if the general impression must be that many manuals place even more emphasis on such factors today than in the 60s and 70s.

Many groups have investment classes for "security and quality improve-ments", "work environment", or simply "non-profitable investments", investments the effects of which are very difficult to quantify. Three of these groups clearly state that profitability criteria cannot be applied to these classes. One of them writes about the class "replacements and environmen-tal investments";

> for these types of investment no economic calculation is in principle needed, as the unquantifiable factors are of such great importance.

We see here that also replacement and environmental investments are not always calculated. Other types and classes of investments which some companies do not always calculate are investments necessitated by safety standards and requlations, emergency, mandatory and absolutely necessary investments as well as investments deemed indispensable for strategic reasons. However, there is no corporation in today's sample which tries to weigh together the qualitative factors into a criterion, as in the earlier studies. This weighing is obviously done by the decision makers, in the process of preparing and reviewing the investment request.

6 Profitability criteria

Both theoretical and empirical research on capital investments have focused heavily on the decision phase, particularly the criteria used to evaluate and decide on investment proposals. It is supposed that investors evaluate the net present value (NPV) of those investment options which arise and choose to go along with all investments which are expected to yield a positive NPV. An enormous number of empirical tests of this assumption have been performed, some of which will be mentioned in this chapter.

Capital budgeting evaluation techniques

Table 6.1 shows that 90 per cent of the twenty-nine major groups, i.e. 26 out of 29, in 1990-91 use an internal rate of return (IRR) or capital value based method for some of their investments. Two small, domestic market based, machinery engineering groups did not use a discounted cash flow (DCF) technique. One well known multinational which earlier used only the simple or discounted payback period (PBP), later supplemented its routines by introducing the NPV for all investments above a certain limit Thus all major Swedish groups participating in this study today use a DCF technique.

Comparisons with the earlier studies by Renck (1966) and Tell (1978) show that the changes have been surprisingly small. Nevertheless, the companies in the surveys are only partly the same. The number of companies in each industry is about the same, but many of the groups have been heavily restructured during the last thirty years. There is a remarkable stability in the use of capital budgeting techniques. A company obviously does not change its routines from one year to another unles it has been taken over and is forced to adopt the administrative routines of the acquiring firm.

Table 6.1
Profitability criteria according to the manuals

	1964	1977	1990
Payback	79 %	87 %	100 %
Simple payback	46	60	79
Discounted payback	32	27	33
Simple payback only	n.a.	7	7
Discounting methods	n.a.	n.a.	93
Discounted cash flow techniques	62	93	90
Internal rate of return	54	53	45
IRR	50	50	45
Modified IRR	4	10	0
Capital value methods	28	n.a.	67
Net present value	11	33	52
Terminal value	0	0	3
Profitability index	14	20	21
Annuity	25	10	14
Annuity index	7	10	7
MAPI	11	10	3
ARR	4	3	0
Break even analysis	0	0	3
Number of criteria per manual	2.04	2.20	2.62
Number of manuals	28	30	29

Notes: The Table is based on Renck (1966), Tell (1978) and the forms and manuals of 29 groups. Since 1990-91 one of the groups has introduced the NPV criterion for major investments.

Today's manuals often assume that the user know how to calculate the PBP or discount a cash flow, and we assume that the reader also knows. We shall, therefore, not describe the methods, the assumptions on which they rest, their theoretical underpinning and the criticism they have met. However, a few criteria are used in Swedish industry which the textbooks do not always describe and which therefore need explaining; some comments on the criteria used also need to be made.

The payback criterion All groups use either the simple or the discounted payback criterion. The simple PBP has become an increasingly popular criterion; at least according to the manuals, because it cannot be ruled out that the simple payback criterion was also formerly used by all groups in the sample although this is not stated in their manuals.

Today, the simple payback criterion is used as the only criterion for investments below a certain limit, and for medium-sized and major investments as a supplement to a DCF type of criterion. Several manuals and interviewees emphasized that it is not exactly a measure of profitability, but more of liquidity and risk, and it is probably used more in the latter sense in connection with major investments. The limit for when a DCF technique is needed ranges from SEK 30,000 to 100,000, and the limits do not necessarily coincide with the limits of authorization. One multinational which uses the discounted PBP for medium-sized investments, has in fact a limit of SEK 5 million for the use of the NPV, and another group which lacks fixed limits of authorization seems to use an often equally high limit for the use of IRR in relation to the simple PBP. The limit for when a DCF evaluation is needed is in some groups higher for replacement, than for expansion investment, with the result that most replacement investments in many groups are evaluated using only the simple PBP. The discounted PBP, on the other hand, is in ten groups used for medium-sized investments.

The PBP is a ratio criterion. It therefore becomes important clearly to define whether running in costs, working capital, salvage value, etc. should be assigned to the numerator or the denominator, to prevent manipulation of the result and enable comparison of different requests.

The manuals do not give precise information on exactly how today's companies do. Only six groups state how the simple or discounted PBP should be calculated and all use the same two formulas. When Renck (1966) did his study all but four users of these criteria supplied a formula for its calculation, and many of these formulas diverged in one way or another. For instance, of the five companies using the discounted PBP in 1964 all presented somewhat different formulas for its calculation. In those days, there were also companies which simplified the evaluation by making assumptions about how the cash flow would develop over time. There are of course also today groups which define the numerator and denominator slightly differently, and one otc-group which calculates a simplified cash flow, but the differentials between the users have no doubt been dramatically reduced in the last thirty years, and a standard approach has been developed.

The net present value criterion The NPV criterion has also become increasingly popular, although not as popular as the Table may imply. Some of the groups which use the IRR use the NPV or the profitability index (PI) to interpolate the correct IRR. Both criteria are requested on their forms, but the IRR appears to be the principal criterion for these groups. The criterion is mainly used for major investments, expansion investments, and invest-

85

ments in new areas, long-term and so-called strategic investments, for which it is important carefully to evaluate the expected streams of revenues.

The profitability index criterion The PI criterion is used by six groups and exists in two different versions:

$$PI = NPV/I$$

and

$$PI = (NPV-I)/I$$

where I stands for the initial outlay, or more correctly the present value of all capital outlays.

The first variant is used by two and the latter by four groups. In the first case, the investment is profitable if the ratio is greater than nil; in the second case, if it is greater than one. The profitability index can be used to interpolate the IRR, so its use may be expected to be over-estimated.

The annuity criterion The annuity criterion is used by three of the groups to evaluate replacement investments, often by disregarding the revenue side.

The annuity index criterion The annuity index (AI) may need an introduction as it is seldom mentioned in Anglo-Saxon books or articles. The variant used by two groups today was partly developed by a Swedish group and is defined as follows:

$$\frac{NPV \times \text{ the annuity factor}}{\text{Average capital tied-up}}$$

The yield thus calculated should exceed a predetermined excess return requirement. Observe that a measure of the cost of capital is used to discount the cash flows to a net present value and to distribute the annuities. The method is termed excess return method and the percentage calculated excess return number.

The internal rate of return criterion Both in Sweden and the U.S. (Canada and Miller, 1985) early adopters of the DCF technique preferred the IRR criterion, late adopters the NPV. Some companies in Sweden used the discounted PBP for a while. In Sweden the IRR held a strong position in the forest industry, perhaps just because these capital-intensive companies were among the first to introduce this new planning tool.

What in Table 6.1 was called the modified IRR is a joint category for companies using a predetermined rate for intermediate cash flow. We shall consider this type of criterion as it has some interesting features, and writers on capital budgeting seem to have overlooked its use. Fremgen (1973, p. 22) arrived at the result that 29 per cent of U.S. major firms "made an explicit assumption about the rate of return to be earned on reinvestment of cash receipts", and that "[a] few firms, however, attempted explicitly to estimate either a future rate of return or the future cost of capital and to use this as their assumed reinvestment rate on the current investments" cash receipts'. This method has appeared now and then in the literature, and a later panel discussion showed that there are major U.S. groups still using this practice of estimating a reinvestment rate (Weaver *et al.*, 1989).

The technique of using one rate for receipts and another for payments was previously recorded by Solomon (1956), Baldwin (1959), Heister (1962), Henke (1973), Kruschwitz (1976), Lin (1976), and Lüder (1976) while new articles appear now and then where variants of the technique are described under different names. Especially Henke's (1973) pioneering work should be mentioned.

However, as Henke (1973) and Kruschwitz (1976) have shown, the modified IRR criterion is only one of a group of criteria using different rates for payments and receipts. The ordinary DCF models assume that all payments are evaluated on the basis of the same hurdle rate. However, the same criteria can also be calculated assuming that payments to and from the project are evaluated with different rates. This so-called bank model can be useful in certain situations to model cash flow streams, but there are questions about its coupling to the theory of the firm (Göppl and Hellwig, 1973; Henke, 1974).

Still another group of DCF criteria was developed by Teichroew, Robichek and Montalbano (1965a; b) assuming that different rates should be applied to payments when the NPV etc is positive and negative respectively. This model can also be useful in certain situations to model a cash flow, but the calculations demand a computer programme.

The accounting rate of return criterion The ARR criterion has been very common among U.K. and U.S. groups. Several surveys have shown a user frequency of about 50 per cent. However, it has never seen much use in Sweden.

It was pointed out earlier that companies often use slightly different procedures for calculating their investment evaluation criteria. A good example thereof is Abdelsamad's (1973) study of the use of the ARR criterion. He could list 24 different ways of calculating yearly payments and receipts, 36 ways of calculating capital expenditures, and 11 different names for the same criterion. The only feature which many of these definitions had in common can be claimed to have been that the criterion was a ratio between yearly payments and receipts, and capital expenditures.

It should be noticed that the ARR criterion resembles the annuity index, or more precisely an undiscounted annuity index. Furthermore, that Swedish companies might calculate the return on assets (ROA) or the return on capital employed (ROCE) for companies and profit centres during the first years of a major capital investment or venture in a new area. The author has seen several examples of this although only one manual states how such an calculation should be made. However, there are also five manuals instructing the requester to submit an analysis of the balance sheet and a statement of income of the company when requesting such investments. Observe, however, that such appraisals are only done with regard to the company or unit making a major investment, and not for the ranking of individual investment requests or for the great majority of small and medium sized investments.

In interviews with top executives Gandemo (1983) observed that major Swedish capital investors in the early 80s had started to attach more weight to ROA and ROCE type of measures when evaluating major investments, and that these measures were adapted to the preconditions of the company and the local market. These observations have been confirmed. The demand imposed by multinationals on companies on different markets varies considerably, and the impact of major investments and investment programmes on the income statement of the local company has become an important criterion in many groups according to the maxim; How well they manage to choose and implement the right investments will sooner or later be seen in their ROCE.

Country differences

There are a great many postal surveys of capital budgeting techniques and investment criteria from the Anglo-Saxon countries. The user frequencies of the most common criteria in major Anglo-Saxon companies according to some of the studies made in the 80s are summed up in Table 6.2. Figures for the annuity, annuity index and other less common criteria are ignored as few studies have mapped their use.

The most striking difference between Anglo-Saxon and Swedish-based groups is no doubt the total absence of the ARR criterion in the manuals of Swedish groups, a remarkable difference not least as 67 per cent of the neighbouring major Finnish groups in 1973 were reported to use the ARR (Honko and Virtanen, 1975). How this difference has emerged is unknown but both the groups which formerly used the ARR had ties with the U.S., so that they may have adapted this criterion from American manuals. One can also surmise that Anglo-Saxon groups more often use both the IRR and NPV criteria. Apart from those observations the user frequencies are similar for major groups in Sweden and the Anglo-Saxon countries.

Multiple criteria

All but four of the twenty-nine groups which specify their criteria used more than one investment criterion; today only three, since yet another group introduced the NPV. The other twenty-five groups use, judged by their manuals, two or more criteria, according to Table 6.3.

Table 6.2
Profitability criteria in major groups

Country Year (study)	PBP	ARR	DCF	IRR	NPV	PI
Australia 1989 (a)	44 %	33 %	-	72 %	75 %	23%
Japan -1986 (b)	84	35	-	16	15	-
Japan -1988 (c)	86	68	-	20	28	-
Japan 1988 (d)	52	36	-	4	6	-
Korea 1989 (c)	75	53	-	75	60	-
New Zealand 1988 (e)	84	78	-	70	75	35
The U.K. 1980 (f)	55	56	51	-	-	-
The U.K. 1981 (g)	81	49	-	57	39	-
The U.K. 1984 (h)	92	44	-	68	51	-
The U.K. 1986 (i)	92	56	-	75	68	-
The U.K. 1989 (j)	78	31	73	58	48	-
The U.S. 1980 (f)	56	41	84	-	-	-
The U.S. 1980-81 (k)	80	59	86	66	68	-
The U.S. 1985 (l)	76	59	90	80	83	-
The U.S. -1987 (c)	71	46	-	69	64	-
The U.S. 1991 (m)	78	30	100	100	52	-
Sweden 1964 (n)	79	4	62	54	11	14
Sweden 1977 (o)	87	3	93	53	33	20
Sweden 1990-91	100	0	90	45	52	21

Notes: (a) Freeman and Hobbes (1991); (b) Kato (1986), see Shields *et al.* (1991); (c) Kim and Song (1990); (d) Yoshikawa, Innes and Mitchell (1989); (e) Patterson (1989); (f) Scapens and Sale (1981); (g) Pike (1982); (h) Mills and Herbert (1987); (i) Pike and Wolfe (1988); (j) Sangster (1993), large Scottish firms; (k) Moore and Reichert (1983); (l) Reichert, Moore and Byler (1988); (m) Remer, Stokdyk, and van Driel (1993); (n) Renck (1966); and (o) Tell (1978). All studies are based on large companies in the country concerned, e.g. Fortune 500 companies. Discounted PBP is in the Swedish studies counted as a PBP and a non-DCF criterion. There is doubt as to how the other studies have treated discounted PBP.

Most companies have different routines for different types of investments. They can for instance have different procedures for pre-approval review, a committee which assesses and ranks a specific type of investment, and

89

requirements for the investment request and the criteria used. The most common distinctions are those between minor and major investments, and between replacement and expansion investments. This means that all investments are not compared using the same decision procedures and set of criteria, as investment theory prescribes.

Table 6.3
Combinations of criteria

		A	B	C	D	E	F	G	H	I
A:	Simple PBP	2	2	1	11	5	2	2	1	12
B:	Discounted PBP	2	-		7	4	2			5
C:	Terminal value	1		-						
D:	NPV	11	7		-	5	2			5
E:	PI	5	4		5	-	2			3
F:	Annuity	2	2		2	2	-			1
G:	Annuity index	2						-		
H:	MAPI	1							-	
I:	IRR	12	5		5	3	1			-

Notes: Among the 29 groups naming potential criteria two use only simple PBP and two discounted PBP, while the other 25 use two or more criteria. The Table shows the combinations which exist.

Renck's (1966) companies used on average 2.04 criteria, Tell's (1978) 2.20 and our sample 2.62 (see Table 6.1). However, confining ourselves to the number of criteria used due to the size of the initial outlay we shall instead arrive at the figures 1.64, 1.67 and 1.83, and if we make the reasonable assumption that the simple PBP criterion is used in all groups for the smallest investments the latest figure has to be adjusted upwards from 1.83 to 2.35. This means that the average group uses one criterion for minor, and another for major investments. Furthermore, that some groups use a third criterion for medium-sized investments and that the most common criterion in that role is the discounted PBP.

These figures are in line with postal surveys of U.S. groups which show 2.24 (Petry, 1975) and 2.56 (Hendricks, 1983) criteria per group. Large groups use more criteria (Petry, 1975; Hendricks, 1983) and more so-called advanced project evaluation techniques (e.g. Schall, Sundem and Geijsbeck, 1978; Stanley and Block, 1984; Mills and Herbert, 1987; Pike and Wolfe, 1988; Patterson, 1989). Other postal surveys (e.g. Mao, 1970; Brigham, 1975; Moore and Reichert, 1983; Yard, 1987, Reichert, Moore and Byler, 1988) have shown that, for instance, utilities, chemical, petrochemical, and other capital-intensive industries use more advanced techniques, and that

U.S. multinationals use more sophisticated evaluation techniques than non-U.S. multinationals (Kim, Crick and Farragher, 1984).

It is true that smaller firms use less advanced criteria. A study of small U.S. firms (Runyon, 1983) showed, for instance, that 45 per cent used the PBP, 24 per cent the ARR and only about 15 per cent a DCF technique. However, as McIntyre and Coulthurst (1986) found in a British study of medium-sized companies, the PBP dominates both in independent and in subsidiary companies. The interviews too have shown that there are major groups which use only the PBP for investments decided by company and divisional managers, viz. in divisions which are larger than some smaller groups which use a DCF criterion. Thus it is true that several studies have demonstrated that the use of advanced evaluation techniques correlates with firm size, but this does not necessarily imply that companies in major groups use more advanced evaluation techniques than independent companies of the same size when evaluating similar investments.

The primary criterion

It has been observed that many groups use several criteria, and several postal surveys have therefore asked their respondents not whether they use a certain criterion, but which is their primary measure. Some of these studies made during the 80s are summed up in Table 6.4. This shows that the IRR is used as a primary criterion far more often than the NPV. One explanation can be the already mentioned tendency to use the NPV only for major and expansion investments, and also the use of the NPV to interpolate the IRR.

However, surveys of primary measures are difficult to interpret. Many groups have different primary measures for different types of investment. Klammer and Walker (1984) have observed this and in their surveys asked for primary measures for specific kinds of investments, but this is not the whole truth. The present analysis shows, as can be seen in Table 6.5, that far from all manuals specify a primary criterion. Only 18 of the 29 manuals clearly state that one specific criterion should be used in connection with a certain type of investment. Five manuals state that two or more criteria should always be used, and six entrust this decision to the appraiser. There may be an informal practice and lower levels can of course issue more specific instructions, but this also means that the primary measure may differ within the parts of a group. Be that as it may, the main point is that in 38 per cent of the cases corporate level does not in its written routine clearly specify a primary criterion or for which type of investments a specific criterion should be used.

One of the manuals gives no guidance at all. It merely states that the PBP and a DCF criterion should be used. Three other manuals name different criteria but make no mention of when they shall be used or if they all are to be calculated, and two scrutinize the pros and cons of the different criteria after which they leave the decision to choose technique to the appraiser. We can of course in the latter two cases guess which criteria are used, but can never be totally certain. The choice seems to a large extent to rest with the appraiser.

Table 6.4
The primary criterion in Anglo-Saxon companies

	PBP	ARR	IRR	NPV	Other
Canada 1980 (a)	25 %	22 %	38 %	11 %	4 %
Canada 1985 (a)	19	25	40	9	7
The U.K .1981 (b)	37	28	-	-	-
The U.S. 1988 (c)	21	4	58	13	6
The U.S. 1991 (d)	12	8	35	41	5
The U.S. MNC 1979 (e)	10	14	60	14	-
The U.S. MNC 1981 (f)	5	11	65	17	3
The U.S. MNC 1983 (g)	12	14	62	9	3
non-U.S. MNC 1983 (g)	31	15	34	10	10

Notes: (a) Blazouske, Carlin and Kim (1988); (b) Jones (1986); (c) Cooper, Cornick and Redmon (1992); (d) Reimer, Stokdyk and van Driel (1993); (e) Oblak and Helm (1984); (f) Stanley and Block (1984); and (g) Kim, Crick and Farragher (1984).

Table 6.5
The primary criterion according to the investment manuals

4	delegates to lower levels to choose criteria
2	describes the pros and cons of different criteria before leaving the choice of criteria to lower levels
5	State that two or more criteria should always be used
7	IRR
4	NPV
1	Net terminal value
2	Annuity index
1	MAPI
2	Discounted PBP
1	Simple PBP

Note: Eleven of the manuals, or 41 per cent, do not specify that *one* specific criterion must be used to evaluate medium-sized and major investments, and five, or 21 per cent of these, specify that two or more criteria should always be calculated apart from the simple PBP.

Another obstacle is the use of diverse business structure. Already Renck (1966) and Aggarwal (1980) drew our attention to the fact that major corporations may follow different routines in different parts of the organization. In fact, one of the changes since the last study seems to be that some groups have decentralized to business areas and divisions to develop their own administrative procedures. Both the manuals and interviews have given several examples of this, at the same time as the interviewees in such groups had vague ideas on exactly what kind of techniques and criteria may exist on lower levels. However, there also seems to be another factor counteracting the spread of diverse criteria, namely that lower levels might prefer to use the same criteria as other parts of the groups to be able to compete for funds on more equal terms, but this is mere speculation.

7 A few issues in capital budgeting

Inflation

Theory Appraisals adjusted for price-level changes can be made both in real and in monetary terms. The NPV will be the same provided that real or nominal values are used consistently. A real discount rate must be used when the cash flow is expressed in real terms, and vice versa. This applies also for evaluating changes in working capital and inventories.

Cash flows expressed in nominal terms can be transformed to real terms with the help of a relationship known as the Fisher effect: $(1 + i_r)(1 + i_{inf}) = (1 + i_n)$, where the nominal discount rate i_n consists of a real discount rate i_r and a measure of the changes in a general price-level i_{inf}, generally approximated with the consumer price index. The Fisher's effect states that the real rate of return is independent of the rate of inflation, and it is one of several models of the connection between real and nominal rents.

A great number of tests of the Fisher effect indicate that the rents for loans and bonds do not adjust perfectly to changes in the rate of inflation, and that the adjustment is still less good for the stock market. It is partly because such an adjustment takes time, partly questionable that a complete adjustment will ever occur.

When using a real rate of interest we must also express the elements of the cash flow in real terms. The price of a service or of goods used or produced by the investment can be expected to change from one period to another by the rate of i_{nx}: $a_t + a_t i_{nx} = a_t(1 + i_{nx}) = a_t(1 + i_{rx})(1 + i_{inf})$. Removing the term $(1 + i_{inf})$, we can express this price change in real terms as $a_t(1 + i_{rx})$, where i_{rx} can be either positive, or negative.

In theory it is easy to make these corrections, but in practice it is of course far more difficult, as inflation redistributes capital between savers and borrowers, between companies, the state and individuals. It is difficult to assess these redistribution effects, but one type of effects which distorts investment appraisals comprises those given by the systems of accounting and taxation as

- depreciations are made on historical purchasing prices.
- interest income and expenditures are taxed by their nominal value, which benefits borrowers.
- the use of FIFO (first-in-first-out) leads to fictitious profits on inventories being taxed.
- the need for working capital increases by inflation.

As depreciations are made on historical purchasing prices companies do not retain enough capital to replace their investments in times of inflation. This effect is to some extent mitigated by the practice of writing off assets earlier than they are used up.

Taxes are paid on nominal values of interest incomes minus interest expenditures. This makes companies in a net debt position into winners in times of inflation as they pay less tax than they should.

The use of FIFO valuation of inventory has the same effect as depreciation on historical purchasing prices, viz. that inflationary profits are taxed. This effect could be lessened by the use of LIFO (last-in-first-out) or by appreciating the value of inventories by an index.

The need for working capital increases with inflation for several reasons. Prices become more volatile with inflation, leading to more adjustment investments and investments in inventories. The need for working capital also increases as the yield from working capital and receivables unprotected for inflation decrease, which by itself causes companies to cash in their receivables faster and better utilize accounts payable.

Several attempts have been made to model and assess these distorting effects of inflation (Lintner, 1975; Ehrbar, 1979; Modigliani and Cohn, 1979; McCauley, 1980; Segelod, 1989). Tests made on U.S. data show that the U.S. industry as a whole has not been able to compensate itself for the growing need for working capital when inflation has increased. The other factors seem by and large to have cancelled each other out. However, the problem still remains that some industries, and especially capital-intensive industries, lose out and other industries win on inflation and price changes depending on the composition of their assets, investments, need for working capital and inventories (Nelson, 1976; Tideman and Tucker, 1976; Kim, 1979).

Practice In the 50s and 60s the rate of inflation varied between one and six per cent in Sweden, apart from during the Korean War when it reached 16 per cent. The cash flows were expressed in real terms and discounted with a nominal rate of interest as market rents are nominal. In major projects the cash flow forecast was sometimes adjusted for estimated future relative price changes in prices and costs for labour and different kinds of material used up. Renck (1966) found no exceptions to this practice.

By mixing real prices and nominal rents the profitability requirement became high. Most appraisers had vague or poor ideas about how changes in prices and the general price level could be considered in an appraisal. However, this did not have only negative consequences. As follow-ups were made in different monetary values an incentive to cut costs by a few per cent per year was also created; an assignment of economizing which many or at least some project managers seem to have been able to fulfil without actually knowing that they had such an assignment (Lundberg, 1961; Segelod, 1986).

The Swedish inflation took off when OPEC multiplied the oil price in 1973-74 and established itself on a much higher level of seven to 15 per cent for the rest of the decade, after which it nevertheless declined. This obliged investors to consider inflation in their appraisals, and when Tell (1978) did his study already 17 out of 30 companies included passages on inflation in their investment manuals (see Table 7.1). However, the hurdle rates remained the same and neither Tell (1978), nor later studies by Segelod (1986), Yard (1987) and Andersson (1988) could reveal a clear difference between real and nominal discount rates. Obviously the knowledge about appraisals in real and nominal terms was still vague, an impression which the author and other researchers (Bergendahl, 1980) repeatedly have had confirmed by studying and reviewing investment appraisals in both the private and public sector.

Table 7.1
Inflation in investment appraisals

| | Sweden | | The U.S. | |
	1977	1990	1981	1986
Use cash flow expressed in				
nominal terms	27 %	24 %	44 %	50 %
real terms	23	10	7	16
nominal or real terms	3	14	-	-
The manual				
unclear on this issue	3	0	-	-
does not treat inflation	43	52	49	30

Notes: Swedish figures based on whether the cash flow is specified in real or nominal terms in the manuals of this and Tell's (1978) study, U.S. figures on postal questionnaires by Hendricks (1983) and Pohlman and Santiago (1988).

Today about half the investment manuals contain passages on inflation and one fourth instruct their users to express the cash flow in nominal terms. Equally many groups require a cash flow expressed in real terms, or in real or nominal terms depending on the type of investment. However, hurdle rates are based on nominal rents and none of the groups supplying information on how they determined their hurdle rate translated this hurdle rate into a real rate. Those interviewed in groups using cash flows expressed in real terms were well aware of this contradiction but did not consider it crucial as most investments were short-term in nature. Studying the 52 per cent of the manuals which do not consider inflation we can identify two different categories of groups. First, we have the smallest groups in the sample, and secondly, the more multinational groups.

U.S. Studies based on postal questionnaires (Hendricks, 1983; Pohlman and Santiago, 1988) and manuals (Mukherjee, 1988) tell two wholly different stories when it comes to inflation. Mukherjee (1988) could in his study of U.S. manuals conclude that

> [o]nly a handful of firms specifically require that all project cost estimates reflect the expected effects of inflation. (Mukherjee, 1988, p. 31)

In direct contrast, postal surveys show that 51 per cent (Hendricks, 1983) and 70 per cent (Pohlman and Santiago, 1988) of the same Fortune 500 companies did consider inflation. Furthermore, 46 per cent of Hendricks' respondents claimed to specify company-wide forecasted rates of inflation, 44 per cent to leave the determination of inflation rates to divisions and lower levels, and 10 per cent to use both these procedures. We can here recall the statement in Chapter 3 that Swedish multinationals were very cautious in letting companies make their own assumptions about inflation and exchange rates.

Major British companies seem still more aware of inflation. Pike and Wolfe (1988) found in a postal survey that 98 per cent of their respondents considered inflation in 1986 as compared with 74 per cent in 1975, and that 79 per cent did so "mostly" or "always". The most common practice, followed by 69 per cent of the firms, was to specify "cashflows at constant prices and using a real rate of return" (Pike and Wolfe, 1988, p. 60). How this "real rate of return" was determined is not recorded.

When inflation is considered The cash flow must be expressed in nominal terms if we are to consider taxes or finance, or follow the investment up, a fact which is also pointed out in some of the manuals. Why then do not all companies make all their appraisals in nominal terms?

It was earlier said that some groups used a nominal rate to discount a cash flow expressed in real terms because they only had short-term investments. One reason why not all appraisals are made in nominal value could of course be that the investments envisaged by the manual are not particularly vulnerable to inflation. Inflation tended to affect adversely capital-intensive companies with large and long-term fixed investments and a low debt equity ratio, at the same time as labour-intensive companies with short-term investments could be expected even to benefit from inflation (Nelson, 1976; Tideman and Tucker, 1976; Kim, 1979). It should then be more important for the capital-intensive forest, steel and power industries to consider inflation, than for the service industry and perhaps also the pharmaceutical industry where investment in R & D predominates.

A second reason advanced by the interviewees for expressing cash flows in real terms has been that decision makers find it difficult to relate a cash flow in nominal terms to their own experience; especially cash flows for long-term projects.

A third reason advanced pertains to the decentralization of investment appraisals. Decentralization of the evaluation of investments presupposes some kind of centralization of the assumptions made, or as one respondent in a well-known multinational group expressed it.

> We have not said that one may not do that [consider inflation], but it becomes very dangerous if too many people are allowed to make their own prognoses of inflation, exchange rates, etc. That is not encouraged at all. If it is a very long-term investment with a cash flow we have to analyse for several years, then we can decide on inflation assumptions and such things in cooperation with its accounting and finance depart-ment. It is really nothing you can allow a lot of people to do because then we will receive very odd figures to compare.

This group invests in very many countries all over the world, and it would therefore be difficult to control inflation rates centrally. The first sorting of proposals is therefore made disregarding inflation, and if the rate of inflation of the country is too high the appraisal is made in U.S. dollars. If it later proves necessary to consider taxes, different financial options, or the effects of inflation, then this appraisal will be made in cooperation with the proper staff unit. This is the prevalent approach, but there are of course exceptions. Thus, later interviews revealed that one of the multinational engineering groups with investments in a great number of countries determined inflation and exchange rates to be used in preparation for the annual budgetary control process; however, that group too used U.S. dollars if the inflation rate was too high.

It was earlier stated that inflation adjustments were more common accord-ing to postal surveys, than studies of investment manuals. Furthermore, that postal surveys show an increasing use of inflation-adjusted appraisals, and Swedish manuals a decreasing use. One reason for these differences can be that respondents on corporate level express themselves about what they do on corporate level rather than what they have decentralized by means of an investment manual. Only "a handful" of U.S. manuals considered inflation according to Mukherjee (1988); nevertheless postal questionnaires completed at the head office show that most of the same Fortune 500 companies do consider inflation. Either the answer is a reflection of what the respondents think is the proper procedure or, as is more probable in the light of this study, relates to the kind of investments which are reviewed and appraised at corporate level. This also accords with the first reason advanced by the interviewees that they mostly had short-term investments. Major investments and long-term investments, viz. the kind of investments which suffer from inflation, will be referred upwards and an appraisal corrected for anticipated changes in prices, the general price level and exchange levels eventually in a later phase and then in cooperation with staff people. Assuming that also major U.K. and U.S. groups have similar administrative procedures we cannot take the postal surveys as proof that major U.K. and U.S. companies more often adjust their appraisals for inflation. The differences in user frequencies may just be a reflection of the degree of decentralization of investment appraisals, and the interpretation of the question made by the respondents.

Taxes

Theory The taxation system affects the return of investments of the firm in two different ways. It affects the payments and receipts of the cash flow through value added, payroll, property and energy taxes, and different types of support to less developed areas and other investment promoting state incentives, and also reduces the NPV of the investment as the profit of the company is taxed. The first type of taxes and subsidiaries can be evaluated by treating them as payments and receipts, but the second corporate income tax is more difficult. It is not the investment project that is taxed, but the company, and how much tax a company will pay is in itself a decision variable as the amount can to some degree be planned. Swedish tax legislation is, and has been, very generous in allowing companies to choose principles of depreciation, and transfer profit from one period to another so as to minimize their tax payments.

The principle of evaluating the after-tax IRR or NPV is simple. The after-tax appraisal has to be made in nominal prices and rents. Payments of taxes and subsidiaries are included in the cash flow. The net cash flow for one year t expressed in nominal value is obtained by subtracting the tax payments for year t (T_t) from the gross cash flow of year t (G_t). If the taxable income of year t is Tp_t and the tax rate s_t then this can be expressed as

$$G_t - T_t = G_t - s_t Tp_t$$

The taxable income is reduced due to depreciations according to tax legislation (D). Therefore, for a certain year t the profit can be expressed as

$$Tp_t = G_t - D_t$$

99

Combining these two equations we have

$$G_t - T_t = G_t - s_t(G_t - D_t) = (1 - s_t) G_t + s_t D_t$$

The after-tax rate of interest i_e is given by the expression

$$i_{after} = (1 - s) i_{before}$$

where i_{before} is the pre-tax rate of interest and s the tax rate.

A still simpler method is to consider taxes only by adjusting the hurdle rate (Lüder, 1976). This method was used by 11 per cent of those major Finnish groups which made after-tax appraisals (Honko and Virtanen, 1975). However, there is no report of its use within major Swedish groups, perhaps due to the influential work by Johansson (1961) on inflation and taxes in investment appraisals.

Practice When Renck (1966) did his study about half the companies made after-tax appraisals for some of their investments, and as certain interviewees expressed the need for such appraisals he arrived at the conclusion that "[t]he development seems to be going towards more companies making after-tax appraisals" (Renck, 1966, p. 90). For some reason, however, the development became the opposite. Tell (1978) could observe that fewer companies always considered taxes according to their manuals, and this trend continued (see Table 7.2). Today only three manuals recommend after-tax appraisals for all types of investments that they cover. In addition eight manuals instruct their user on how to treat value added taxes and certain other types of taxes and subsidiaries which may be included in the cash flow estimation.

Table 7.2
Corporate income tax in investment appraisals

	1964	1977	1990
Appraisals are made pre-tax	50 %	40 %	66 %
Appraisals are made after-tax			
for all investment requests	25	47	10
for certain investments	25	13	24
Total	100	100	100

Notes: The figures are based on Renck (1966), Tell (1978) and 29 investment manuals.

The reduced space allocated to the effects of taxes can be explained by the growing decentralization of investment appraisals and the consequent increasing need for simpler and fewer instructions. For the interviews showed that most groups which do not consider the tax issue in their manuals in fact make after-tax appraisals if taxes are expected to alter the assessment of the investment. It is difficult to know how many groups make after-tax appraisals for certain investments, but the interviews indicate that all groups have evaluated leasing or acquisitions at one time or another, and to do so they must evaluate taxes. These evaluations however were not then decentralized, but made by a staff unit.

The development has proceeded from some companies regularly evaluating taxes towards most companies making after-tax appraisals only when the tax situation might affect the decision. Such situations arise for instance in connection with the evaluation of acquisitions, leasing, investments which can be financed in different ways, or those in countries with different tax legislations. In current practice companies start by making a pre-tax appraisal, without considering inflation. Then in a second stage, inflation and taxes are considered if this is deemed necessary for the decision. However, these more advanced calculations are made by, or in cooperation with a staff unit, and today's manuals are therefore rather silent or brief about these issues, a silence which they share with the many postal questionnaires from Anglo-Saxon countries mentioned in this study.

Risk

The use of formal risk analysis Investment appraisals are based on estimates, some more uncertain than others. Many variables can affect the outcome of an investment, and many groups use some form of risk analysis to visualise these risks . Postal surveys of major Australian (Freeman and Hobbs, 1991), Canadian (Baumgartner and Irvine, 1977; Blazouske, Carlin and Kim, 1988), New Zealand (Patterson, 1989), U.K. (e.g. Pike and Wolfe, 1988) and U.S. (e.g. Klammer and Walker, 1984; Stanley and Block, 1984) firms show a growing use of such methods as sensitivity analysis and increased hurdle rates, lately also of computer simulation and beta analysis (see Table 7.3).

The most common technique in Swedish and Anglo-Saxon groups is no doubt sensitivity analysis, and variants of this technique such as the analysis of critical values and pessimistic and optimistic forecasts. Many Anglo-Saxon companies are also reported to increase their hurdle rates and shorten their PDP requirements to adjust for project risks. This practice is far less common in Swedish groups. It may well be that this is an effect of the method of investigation inasmuch as such evaluations are done in the assessment phase. Not surprisingly the interviews also indicated that risk is an important factor influencing the shortest acceptable PBP. However, as has previously been pointed out, the same interviews did not give any examples of adjustment of the hurdle rate to cater for project risk, although it is surely easier to have a riskier investment approved if the expected IRR is high.

Table 7.3
The use of formal risk analysis

	Sweden		The U.K.		The U.S.	
	1977	1990	1975	1986	1970	1980
Sensitivity analysis	33 %	46 %	28 %	71 %	30 %	48%
Best/worst estimates	23	10	-	-	-	-
Analysis of critical values	23	10	-	-	-	-
Reduced payback period	-	7	25	61	19	20
Increased hurdle rate	-	7	37	61	25	35
Probability analysis	17	3	9	40	12	21
Computer simulation	23	10	12	40	-	-
Beta analysis	0	0	0	16	-	-
Use formal risk analysis	80	57	26	86	-	-

Notes: Measures for the U.K. are taken from Pike and Wolfe (1988), for the U.S. from Klammer and Walker (1984), and for Sweden from Tell (1978) and the analysis of 29 investment manuals.

Analyses of manuals and interviews The development towards the use of more advanced evaluation techniques has pleased observers of the practice within industries:

> The dramatic increase in the formal analysis of risk required by firms (from 26 per cent in 1975 to 86 per cent in 1986) is perhaps the most encouraging finding from the entire study. (Pike and Wolfe, 1988, p. 93)

Industry has adopted the techniques recommended by business schools, and learnt to act more rationally. This will ensure better investment decisions. It is regrettable then that the development has been the opposite in Sweden, at least if Swedish groups are judged by their investment manuals. From having been as advanced as those of their U.K. and U.S. competitors their risk evaluation techniques seem to have deteriorated during the 80s, at the same time as U.K. and U.S. groups have improved theirs. The question arises: Why have they gone against the stream, or have they? To answer this question we shall analyse the manuals and interviews more closely.

Interviews on corporate level The investment manual is intended for people developing an investment request and can therefore be expected to reflect the evaluation techniques and criteria used in investment requests for, particularly medium-sized investments. Investments below a certain level of investment outlay do not need a request, and requests for major investments are often accompanied by tailor-made appraisals. The differences between Anglo-Saxon and Swedish groups could therefore be explained by the survey methods. A postal survey directed to corporate level will not necessarily reflect what is stated in the manual, but can also reflect the practice - if there is such - developed on corporate level for investments which are evaluated by corporate staff or need group level review and approval.

To form an idea about whether corporate level used different and more advanced evaluation techniques and criteria the interviewees on corporate level were asked whether they had seen any of the techniques listed in Table 7.4 in use in connection with investment decisions. This should give answers comparable to those received by postal questionnaires.

Table 7.4
Evaluation techniques used on corporate level

	Number of users	Expressed as a percentage
Sensitivity analysis	14	100 %
Balance sheet analysis	12	86
Company model	7	50
Analysis of flexibility	6	43
CAPM	0	0
BCG type matrix	9	64
Competitors costs	5	36
PIMS	4	29
Mathematical programming	1	7
Production cost criterion	13	93
Marginal criterion	6	43

Notes: Interviews were made on corporate level in 19 of the largest groups, whereof 14 used an investment manual. The respondents in the 14 groups using manuals were asked whether they had seen any of the techniques and measures in the Table being used for investment planning in their group.

The interviews showed that all major groups with an investment manual had used sensitivity analysis to evaluate risks, so if this technique is only applied in about 50 per cent of the groups to evaluate medium-sized investments, its use with major investments is definitely more frequent. Another risk evaluation technique which was very common was balance sheet and income statement analysis. It was used in connection with acquisitions, major investments and investment programmes, investments which could have a strong effect on the balance sheet and income statement of the investing company and perhaps even the group; seven of the groups had a company model which they had used in this way to evaluate these types of investments.

Gupta and Rosenhead (1968) have developed the concepts of robust decisions and stability. A robust investment decision is a decision which does not necessarily promise the highest NPV in one possible future but an acceptable NPV in several possible futures. When

> there are a number of end-states whose outcomes (on the basis of current information) are not much inferior to that of the 'best' end-state, to make initial decisions which permit the achievement of as many as possible of these end-states. We have called such initial decisions 'robust.' Where there are several robust decisions, an appropriate discriminatory factor is 'stability' - that is, the ability of the system (as amended by the initial decision or decisions) to perform well should the subsequent stages of the investment plan be delayed or cancelled. (Gupta and Rosenhead, 1968, p. B-28)

Such an analysis of flexibility cannot be rigidly performed by some kind of sensitivity analysis. It is necessary to consider connections to possible future investments and to other investments of the group. Furthermore to evaluate what may happen if, for instance, it takes a long time to run in a new plant, the project has to be abandoned, or there is a price war; What disasters can ensue, and what remedies can be adopted if they do? Such specific analysis of the flexibility of major investment decisions has been done in six of the groups, and the managers responsible for investment procedures in two of them said that they intended to improve their manuals in this area. Many manuals already have such instructions, ranging from check-lists of events which may affect an investment to general instructions to the appraiser to describe major investments in their context and show how certain major changes in the preconditions can affect the outcome of such investments. It is difficult to draw the line, but a count showed that 55 per cent of the manuals could be said to contain such instructions in one form or another.

Other techniques which had seen use was the BCG type matrix to allocate capital between businesses, and previously the PIMS project and mathematical programming but the PIMS project had now lost its role and mathematical programming had only been tested in one of the groups and many years ago at that. However, five groups regularly appraised the costs of their competitors and two more had tried to do so but without much success. Two kinds of criteria which are rarely mentioned are production cost and marginal. Almost all groups had had investment decisions based on a comparison of the production cost of the old and the new machine or plant. Six of the groups had also once perceived the marginal between costs and revenues between, for instance, the old and the new plant, as a criterion influencing the decision to invest. This kind of criterion has been observed in the refinery industry; by making this investment the marginal between what we

104

pay for crude oil and what we shall receive from the refined product will be increased by so much.

Table 7.4 is interesting in another way. It probably has more to say about the teaching in capital budgeting, than about the companies studied. During the 60s and early 70s the academic profession made a great effort to teach industry to use mathematical programming, yet only one of the groups has even tested it. Partly in consequence of these poor results several teachers entered the finance field and started to teach so-called modern finance with portfolio theory and the CAPM, so far however without success. Instead companies continue to use and develop techniques and criteria to which business schools pay very little attention, e.g. how to analyse the flexibility of an investment and its impact on the balance sheet and income statement of the company. The interviewees were familiar with mathematical programming and modern finance. They have studied these models at business schools or on executive courses, but consider them too academic.

An analysis of manuals A more thorough analysis of the manuals showed that these in fact contained many instructions which could be classified as measures to handle uncertainty. Large investments, for instance, need more exhaustive investment requests according to all but one of the manuals (see Table 7.5). Nevertheless a more characteristic feature consists in the heavier emphasis placed on qualitative factors, particularly in investment requests for major investments. Most manuals instruct their user to describe the circumstances around the investment, or in other words to put the investment in its context, and nine of the manuals can be said strongly to emphasize this point by helping the appraiser to identify important aspects of this context, etc. It is of course difficult to classify such instructions. A subjective trait is inevitable and some investment manuals are for various reasons more comprehensive than others.

Only thirteen of the manuals require a sensitivity analysis to be done, but no less than sixteen instruct the user in one way or another to analyse the flexibility of the investment, especially if the investment is major. Eight of the manuals have detailed instructions telling the requester not to forget the additional investments which the investment might bring, and four manuals instruct the user to analyse how the throughput time is affected by the investment. The last-mentioned passage seem to be a result of the just in time thinking of our days.

Twenty-five of the manuals require the requestor to submit a cash flow projection for all investment above a certain investment outlay limit. Almost as many ask for the PBP to be calculated, and five for an analysis of the impact of major investments on the balance sheet and income statement of the investing company. The paucity of manuals stipulating balance sheet analyses is due to the fact that the finance function will be contacted notwithstanding when the finance of major investments is decided.

Table 7.5
Some methods of handling uncertainty in requests

The investment and its context
28 Large investments demand more exhaustive requests, more advanced evaluation techniques and heavier emphasis on qualitative factors
25 The investment must be put in its context
9 The need to put the investment in its context is especially emphasized

Evaluation of risk
13 Sensitivity analysis

Evaluation of flexibility
16 The flexibility of at least major investments should be evaluated
8 Contingent investments should be considered
4 Changes in the throughput time should be analysed

Evaluation of financial risk
25 Cash flow projection
23 Pay-back period
5 Balance sheet and income statement analysis

Measures of control
24 Limits of authorization
21 Request must be signed by reviewer
20 Pre-approval review by staff
4 Responsibility emphasized

Notes: The Table is based on analysis of 29 investment manuals. As some of the manuals are incomplete as regards the description of the capital budgeting process the total number of groups demanding, for instance, pre-approval review is probably higher than the Table indicates.

One of the principal purposes of the manual was to create a unitary investment request with which investments could be compared. Twenty of these manuals stipulate that all investments be requested by one or several staff units. Twenty-one manuals also state that the request must be signed by one or several people, the project manager, the maker of the request, managers on different levels and staff units reviewing the request; four of them contain very detailed regulations, covering several pages of job descriptions, on who is responsible for what in the capital budgeting process of the company.

Analysing the manuals this way reveals that the evaluation procedures are not as unsophisticated with regard to risk and uncertainty, as Table 7.3 and a survey of risk evaluation techniques might indicate. It is true that the more advanced risk evaluation techniques which require the estimation of probabilities and the use of computers are conspicuous by their absence, but

106

this does not mean that these groups and manuals do not expect their users to evaluate risks and uncertainty. They do so in several different ways: by putting and analysing the investment in its context, evaluating possible outcomes, effects on the company and future possible investments, and different measures of control whereof the manual in itself of course is one.

Decentralization and flexibility According to both the interviews and the manuals Swedish groups seem to attach less weight to risk analysis today than during the 70s. The interviews and the analysis of the manuals show two different lines of development which may explain this diverse development, namely

- an increased decentralization of investment appraisals and the role of the investment manual as an instrument of decentralization and control.
- less weight attached to formal risk analysis of individual investment projects in favour of an increased importance attributed to the analysis of investment programmes, their flexibility and impact on companies.

Some of the manuals analysed in this last study are couched in more general terms than their predecessor, in order to be able to serve as a framework for manuals and instructions developed by lower levels. This decentralization can explain the development toward less advanced risk evaluation techniques. Decision makers and higher levels might prefer discrete to probability values; it is then easier to transfer responsibility for both when it comes to making the estimates and answering for the outcome of the investment, which, of course, does not mean that it is disadvantageous to undertake an analysis of the risks, showing that the appraisers have done their homework well.

Advanced methods, on the other hand, presuppose an appraiser familiar with such techniques. Such knowledge is best found in staff units and postal surveys (Weston, 1973; Moore and Reichert, 1983) have not surprisingly also shown that corporations with a long range planning function are more likely to apply advanced evaluation techniques. However, staff units are small in Swedish groups, having been decentralized or abolished during the last decades of decentralization.

The introduction of the computer presumably contributed to the introduction of more advanced risk evaluation techniques, but it is difficult to know whether this is so. In the 70s some groups had computer programmes for the evaluation of investments, but these programmes were decentralized when the personal computer took over. Some of the interviewees maintained that some companies use spreadsheet programmes to analyse investments, but as central control of these programmes is limited, they had very vague ideas of the extent to which such programmes were indeed used. Two of the groups had in 1990-91 developed electronic forms for investment requests, but all the rest relied on traditional forms, the post office and fax machines, to distribute and send their investment requests.

The other type of explanation had to do with the tendency of companies today to attach less weight to the formal risk analysis of individual investment projects, and more to evaluating their flexibility and to placing individual investments in their strategic and financial context. A shift of interest may be observed from individual investments towards their effects on the development of the company.

The exact consequences of an investment decision are uncertain. Some of the consequences are known and some of these known consequences are assessable. Risk analysis concerns the class of known consequences. It is a rationalistic planning philosophy, assuming that the uncertainty surrounding an investment decision can best be handled by predicting and preparing for the future.

However, to predict and plan the future is only one way of handling uncertainty (see e.g. Meffert, 1969; 1985; Mascarenhas, 1982; Aaker and Mascarenhas, 1984; Skromme Baird and Thomas, 1985; March and Shapira, 1987; Allaire and Firsirotu, 1989; Segelod, 1991b). If the supply of raw material is uncertain the risk of shortage can be controlled by integrating backwards or signing a long-term contract with a supplier. Companies can insure against some types of risk, they can avoid certain risks and they can build resources and design the organization so that they can adapt to changes as soon as they appear. The insurance option is limited to uncertainties of which the historical probabilities are known and used when the ability to control the outcome is limited. Swedish groups are relatively small. While they try to dominate certain market segments etc, they appear primarily to respond to the faster development and higher uncertainty which they have perceived by adapting, rather than by planning for the future, a change in planning philosophy recorded already around 1980 by Gandemo (1983).

Everything cannot be foreseen and it is impossible to plan for every eventuality in a rapidly changing evironment; firms have therefore come to rely on the ability of the organization to deal with new situations when they arise; to learn and unlearn. The stronger emphasis on choosing flexible investments is one way of creating such adaptability, and the aforesaid decentralization is another way of improving a firm's ability to respond to faster market changes; the decreasing observed emphasis on risk analysis could therefore very well be a reflection of these changes in the way major Swedish groups try to handle uncertainty.

Ex post review

The purpose of follow-ups We started out in Chapter 3 by listing a number of measures used to control investments prior to the decision to invest, and we then examined these measures one by one in the following chapters. The time has now come to survey the use of measures for ex post control of investments, viz. measures to control investments once the investment decision has been made. Limiting ourselves to individual investments ex post review might stand for

-   the monitoring of investments during their implementation,
-   post-completion review or post audit of investments,
-   the updating of the investment request on which the decision to invest was based.

Why should investments be followed up? The manuals are terse on this point. Only nine of the twenty manuals which mention ex post review give a reason for making reviews. They state that lower levels should follow up all investments, in four cases all investments above an expenditure limit, or those the company management finds strategically important, in order to

-   supply data for financial planning (three manuals),
-   supply data so that the investment projects can be implemented in an optimal way (two manuals) and achieve their   strategic goals (four manuals),
-   improve future investment appraisals and requests (five manuals), decision procedures (one manual), and investment projects (two manuals),
-   assign greater responsibility for investment requests and implementation (four manuals).

Empirical studies of reviews have shown that investments are followed up for many different reasons (See e.g. Hägg, (1977; Neale and Holms, 1990; Neale, 1991). Neale (1991), for instance, recorded the following objectives derived from post-auditing in a postal survey of U.K. firms:

1.   To enable better capital expenditure decision-making
2.   To encourage a more realistic assessment of project viability
3.   To ensure improvements in future planning
4.   To delineate and remedy difficulties in early project life
5.   To evaluate management expertise in project appraisal
6.   To reduce management autonomy at local level (Neale,1991,p.86)

The first three objectives aim at improving the planning and decision-making process, and the latter three at controlling the result of the investment project. The first objective was perceived as the most important, the last as the least important, and the four in between of about the same importance. A similar study of Norwegian firms (Steen and Fjell, 1990) showed that these firms put even more emphasis on review as a means of improving the quality of future decision-making, than British corporations did.

The use of follow-ups Postal surveys in the U.K. (Scapens and Sale, 1981; Pike, 1982; Mills and Herbert, 1987; Pike and Wolfe, 1987; Neale, 1991) and the U.S. (Scapens and Sale, 1981; Klammer and Walker, 1984; Posey,

Roth and Dittrich, 1985) have shown an increasing use of follow-ups. From the 50 per cent recorded by Istvan (1961a) in the late 50s to Posey, Roth and Dittrich's (1985) 95 per cent that monitor their investments, 83 per cent that makes a post-completion review and 51 per cent that update the profitability appraisal of the investment request. U.K. industry was a little slower to adapt ex post review practice, but caught up in the 80s. Neale (1991) found that 92 per cent monitored all major projects and 43 per cent some projects, as compared with 55 per cent in 1980 (Scapens and Sale, 1981). Post-completion review or post-audit, as it is often termed, was done by 88 per cent for all major projects and 18 per cent for some projects, as compared with 36 per cent in 1980.

The use of ex post review like that of DCF techniques no doubt increased, even if it is more difficult to compare studies of ex post review. Many of the studies do not clearly distinguish between the monitoring of current projects, the checking against the original capital expenditure budget of the investment project, the post-completion review made when the project has been run in, and possible post-audits made by independent audit units; only a few of them link any of these types of review to the kinds of investments reviewed and by whom the review is made.

Turning to Swedish companies Tell (1978) found that 50 per cent of his investment manuals stated that a post-completion review should be performed and 53 per cent that investment requests should be updated. Today the same figures are 66 per cent and 55 per cent. However, these figures may be an under-estimation as they are based on the fifteen manuals that in 1977, and the twenty-two manuals in 1990 which mention review. Comparisons with the subsequent interviews also revealed a somewhat different picture.

Studies of major U.K. and U.S. corporations show that the responsibility for executing the review rests with corporate and divisional levels in about 50 per cent per cent of the cases each (see Table 7.6). This is very different from the nineteen major Swedish groups in which interviews were made. One of these groups had divided the responsibility between corporate level and the company in which the investment was done, and another had decentralized ex-post review to the divisions. All the other groups had decentralized the responsibility for following up investments to the company or project manager. Only in the smaller groups on the otc-list did this responsibility rest with corporate level.

This far-reaching decentralization of follow-ups makes it very difficult and unreliable to survey issues connected with review from corporate level. All nineteen groups had routines stating that all investments, sometimes all investments above a certain limit of initial outlay, should be followed up by the company or project manager, and reported to the decision-level which approved the same investment. Thus, according to the formal routines, 100 per cent of these groups followed up at least some of their investments, but it is difficult to discover the extent to which these instructions were obeyed.

Table 7.6
Responsibility for performing post-completion review

	Corporate level	Decen- tralized	Another division
Sweden 1990	5 %	100 %	0 %
The U.K. 1980	51	46	1
The U.S. 1980	44	50	1

Notes: U.K. and U.S. data based on Scapens and Sale (1981), Swedish data on interviews in 19 of the major groups.

The high degree of decentralization has been explained by the small staff units used by Swedish groups in general. Moreover there is reason to believe that the widespread use of project management technique to plan and implement investment among the groups with investment manuals makes it natural to decentralize the follow-up to project or company management; be that as it may it is they who must carry on the experiences gained to future investments. However, it should also be observed that if corporate staff wish to follow up the budget of the investment, they can often find such data in their computerized accounting system, provided that they consider it worth while to collect this information.

The pros and cons of decentralized review are of course open to discussion. Hägg (1977) discusses these issues in terms of knowledge and objectivity. Those who have implemented the project are better informed about the details of the investment, at the same time as a neutral person might be more suitable to make an objective post-audit. This follows Kooken (1961, in Hägg, 1977) who maintained that the review should be made by an independent auditor if an objective assessment was envisaged, and local people if the purpose was to improve their future appraisals.

The monitoring during implementation The administrative principles for review were broadly similar in the nineteen major groups. When an investment and its budget has been approved a project manager is assigned to the project. He or she is given responsibility for the implementation, monitoring and post-completion review of the project.

Estimated investment outlay tends to rise during the planning process, and in some projects also after the budget of the investment has been approved. Mention is made of an optimistic or upward bias in capital budgeting proposals (Cyert, March and Starbuck, 1961; Statman and Tyebjee, 1985; Segelod, 1986; Pruitt and Gitman, 1987; Tyebjee, 1987). Many budget items contain certain reservations for additional expenses and there is often also an item termed 'contingencies'. If these reserves prove to be insufficient, project management can usually make some savings by lowering the level of ambition, redistributing funds between projects, postponing part of the project, etc. However, if the cost escalation is too great additional funds must be appropriated. Consequently, five of the manuals instruct project management to make requests for additional funds immediately if the final outlay exceeds the projected, usually with more than ten per cent.

> If during the implementation of the project the investment outlay is projected to exceed the budget with more than ten per cent or 0.5 MSEK a request for additional funds shall be made. The request shall be sent to the same instance that approved the original budget. It is important that expected overruns are reported as soon as possible so that the decision-maker is given the opportunity to act. Requests for budgets already overdrawn can never be accepted.

Investments are monitored as project management need to know where they stand with regard to the budget and the time table, and financial managers need the information for their financial planning. Today computers are used to monitor payments, but in 1964 major investment projects were reviewed manually perhaps four times a year. However, neither the manuals nor the interviews reveal the extent to which investments are monitored, but it may be assumed that the budget of the investment is monitored regularly as corporate level reviews the capital budget regularly. More about this later on.

Post-completion review It usually takes some time to run in a new machine, to achieve planned product quality and production volume. Due to the length of this running-in period, often specific to the technology in question, post-completion review is made six to 24 months after starting operation. Such a review and final inspection comprise not only an estimate of the actual investment expenditures, but also an assessment of how well product and production goals have been achieved.

It is difficult to know the extent to which post-completion reviews are made. Some groups state that all investments shall be followed up, a few have a limit ranging from 0.3 to 5 MSEK. In the latter group corporate level only state that investments which needed group level approval should be followed up. However, it is not forbidden for lower levels to follow up also smaller investments if they find it necessary.

It is also difficult to know the extent to which these instructions are obeyed. Some of the interviewees said that they are aware that some divisions are better at following up their investments, and some that they did not receive post-completion reviews for all the investments which corporate level had approved. The problem consisted in that group staff lacked means of sanction. Those who want to carry out an investment have to follow the instructions and produce an investment request before they are allowed to act, but when it comes to ex post review there is no such carrot.

Updating the investment request Sometimes the investment request on which the decision to invest was made is also updated in connection with the post-completion review. This more ambitious form of review can be expected to be even less frequent.

Some of the manuals stipulate that the investment request always be updated, and about 50 per cent of the manuals were accompanied by forms used both for summing up the investment request and for the post-completion review. These forms also give room to estimate the probable PBP and IRR etc at the time of review, but the interviews indicate that such reviews are made less often than post-completion reviews.

> Yes, post-completion review but not profitability review. We do not look in the mirror. It is the future that is interesting. An exception is major projects that are carefully audited. Apart from that it is considered to difficult to evaluate independent projects.

Group level review of investments

Several researchers have found that ex post review, just like pre-investment planning, can serve different purposes for different actors. Barry (1984), for instance, found that the economic and financial consequences of the review were considered as more important by higher levels, while business level was more interested in technical, product and market consequences. The interviewees on corporate level have especially stressed the role of ex post review to achieve financial and strategic control. Some also said that they make inspections to see that the instructions to make post-completion reviews are obeyed by the companies.

Financial control The major nineteen groups all had a one year capital expenditure budget. Three of them had supplemented this short-term budget with a three years budget and two with a five years budget. This means that 14 of the 19 groups or 74 per cent only had a one year capital expenditure budget on corporate level. This includes several of the well-known multinational machine engineering groups. The forest and steel groups had longer budgets, and longer budgets probably also exist on lower levels in many of the other groups; One of the interviewees could report in detail on companies which had all from a one to a five years budget.

Similar studies of major U.K. and U.S. groups have shown that most groups supplemented their one year capital expenditure budget with a looser three or five years capital budget or plan (see Table 7.7). Some of the Swedish groups had more long-term planning in the 70s, but this difference is still difficult to explain, and several of the interviewees expressed astonishment that so many U.K. and U.S. groups on corporate level were still projecting a long-term capital budget. However, if the economic situation were to demand the projection of such a budget they could compile one.

Table 7.7
Corporate level capital budget

Corporate level capital budget	1 year	>1 year
Sweden 1990-93	74 %	26 %
The U.K. 1981 (a)	36	64
The U.K. 1986 (a)	36	64
The U.S. 1960 (b)	57	43
The U.S. 1970 (b)	31	69
The U.S. 1980 (b)	25	75
The U.S. 1981 (c)	18	82

Notes: Based on interviews in 19 major Swedish groups and (a) Pike and Wolfe (1988), (b) Klammer and Walker (1984), and (c) Hendricks (1983).

In 1990-91 after a long boom corporate level monitored their capital expenditure budget one to 12 times a year; median four times a year. Later interviews in 1993 showed that several of the groups had gone over to more frequent reviews during the recession. In fact, today many of the largest groups review their capital budget every month. These reviews are used to determine the group's need for capital requirements during the next few months and year, and as the data mostly come from the investments implemented we may presume that individual investments are monitored equally often.

One of the nineteen groups had repeatedly overdrawn their capital expenditure budget, due to frequent cost overruns among many of their smaller projects. The other eighteen groups had either managed to meet their budget or finished with a surplus. These two groups of groups seem to be about equally large. The finish-ing below budget was explained by delays in the start of many projects. One of the respondents said that these underruns had appeared with such regularity that they had learned to take them into account in their financial planning.

Strategic control Postal surveys in Norway (Steen and Fjell, 1990) and the U.K. (Neale, 1991) have shown that by far the most important criterion for post-completion review is the size of a project. About 90 per cent of the respondents in these two surveys answered that size is an important criterion, as compared with 10 to 30 per cent for the degree of risk, typicality of the project and project chosen at random. This is in accord with our manuals and also with the interviews if we assume that size, riskiness and typicality are measures of the perceived strategic importance of the investment.

It is not altogether true to say that corporate staff do not review individual investments, but only such that the board and top management perceive as strategically important, or have felt uncertain about and therefore want to see evaluated. Thus, they review acquisitions and investments in new markets and technology, and the absolutely largest investments, viz. investments which change the domains of the group. However, such strategic investments often consist of a number of investments and take a long time to implement, so that we may say that it is more important to review strategies or approved directions of investments than individual investments and that review of individual investments serves to monitor how decisions on new strategies progress. The emphasis on strategic control makes pre-approval review more important than ex post review as it is easier to influence a strategic direction before an investment is implemented than afterwards.

The ex post review is of less interest than the ex ante review as they are of less value to the strategy.

There are cases in which corporate staff have evaluated the progress of decisions to enter new geographical markets, new technologies, decisions to invest in FMS and computerization, and of course acquisitions. Top management wished to know whether the route they chose was the right one. Should they continue on their present course, or should they change track. "We want to make sure that we are on the right track", as one financial manager expressed it. As in all reviews there is a strong aspect of learning in this monitoring. Information on how strategies progress gives management feedback to learn more about how the same strategies should be designed.

Strategic control can also be claimed to include the development of new, better administrative routines. Chandler (1962) tought us that structure follows strategy. When new businesses are entered, new technology introduced and new strategies chosen, new administrative routines must sometimes be developed to match the new strategy and make it effective. Good examples of new technologies which needed such new routines are investments in flexible manufacturing systems and computerization. As companies have found it difficult to justify FMS investments, and doubts have been expressed about computerization, these issues have been referred upwards and corporate staff have participated in their evaluation. This later resulted in new routines and additional instructions for the evaluation of such investments, and the issue has once again been decentralized. A similar reversed U-turn is perhaps awaiting investments in information technology, which has been referred upwards in many groups. The decision to invest in these new technologies is clearly strategic, but the implementation of this strategy yields a large number of typical projects in which handling can be standardized.

Educating the companies The responsibility for the post-completion review of individual investment projects is, as earlier said, decentralized to the company and project management. Corporate staff rarely engage in these reviews, but a few of the respondents said that they make random tests to see that such reviews are really done or specifically ask for reviews of projects about which they were uncertain.

> We follow individual investment projects especially when they are a little odd, unusually large or when we have not really believed in the appraisal to show that we are aware of what we sign. It varies from company to company depending on how good they are at following up their investments.

> It is more a matter of educating the companies to see what is profitable and what is not.

Post-completion reviews are to be sent to the decision-station approving the investment request, but, as stated above, some of the interviewees admitted that they do not receive reports of all investments that they have approved. The problem is that the means of sanction are weak. To have an investment financed you have to compile an investment request, but there is no similar mean of sanction for making a post-completion review.

8 Resource allocation and organizational structure

We have now gone through various aspects of the formal resource allocation system, viz. the investment manual, profitability criteria, the treatment of taxes etc., issue by issue; how many groups with a manual use a specific criterion and calculate the after-tax return, and how many do not. The all-embracing aim of the many postal surveys in this field has been to survey user frequencies, and these sections were written with this in mind. We shall now turn to connections between the resource allocation system and the organizational structure.

It was said above that no two groups have the same administrative routines for investments. The scope of the manuals varies as does the emphasis placed on different means of control. At the same time there are no doubt similarities between groups in the same kind of industry. The multinational engineering groups, for instance, show strong similarities, when compared to groups in the retailing or the forest industry. The routines form a system the logic of which becomes evident only when it is placed in its proper context; the characteristics of a resource allocation system are related to the investments it is expected to handle and the markets and technologies which these investments represent.

The analyses of the manuals and particularly of the interviews have made it clear that groups belonging to the same industry show some remarkable similarities; we shall describe these similarities, and the dissimilarities, in this section.

The account will take its point of departure from the multinational engineering groups. These groups have well developed resource allocation systems and manuals, and also a dominant position in Swedish industry and in this study; as described in Chapter 1 about half the manuals came from the engineering industry. Due to these groups' dominant position the account of their routines also constitutes a summary of the findings in earlier chapters.

The subsequent descriptions of groups in other industries are then derived from this account of the multinational engineering groups, which also means that the presentation of these categories of firms can be confined to the differences relative to the engineering groups and thereby shortened. Some of the categorisations are based on only a few groups and should, therefore, be seen as tentative. A brief introduction and summary of the main features of the categories of companies which are described in this chapter, is the following:

1. *Multinational engineering groups* Fixed, R & D, and market investments of about the same size. Investment proposals come from below, but corporate management can sponsor strategic initiative. Two of the groups handle major investments in a strategic process, the others use limits of authorization which may be differentiated with regard to the type of investment, and a well developed system of pre-approval review. The manual is important and also valid for certain expense type of investments. The description is based on interviews in six groups and analyses of nine investment manuals.

2. *Small engineering groups* The manual is intended only for fixed investments. Both the manual and capital budgeting procedures are simpler than in larger groups. Based on interviews in four groups and six manuals.

3. *Forest and steel groups* Large investment projects predominate and the manual is adjusted for these types of project. Based on interviews in three groups and eight manuals.

4. *Trade and retailing groups* Intangible investments predominate. More short-term investments and simpler evaluation techniques than in the engineering groups. Based on interviews in three groups and one manual.

5. *Capital intensive groups* Large recurrent investments predominate. Investment proposals come from below. The corporate management sponsors strategic initiative and is represented on the investment committee which ranks investments. The manual is very thick and the profitability criterion only one of several criteria influencing the decision to invest. Based on interviews in one group. Two additional groups supplying manuals could perhaps be assigned to this category.

6. *R & D intensive groups* Both R & D and market investments are very large. Major commitments are decided in a strategic process, minor in the subsequent budgetary control process. Relatively centralized decisions on new products and markets generate investments on lower levels in production equipment. The evaluation techniques used are quite simple and the importance of the investment manual has diminished as

118

the volume of intangible investments has increased. Based on interviews in two groups and manuals from three groups.

7. *Shipping groups* Ships are very large investments. Appraisals and decisions are made within a small management group. There is no manual.
The appraisals can be either simple or advanced. Similar conditions
prevail in real-estate companies and small companies where the functions of ownership and management have not yet been separated.
Based on interviews in two groups.

8. *Service groups* Intangible investments predominate. Some groups have
different investment committees for different types of investment.
There is usually no investment manual and for most investments only
simple evaluation techniques are used. Based on interviews in seven
groups, or ten groups if the three trade and retailing groups are
included in this category.

Multinational engineering groups

Investments The engineering industry invests about 3 to 8 per cent annually
in fixed investments, and an equal amount in both R & D and market development. In fact, the figure may be slightly higher for market investments
and lower for R & D, as these figures refer to investments in Sweden.

Structure The multinational engineering groups are divisionalized. The
larger groups have several hundred companies, or business boards, divided
among divisions which belong to different business areas, and a great many
profit centres spread out in many countries and on several continents.
Starting as national companies they have gradually developed a complex
multinational structure with multiple centres, sometimes with divisional, and
business area, head offices outside Sweden. The staff units on corporate
level are today small, and especially technical staff units have been
decentralized, transformed into staff companies or wound up.

The path of the investment request There is no formal group of people
initiating new investment ideas. Instead there is a steady flow of investment
requests, emanating from the companies. One exception is acquisitions
which may be initiated by the companies but also by higher levels and board
members. Several of the multinational engineering groups have taken on the
role of restructuring mature industries. This has involved, *inter alia*, coordination of production, marketing and development leading to concentration
and relocation of production, divestments and investments, a process in
which business area and divisional managers have played a key role. In
some cases investment can also be said to have been initiated from the top
as corporate management has advocated investments in certain markets and

technologies, e.g. just-in-time investments and certain types of production equipment.

Investment requests are ranked in the companies and divisions, and are seldom rejected definitively if they reach corporate level. They are more often referred back for reconsideration, which means that they have to pass the review process once more, be postponed and perhaps then out of date.

Pre-approval review Major engineering groups have a well developed system of pre-approval review starting already in the companies. The request and appraisal are usually made on business level by an engineer in cooperation with the controller etc of the company. In the case of major investments the company management is directly involved.

If the initial outlay of the investment exceeds the limit of authorization of the manager he or she has to sign the request and refer it upward for approval. All but one of the multinational engineering groups have fixed limits of authorization which determine how far up in the hierarchy a request must be referred for decision.

During its journey upwards in the hierarchy the request will be scrutinized by different stations of review with regard to the economy, market and technology. A characteristic trait in the review system of the multinational engineering groups is that most of them have different limits and rules for when a staff unit should be informed about an investment or should review the request depending on whether it concerns an investment in production equipment, land and property, telecommunication and computer software or hardware, leasing or special finance. As a group they have the best developed system of pre-approval review, guaranteeing that a request needing group level decision has been scrutinized several times by different specialists.

This review makes it possible to coordinate investments in different companies and to utilize the experience of other group companies which already have made similar investments. The economy function at corporate level can assess the reasonableness of the assumptions and the appraisal, and if they feel uncertain ask for additional information. The burden of proof rests on the requester.

Means of control The corporate level uses several means to control the volume and direction of the group's investments. All groups have a capital budget which is fixed in the annual budgetary control process. There are usually more requests than can be covered by the budget, so that lower units must rank the requests. Other factors which can stop investments and sometimes also limit the volume of investment are shortage of skilled engineers, project and company managers, and the need to distribute investments evenly over time and companies etc. Corporate level only has a one year investment budget, which is monitored several times a year; in some groups every month.

120

Another important means of control is the investment manual; it contains instructions on how individual investments should be appraised and implemented, a draft for an investment request, the formal decision process and areas of responsibility, including limits of authorization which refer important strategic investments upwards.

Many of the interviewees also emphasized other fora for influence, e.g. board representation, staff, executive meetings and travel within the group partly to coordinate investments, partly to pursue strategic initiatives. None of the groups mentioned all these measures of control, and some of them regarded certain measures as being of greater importance than others for their group; this differed from group to group.

The budgetary control process runs during the autumn, and in two of the groups is preceded by a type of annual strategic planning process. Still another group has a formal strategic planning process for use when necessary, and perhaps such irregular processes also exist in some of the other groups, but this is speculation. The groups which run an annual strategic planning process decide the volume of investments, major investments, and investments in new markets and technology within its framework.

The strategic process implies a focus on strategic investments. These investments can then be assessed and decided on before decisions are reached in the budgetary control process on the great majority of small- and medium-sized investments. Those multinational engineering groups which lack a strategic process seem to try to achieve a similar focus by stipulating that the company may not divide up investments reaching over several years. First when a request for an investment programme or major investment has been approved, can requests for the consequential sub-investments be processed. There are also investment committees which rank the requests of a division, and also committees for certain types of intangible investments.

Investment manual All engineering groups have an investment manual. These routines were introduced during the late 50s and the 60s. The manual contains forms, instructions for their filling in and for investment appraisals, a description of the formal decision process and the division of authority. The aim of the manual from the outset was to elicit unitary requests and appraisals, so that the requests could be compared and possibly also ranked.

Today the importance of the manuals for financial planning, strategic planning and control, and the coordination of the investments of the group is also emphasised, as well as their role in creating a common group language with regard to investments. The latter communicative purpose has been stressed particularly in groups which have grown through international acquisitions and therefore been faced with the task of integrating units with different investment procedures and company cultures.

Some of the more heterogeneous groups, whereof some engineering groups, have abolished the group manual, and allowed business areas and

121

divisions to develop their own investment procedures. Other groups have made the manual very general so that it can serve as a framework for detailed manuals on lower levels. Increased heterogeneity and international-ization have therefore contributed to simpler, general routines which can be applied to different types of investments and be understood by everybody using them.

Most groups also seem to have a templet for investment requests presented to the group board, in a few groups also valid for internal boards. This templet describes what data are needed for board decisions and how the information should be presented. The borderline between a detailed templet and a less detailed investment manual is fluid. However, the templet allows more scope for qualitative data and in most groups also gives the requester more freedom to apply methods of analysis deemed suitable for the decision in question.

All engineering groups have today abolished the accounting based definition of an investment and therefore include also certain expenses associated with the implementation of an investment in the initial outlay. Some of the multinational engineering groups have taken yet another step and decided that their investment manual is valid also for certain expense types of investments, and a few others have developed special manuals for acquisitions and R & D.

Investment procedures The multinational engineering groups consistently have more complex investment procedures than the other groups in this study. The manual is most detailed for medium-sized investments. The result of the appraisal is summed up on one form, in some of the groups accompanied by forms specifying the items of the investment budget and the items of the cash flow computation.

All acquisitions, in some groups all acquisitions above a certain limit of authorization, need group board approval. In some groups such approval is also necessary for development projects and ventures in new areas which can alter a business formula previously agreed on for a company.

The larger engineering groups often have rules stipulating that a staff unit should review or be contacted in connection with investments in land and property, machines, telecommunication and computer hardware and software, leasing, the choice of finance for major investments, etc. In addition, certain groups have considerably lower levels of authorization for investments in, primarily information technology.

Requests for expenditures are classified by marking one of the categories of investments listed on the form with a cross. The classes have increased in number and there seem to be two major bases of division. First, the distinction between upkeep existing production equipment, and expansion investments. Secondly, classifications with regard to the type of investment, e.g. machines, computers, markets, R & D, etc. The templets used for major investments lack such systems of classification and in general there do not seem to be any statistics on corporate level concerning how much the group as a whole invests in each class of investment.

Investment criteria The investment criterion for minor investments is the PBP, and for investments over a certain expenditure limit the PBP plus one or more DCF criteria. Many groups use several DCF criteria, and some delegate to the appraiser to choose suitable criteria. The PBP and annuity index are used for replacement investments, and they often only compare the cost sides of the old and the new machine. The NPV criterion is mainly used for major investments, expansion investments and investments in new areas.

The hurdle rate is not differentiated with regard to type of investments. However, the major engineering groups as multinationals, usually differentiate their hurdle rate according to the country of the investing company, a practice that separates them from the less multinational groups which use a unitary group rate. A few of these more multinational groups have taken yet another step by also decentralizing the determination of the hurdle rate.

The hurdle rate varies considerably from group to group, and both this and the payback criterion are used with flexibility, at least for investments needing group level approval. There is no absolute limit which prevents group approval of an investment that shows a PBP longer than the 1½ to 3 years formally required or an IRR lower than the formal cut-off rate. If the expected profitability is unusually low then the strategic reasons and other arguments must be stronger instead. The interviewees have given examples of occasional investments with an estimated PBP of 7 to 8 years which for strategic reasons have been approved by the corporate level.

In general terms the hurdle rate seems to be of more importance for investments decided on divisional level, than for those needing corporate level approval. Soft data become relatively more important than, for instance, the IRR for investments in new markets, products and product lines, while for major investments and investment programmes the fund-flow is crucial; does the company have the financial and managerial strength to carry out such an investment.

Most groups have a long-term ROI type requirement determined by the group board which extends over one business cycle. This requirement is later broken down according to the preconditions for operations in different countries and part of the group. The requirement can vary considerably depending on local market conditions and is usually seen primarily as a commitment by the unit in question, and not as an absolute requirement fixed by higher levels.

Investment appraisal and follow-up The appraisal must be made in nominal terms if the intention is to consider taxes, follow the investment up, or consider different ways of financing the project. The first request is in general made without considering taxes, inflation or finance. If such an evaluation is deemed necessary this is usually done later on and possibly in cooperation with a staff unit.

Ex-post review can refer to the monitoring of capital expenditures, the review of implemented projects, and the updating of the original investment request. It is difficult to know the extent to which capital investments are followed up in major Swedish groups, as the responsibility for the review is decentralized to the company or project management carrying out the investment. Corporate level only follows up strategic decisions like acquisitions, investments in new markets and technology, and in some groups also check that lower levels do follow up investments. However, the investment budget is monitored several times a year by corporate level which indicates that also investments are monitored.

At first sight Swedish groups seem to be unsophisticated in their use of risk evaluation techniques. However, further analyses of their manuals and interviews show that in fact several methods are used to evaluate risks and flexibility, so that the apparent lack of risk evaluating techniques in the manuals may be due partly to the role of the manual as an instrument of decentralization, and partly to a stronger emphasis on finding flexible solutions, than on evaluating risks.

Small engineering groups

Interviews were also held in three engineering groups listed on the small business list. Two of these groups used a manual, and both their manuals and their procedures on the whole closely resembled those of the two smallest engineering groups in the main group. The groups were all divisionalized with a volume of investment of about 8 per cent. One of the groups invested more in market development than in fixed investments, the other two had considerably smaller intangible investments than the larger multinational engineering groups.

The investment manual is thinner and intended for fixed investments only. The procedures are simpler. There are no differentiated limits of authorization, few investment classes, much shorter communication distances and more frequent contacts between corporate level and the management of the companies. The investment criterion is PBP, and in one of the groups also discounted PBP. Taxes and inflation are not considered. Acquisitions are evaluated on corporate level, and if taxes, inflation, and finance must be considered then this is done on corporate level. Apart from this the procedures are reminiscent of those found in the larger engineering groups, for instance with regard to pre-approval review.

All groups had a capital budget, which was monitored several times each year. Post-completion reviews are performed sporadically.

The smaller engineering groups are reminiscent in certain aspects of divisions in the larger groups. The distance between the company management and the group management is shorter. This enables frequent, informal contacts, and involves corporate managers more directly in decisions on the companies' major and strategic investments.

Forest and steel groups

The forest and steel groups are divisionalized, but the companies are fewer than in engineering groups of similar size. The steel groups invest just as much as the engineering groups in fixed investments, the forest groups still more, in some years more than 10 per cent of sales. Intangible investments are small compared with the engineering industry. Both the forest and steel industries are process industries. An investment in a new paper mill or machine or steel works may involve milliards SEK. However, due to the market situation such investments have been few since the 70s. The companies have instead developed their plants through contingent investments, which sometimes also led to comparatively large investment projects. The manufacturing process is controlled by computers, and the investments in control equipment are therefore comparatively large, but treated as a part of the machine they control.

Steel and forest groups control their investments in a similar way to engineering groups, but there are differences. The manuals are adjusted to the relatively large investment projects of which these companies have experience, and which they evaluate and implement through a project organization. There are no differentiated limits of authorization. The stations of review are fewer and one of the groups formally lacked staff review completely. Among investment criteria the IRR has a strong position, perhaps because these capital-intensive companies introduced the DCF technique at an early stage.

Major basic investments in these industries can have a very long economic life provided that they do not become obsolete or the firm is outperformed. However, as is usually the case also with major investment projects in other industries, the decision to invest is seldom based on a long-term DCF appraisal alone. Market factors are more important, but an analysis must be performed to show how the company can manage such a major undertaking financially.

One explanation for these differences may be that the competence relating to technology is in the companies, staff companies selling technical know-how and consultancy companies. Investments are projected, appraised, implemented and reviewed within the framework of a project organization controlled by representatives of the investing company and group. Major investment projects need a formal decision to be planned, and several years of preparation before the board will approve their implementation. This enables corporate managers to follow the evaluation process of major investments, and the interviewees also mentioned the importance of board representation as a means of control.

Trade and retailing groups

The interviews also covered two divisionalized multinational groups which, although they have some production, can be classified as commerce, one of them importing and exporting products used in industry, and the other selling both to industry and to consumers. The head offices of these groups are small and the groups decentralized; all decisions and responsibility for operative matters rest on the divisions and companies. The profit centres are relatively numerous and small, as is the need to coordinate investments in different divisions and companies.

The volume of fixed investments is smaller than in engineering groups and dominated by investments in property and new sales outlets. With respect to market investments one of the groups estimated their investments in building up customer relations to at least 20 per cent of sales, the other to about 10 per cent.

Market investments are handled in the budgetary control process. As most investments are small in absolute terms, relatively few requests need group level approval, and when they do the main question usually concerns their strategic fit. One of the groups has an investment manual, but the appraisals are fairly simple even if the DCF technique is used for major investments. Proposals for acquisitions come often from the companies, and are evaluated on divisional level in one of the groups and on corporate level in the other.

Trade and retailing is characterized by a high speed of change; the product can become obsolete, the market and partners virtually disappear. Short break-even times are therefore required and reviews are made often. Key ratios seem to be significant measures of control, as well as executive meetings and frequent informal contacts. Several key ratios are used and it becomes more important to control capital tied up in inventories and working capital, than in production equipment.

An interview was also conducted with the chief financial executives of a non divisionalized multinational retailing company. This means that the purchasing and partly also the marketing functions were centralized. Apart from these structural differences the similarities to the other two groups in this industry were obvious with regard to investment issues.

Capital intensive groups

The resource allocation process of one of the most capital-intensive groups differs from that of the engineering groups. This group has very large capital investments in plants and distribution systems in several countries, distribution areas which are protected by the very high capital cost of entering the distribution area of a competitor. As all the distribution systems use the same technology, partly developed by the group, there is also an advantage in stronger coordination of the technical competency of the group, than in the engineering groups.

Investment requests, proposals of acquisitions and sometimes also strategic initiatives, come from the companies; "They know the market best". Strategic initiatives to invest in a certain technology or strategic directions are frequently pursued from the centre. Strategic issues are treated in the budgetary control process, executive meetings which are held five to six times a year, through board representation and informal contacts.

The volume of investment is determined from the top, and the one year capital budget is supplemented with a three year projection. The investment requests are assessed and ranked in investment committees with representatives of technical staff companies and chaired by corporate staff, previously the vice-president finance and accounting.

Acquisitions need group level approval. There is no limit of authorisation, but development projects are ranked by the head office in an investment committee. There is no ROI type profitability criterion, but a set of target criteria, e.g. the volume of sales and investments, and operating income before depreciation.

The group has a very comprehensive capital budgeting manual and a simple templet for board decisions. The investments are evaluated with the PBP, major investments also with the IRR and an analysis of their impact on the balance sheet and income statement of the company. The cut-off rate varies between 10 and 30 per cent depending on the type, and country of the investment, and the payback period might vary between 1½ to 5 years. Profitability criteria are used with great flexibility and seen only as one of several factors relevant to the decision to invest, e.g. the possibility to forestall competitors, strategies and safety aspects.

This single group has traits in common with companies in the power industry. Power companies too have very large fixed investments and a need to coordinate investments in the power system.

R & D intensive groups

Investments Interviews were also held in two R & D intensive multinational companies, whereof one had a divisionalized structure. The expenditures for fixed investments were of the same magnitude as for the multinational engineering groups, but the investments in R & D considerably larger, and in one of the groups also the market investments.

Planning processes The group with large investments in both R & D and markets, had supplemented the budgetary control process with an annual strategic planning process. The strategic process runs during the spring, precedes the budgetary control process and ends in a five year plan. In the strategic process the investment budgets for both fixed and expense kinds of investments were determined, as well as strategies and major investments. The strategic process involves a number of committees, plans are made for markets, products and human capital, and target ratios are set. The budgetary control process is composed of two steps; a tentative and a definite, and ends in budgets both for fixed investments and for different expense kinds of investments. Apart from the strategic process, executive meetings and investment committees were also considered vital for the control of investments.

Major and long-term investments in new markets, and generation of products, are decided in the strategic process and high up in the group. It can therefore be claimed that investments in production equipment are initiated from the top, rather than, as in most groups, from the companies. As most investments are treated in planning processes relatively few independent investment requests are submitted, and as most investments are also intangible relatively few traditional investment appraisals occur. This change and the predominance of intangible investments has reduced the importance attached to the traditional investment appraisal using a DCF evaluation for the investment decision. As with major investments and investment programmes in other capital-intensive industries there was often a tendency to reverse and rephrase the evaluation issue in terms of how much can we invest in this kind of project, and when can we do so, considering our financial and human resources.

The other group had a functional structure. As in the other group the allocation of funds to R & D projects was centralized, and investments in production equipment were prompted by decisions to market new products.

Investment manuals and requests Both groups have a traditional although relatively simple, investment manual intended for fixed investments. However, the result of the appraisal plays a limited role as investments in production equipment ensue from decisions to invest in certain markets and products, and these investments are rather centralized. The manual is more important for the choice of design and the fixed investments are ranked in the budgetary control process.

Shipping groups

Structure In a sense the two shipping groups are the most investment-intensive groups in the study. During 1990, for instance, they invested about 50 per cent of sales in new and old ships.

The shipping companies treat their ships as companies, but there is no ROI type of profitability requirement, nor an investment manual. Such control measures are unnecessary as all appraisals are made and decisions taken by a small group of managers on corporate level. However, as investments in new ships demand board level decision the presentation made to the board follows a certain templet. There is actually no academic education in shipping. Instead personal competence is built up through on-the-spot training in the shipping industry, and transferred through oral channels.

Investment requests One of the groups had certain investment criteria set by the board concerning what was an acceptable consolidated balance sheet and also what this was after a price fall on the company's assets. A consolidated balance sheet and not solidity was used because of a desire to consider taxes when appraising the risk level. The rate of interest was determined as a weighted average cost of capital for the ship in question, and used mostly to estimate annuities; the cost per day and month of operating the ship. Another requirement mentioned was that the ship had to fit the company's portfolio of ships with regard to markets and segments of ships.

The respondents in the other shipping group put less emphasis on the appraisal and said that it was top management's and the brokers' feeling for what was a profitable investment in the long-term that really mattered. However, they also remarked that with this feeling in place, much work was devoted to handling risks, through the length of the contract of affreightment, the composition of the fleet, maintenance of a high degree of solidity and consolidation, and through increasing the company's ability to detect weak signals from the market and react immediately when the market so demanded. The appraisal too resembled an analysis of risks, rather than a profitability calculus.

One characteristic of the shipping groups was the short or non-existent distance between those making the appraisals and those making the investment decision. In other words, the agency problem was very small, if it existed at all. A similar situation prevailed in two of the other companies studied, one real-estate company and one of the engineering groups on the otc list. The latter group had a dominant owner and chairman of the board, and although the group was divisionalized, all investment requests needed approval by the group board. In this group the functions of ownership and management had not yet been separated. Not altogether unexpectedly, this group was later bought out by the dominant owner.

Service groups

Interviews were held in seven service groups, including two bank groups, service groups producing and selling software and computer services to companies, and various types of consulting services to industries and consumers as e.g. security systems, architectural and general consultants to the building industry, entrepreneurial services, pest control and security systems. As a group these service groups share several features with the trade and retailing groups. Investments in machines and production equipment are small; so is also the corporate effort to coordinate investments in different companies and of different types, although banks seem to do more in this respect.

Investments Some of the service groups had made rather large real estate investments during the last years of the 80s, but fixed investments in machinery etc. were and are small. Investments in markets, computers, employee training and competency development predominate. One of the groups had as a policy to invest 5 per cent of its sales in the development of new competencies. This figure disregards the training which employees receive through the assignments paid for by the customers. Several of the interviewees pointed out that their volume of investment was more likely to be curtailed by the availability of competent personnel than financial restrictions.

Resource allocation The direction of investments is controlled through the annual budgetary control process, financial measures of control, executive meetings and informal contacts. All but one group had a yearly capital budget, the two bank groups also a looser long-term investment plan. There was no investment manual, although both the bank groups had discussed the introduction of one. However, an investment request is needed to reach a decision on issues which are perceived as an investment. The investment request is made by the requester, and since there are no written instructions the requester is free to design the appraisal and request as he or she thinks fit. The PBP is the predominant measure of profitability, if such an evaluation is made. Major investments, financial options and leasing are, if necessary, evaluated with a DCF technique, taking inflation and taxes into account. However, it should be observed that these more advanced evaluations often seem to be made by the finance function, and that practice varies more in groups which lack written routines.

This is in line with Farragher (1986) who found that major U.S. service groups used the same, albeit far simpler evaluation techniques as manufacturing groups, and Neale (1991b) who discovered that post-completion reviews were less common in U.K. service than in manufacturing groups.

Intangible investments are rarely calculated, due to the problems of making such economic appraisals. They are instead discussed and decided locally and within the framework of the annual budgetary control process. Limits of authorization exist in many of the groups but are only valid for fixed investments. Acquisitions are evaluated and decided on corporate level.

The service groups are decentralized, but retain a certain central control over investments, especially of the maintenance and enhancement of their core competency, and the development of new businesses and competencies.

In six out of the seven groups corporate level are engaged in programmes for in-house training, the development of new competencies, or in the systematization and dissemination of information and know-how of common interest to the companies of the group, or the development of new services and products. The banks differ from the other service groups.

Bank group A Few companies have more comprehensive computer operations than the banks. The resource allocation system of one of the banks resembles that of the engineering groups. The volume of investment is determined from above. An investment request with an appraisal is in principle needed for all investments. There are stations which review requests coming from below, and a simple investment manual is to be introduced. Limits of authorization are low. DCF techniques, after-tax and nominal cash flow evaluations are to be made when necessary. The capital budget extends over one year with a projection over three years; furthermore the profit centres are followed up each month. There is also a "market group" working on the long-term investments of the group and business development.

Bank group B As in many other service groups the investment budget is built up from below. There were separate budgets for fixed investments, market investments, employee training, etc., and an investment committee for each of these. These investment budgets extended over one year, were followed up at least three times a year, and supplemented with a three year plan.

If there are more investment requests than can be approved then short-term investments are ranked using simple PBP, and long-term investments by the investment committees. In the latter case the strategic assessment is of more importance than possible appraisals. There are no formal limits of authorization.

The bank formerly had an investment form and certain written instructions for investment requests but the form fell into disuse. The re-introduction of an investment manual is under consideration. The lack of an instrument permitting comparision and ranking of investments is perceived as a disadvantage when an investment budget has to be curtailed. Under the present circumstances they have to use salami tactics when cutting down on investments and this was not felt to give the best trade-off between different types of investments and investments in different parts of the group.

Decentralization versus coordination and control

It is no exaggeration to say that the world economy of today is dominated by large, more or less diversified, multinational groups, and this development draws attention to the function of the head office in these multidivisional groups; Which functions does it perform? By studying the development of the multidivisional firm in the U.S. Chandler (1962) identified two basic; closely related functions which he terms the entrepreneurial and the administrative functions. The first function, the entrepreneurial or value-creating function, stood for the determination of the growth paths, goals, and strategies of the organization and the allocation of resources to pursue these strategies. The second, the administrative or loss preventing function, stood for the monitoring of the performance of subordinate operating units, their use of resources allocated and continued improvements.

Investment decisions are generally considered as one of the principle ways in which the head office can influence the growth path and strategies of the companies, and the products and markets on which the companies of the group will be competing in the future; investment decisions are therefore relatively centralized also in groups where most other types of decisions have been decentralized. This centralization is thought necessary to help the head office exercise this value-creating role.

The descriptions given in the previous section show that there are certain resource allocation system archetypes. No two groups have exactly the same resource allocation systems, but there are marked similarities between groups in one and the same line of industry; similarities which can be explained by the character of the investments and the need to coordinate resources in companies and divisions, and which affect the degree of decentralization, the means of control used and the emphasis put on these means.

We have seen that investment decisions are more decentralized in trading and retailing, and also in some service groups. The service groups are generally decentralized at the same time as they continue to exercise central control over the specification and development of the knowledge and skills that they sell. A good example is McDonald's which is franchising its business formula at the same time as it has retained central control of the set and quality of the services that the franchisees perform.

A different situation prevails in the three investment- and R & D-intensive groups. The investment-intensive group uses the same basic technologies in the capital intensive production and distribution systems that it has built up in several different countries. This makes it profitable to coordinate investments and the investment specific competencies that are essential for their success. The other two groups have very large investments in market and product development, complex investments, fast technical development with short product life cycles. This necessitates stronger involvement from the head office to execute its value-creating role, and an annual strategic process has been introduced with this in mind. Strategies and strategic investments are decided in the strategic process, and other investments necessary for the implementation of these strategies in the subsequent budgetary control process.

The large mechanical engineering groups are to be found somewhere in between these two extremes. Proposals of new products and markets come from below. The corporate level put strong emphasis on that the companies adhere to the business formulas and strategies earlier agreed on and check that the investment requests are in line with these strategies; otherwise the decision has to be referred upwards and a far more comprehensive analysis is made. For the rest they control the quality of the request and supply feedback to the investor, and from time to time also sponsor certain strategic initiatives. Larger groups are forced to put a stronger emphasis on financial measures of control, than smaller ones, and the multinational engineering groups use a great number of control measures. The steel and forest groups seem to attach similar weight to strategic control. However, the structure of investments is less complex, they use fewer measures of control and the pre-approval review system is less well developed or at least different.

After classifying these three categories of groups with regard to degree of decentralization of investment decisions and the need for coordination of investments we arrive at Table 8.1, which freely summarizes the description of these three archetypes. Observe that individual business areas, divisions and companies in certain groups might be run differently.

Table 8.1
Resource allocation in a few industries

Capital or R & D intensive groups	*Multinational engineering and forest groups*	*Trading, retailing and certain service groups*
Investments		
Large volume of investments and large long-term investments demanding central coordination	Large and long-term investments or a great mixture of investments mostly coordinated on divisional level	Relatively small and short-term investments predominates
Structure: Linkages between investments needing coordination		
Substantial	Moderate	Simple
Planning processes		
Top-down planning or a strong influence from the top	Bottom-up planning combining many means of control	Bottom-up planning
The centre active in planning	Strong divisional influence	Strong business influence
Major investments decided before, and outside the budgetary control process	Investments handled in the budgetary control process. A strategic process	All investments handled in the budgetary control process

	or other measures to separate strategic investments might exist	
Consensus important	Clear individual responsibility	

Investment committees for specific types of intangible investments such as R & D, employees competence development, software development, IT and market investments may exist in groups where such investments are important

Ex post review
Individual investments are followed up as decentralized

Group staff may follow up new strategies

Investment manual

Can be very compre-	Manual exists and	Manual exists in some
hensive, but also very	can play an import-	groups, but is simple
simple and play a sub-	ant role, not least	
ordinate role if major	for the forming	
investments are decided	of standards and	
in a separate planning	a common group	
process or intangible in-	language with regard	
vestments predominate	to investment issues	

Investment criteria

PBP used to rank small- and medium-sized investments and DCF technique for major and expansion investments		PBP and in some groups DCF for major investments

PBP and DCF criteria	PBP and DCF criteria	PBP and DCF criteria
only two of several	used with flexibility	used relatively strictly,
investment criteria	by corporate level,	if they are applied
and used with great	stricter to impose	
flexibility	capital rationing	
	on lower levels	

The shipping groups do not fit into this classification as investment decisions are not decentralized. There are, in other words, no agency problems (see e.g. Eisenhardt, 1989; Thakor, 1993) between the managers making the appraisal, those 'pushing' the investment and those making the investment decision. Many of the service groups show similarities with the trading and retailing groups, although corporate level is represented in the investment committees assessing certain important, often company-specific types of investment like investments in software, market and competency development.

One point to be noticed is that the ranking and determination of the investment budget within the framework of the annual budgetary control process constitute a form of monitoring how strategies already approved are progressing, viz. it probably often has more to do with the loss preventing, than the value-creating function of the head office. Strategic investments have usually already been evaluated and decided on before the great majority of investment requests enter into that process. The problem is to identify these strategic invest-ments and events and refer them to the right level of the organization. Those groups which do not have an annual strategic process or direct access to the investment committees do this through limits of authorization, direction for major projects and investment programmes, board representation, executive meetings and various informal channels.

Investments and management styles

The proposed classification is in its external appearance almost identical to that developed by Goold and Campbell (1987a; b; 1988). They studied the role of the centre and management styles in sixteen successful, diversified, British groups, and arrived at a model in which the management styles used by senior management at corporate level are classified into three main categories; those focusing on strategic planning, strategic control, and financial control.

> Strategic Planning companies focus on a few core businesses with the centre actively participating in formulating strategies with the business units, aiming to help the businesses make better strategic decisions, and often initiating strategic thrusts among interrelated businesses. Financial Control companies, on the other hand, mainly delegate strategic decisions to profit-responsible business unit managers, and the centre's role is to agree and monitor demanding, short-term financial targets for the business. Strategic Control companies also have a strong commitment to decentralization and emphasize control against demanding targets for their businesses, but in addition they tend to have extensive strategic planning systems and processes, through which the centre seeks to add value by reviewing, challenging and monitoring business level strategies. (Goold, Campbell and Luchs, 1993a, p. 49).

Goold and Campbell's Strategic planning groups had fewer divisions and companies than the financial control groups; on average twenty-three companies as compared with eighty-eight companies, and the linkages between divisions and companies were more numerous and stronger in their strategic planning groups. Growth had mainly been organic as opposed to the financial control groups which had grown through acquisitions. The strategic control groups were found in between. They had combined organic and acquisition growth and had thirty-two businesses per group, which is no

135

more than, and in some cases less than, a tenth of what some of our multinational engineering groups have.

Corporate level and the centre are more actively involved in shaping business strategies in strategic planning companies, and planning is therefore more centralized than in strategic and financial control groups. In consequence it also tends to measure and react with greater flexibility to, the performance of lower levels. The decentralized financial planning groups rely more on financial measures than on control and interpret them also with less flexibility. Strategic control groups tend to combine traits from these styles and to emphasize strategic control. Then there are various more or less decentralized sub-groups thereof, but most groups seem to prefer one or another of these three main categories.

Contemplating our descriptions we observe that our R & D- and investment-intensive groups have marked similarities with those groups that Goold and Campbell (1987a) term strategic planning groups. The trading and retailing groups, on the other hand, have features in common with financial control groups. The forest and engineering groups are to be found somewhere in between. Some of the engineering groups seem to put more stress on financial control, but on the whole, the main focus is on strategic control even if they have many more businesses than Goold and Campbell's U.K. groups. Some service groups can be classified as exercising financial control, others are perhaps more centralized.

One explanation why many groups favour strategic control might be that they are multinationals and work mostly on mature markets. Such multinationals have to combine flexible responsiveness to the needs of national subsidiaries with central coordination to achieve global competitiveness (Doz and Prahalad, 1984; Bartlett and Ghoshal, 1989), and this tends to make strategic control a feasible style for many multinationals. There are few examples of successful multinationals practicing a strict financial planning style. In general a more flexible approach to local markets and performance measures is necessary.

Goold and Campbell (1987a) are careful to stress that their classification builds on 'management styles' and not on line of industry or formal structure and administrative systems. The latter can, according to them, be similar.

> [I]t is important to stress that many style differences relate less to formal structures and systems than to ways in which they are operated. Budgetary processes, capital approval systems and information flows may look similar. The important differences lie in the attitudes and intentions of top management and, therefore, in the way in which formal systems are used. Our comparisons between the styles attempt to catch the cultural differences between companies as well as the more obvious differences in formal systems and processes. (Goold and Campbell, 1987a, p. 151)

Management styles are, according to Goold and Campbell (1987a), more dependent on the growth path which the group has chosen, than on industry-specific conditions. Top management chooses a management style based on their formula of success, and they also give several examples in which the U.K. groups they studied have changed style from time to time. However, linkages between divisions and companies due to the character of the investments creates a need for coordination which in our groups has been met by increased centralization, why the structure and character of investments, the need for coordination and degree of decentralization are directly reflected in the formal investment routines of the groups studied. Going from strategic planning to financial control, the responsibility of lower units has to be clearly specified and financial measures of control adapted, *inter alia*. Similarly, going from strategic control to strategic planning would no doubt necessitate at least the adaptation of the administrative routines to the new management style. It is difficult to see how else such a change could give the centre more than an illusion of increased influence.

Goold and Campbell's (1987a) classification indicates a basic connection between the stress placed on certain measures of control and the degree of decentralization. It is a simple basis of division, perhaps just because it is often difficult unambiguously to classify individual groups. The multinational engineering groups in particular combine a large number of measures to control their investments. They seem to give precedence to strategic control, at the same time as they also try to varying degrees to exert financial control and strategic planning influence. Other problems are the aforesaid effects of group size and the existence of heterogeneous business structures.

Yet another problem is the fact that decentralization as Shrivstava (1986) and Cummings (1995) have claimed, can be seen as an ideology in itself and therefore be independent of the management styles identified by Goold and Campbell (1987a). Their British financial control groups have about 100 people at the centre, the strategic control groups, and especially the strategic planning groups, considerably more. It is true that the staff units are smaller in the trading and retailing groups than in the investment and R & D -intensive groups, but some of the forest and engineering groups have less than 100 people at the centre. If classified according to the size of their staff units most Swedish groups are financial control groups, although they are not so in reality. They succed in exerting strategic control with smaller group staff units than their British colleagues. Goold and Campbell (1987a) seem to be aware of this as they refer to Pascale and Athos' (1982) description of Matsushita which they classify as financial programming - a more centralized version of financial control - which then had about 3,500 people working at the centre.

9 Requirements and trade-offs between investments

In theory there is a clear, well established connection between the value of a firm and the NPV of its investment projects. The growing use of the DCF technique and other so-called advanced evaluation techniques has therefore been seen as promoting growth and profit and many researchers have asked themselves why not all companies use these superior techniques and even projected their anticipated increased use in the future.

Managers (Neuhauser and Viscione, 1973; Hastie; 1974; Hunsicker, 1980) have often been in greater doubt about the blessing of these techniques. The most common criticism mentioned in Neuhauser and Viscione's (1973, p. 20) survey of managers' opinions of advanced capital evaluation techniques was that they give "an illusion of exactness" when input data is approximate, and that they pay to much attention to quantitative data and therefore tend to "neglect vital elements of experience, opinion, and other less quantitative" data.

However, there have always also been academics who criticised the obsession of the profession with formal evaluation techniques and favoured a broader perspective on investment decisions (e.g. Walker, 1961; Haynes and Solomon, 1962; Pinches, 1982). It has been argued that an investor is unlikely to have such good information about the investment projects of a firm that the value of its projects will equal the value of the firm (Danielsson, 1967; Findley and Williams, 1980), and that firms do not try merely to maximize shareholders wealth but pursue multiple objectives (Cyert and March, 1963; Skeddle, 1973). Critics have also referred to the difficulties of estimating the future cash flow of an investment and maintained that the uncertainty surrounding the cash flow projection often makes it impossible to base a decision to invest on the NPV alone (Skeddle,

1973; Vandell and Stonich, 1973; Gold, 1976) and that such a practice tends to favour short-term investments (Gold, 1973; Skeddle, 1973; Gold and Boyland, 1975; Hayes and Garvin, 1982). Furthermore, that the DCF technique necessitates concentration on evaluating individual projects instead of their contribution to the future of the firm as a whole (Walker, 1961; Hayes and Solomon, 1962; Gold and Boyland, 1975; Pinches, 1982).

This criticism gathered fresh momentum and took a partly new turn in the 70s when American companies began to be outperformed by Japanese firms. Studies by, for instance Hodder (1986), showed that Japanese corporations used very simple evaluation techniques like the ARR and the simple PBP. These were more inclined to challenge the assumptions on which the investment decision was based and to create consensus for the decision. Several studies were now initiated which confirmed the assumption that the Germans and especially the Japanese invested more in capital-intensive industries, and that U.S. industry was losing market shares, especially on high growth capital-intensive markets (Jacobs, 1991; Porter, 1992a; b). The U.S. industry was aging and comparative studies showed that Swedish industry had aged in a similar way. German industry was seen to be following the same path with a delay and the U.K. has long suffered from aging in parts of its industry (Porter, 1990).

This short-term behaviour of U.K. and U.S. groups has been blamed on a higher cost of capital, unduly high hurdle rates (e.g. Pearson, 1986; 1987; McCullum, 1987; Reimann, 1990; Lefley, 1994), the use of DCF techniques (e.g. Hayes and Abernathy, 1980; Hayes and Garvin, 1982; Hayes, 1985; Baldwin; 1991), undue focus on measurable effects, and later also on the bottom-up type of resource allocation system used in U.K. and U.S. groups as a whole (e.g. Hayes, Wheelwright and Clark, 1988; Carr, Tomkins and Bayliss, 1991; 1994a; b; Baldwin and Clark, 1992; 1994; Currie, 1992; Porter, 1992a; b; Jones, Currie and Dugdale, 1993). This led Porter (1992a; b), for instance, to recommend a

> [m]ove to universal investment budgeting. Conventional approaches to capital budgeting were never ideal for evaluating investment choices; they failed to deal with the changing nature of investment. A new system is needed to evaluate investment programs instead of just discrete projects; to treat all forms of investment in a unified manner; and to evaluate investments in two stages - first, determining the asset positions needed for competitiveness and second, evaluating exactly how to achieve those positions. (Porter 1992b, p. 82)

We shall evaluate these claims, starting by studying hurdle rates and PBP in Sweden, the U.K. and U.S., and try to discover whether requirements have been sharpened as some proponents claim. It will be shown that companies use different rates for different types of investments and we shall therefore clarify the distinction between creating and exploiting investments, and give examples of how this distinction applies to different types of investments and how the ability to generate profit can vary depending on the type of investment. Then, after this disgression, we shall return to the question of whether the use of DCF technique affects the propensity of the firm to make long-term investments.

Requirement levels in the past and the present

Hurdle rates Lundberg (1961) seems to have been the first to study requirement levels in Swedish industry. Through a postal survey from 1957 and almost 200 interviews he could conclude that the PBP for new machines intended to rationalize production varied between one and five years. Furthermore, that the DCF technique was sometimes used for expansion investments, and that the discount rate then was at least 10 per cent or on average about 20 per cent. The interviews gave him the impression that 30 to 40 per cent was a not uncommon rate of return requirement for short-term investments intended e.g. to rationalize production, and 15 to 20 per cent for major investment programmes. However, the cut-off or hurdle rate could be substantially lower for certain types of investment, for instance 6 to 8 per cent for power plants and 3 to 4 per cent for afforestation.

Today the hurdle rate varies between 9 and 30 per cent for the 16 groups which supply such information, with an average of 16 to 17 per cent. The figure differs depending on the principle used to determine the discount or cut-off rate. As previously explained for in Chapter 5 the less multinational groups determined their hurdle rate as a weighted average cost of capital based on accounting measures, while the more multinational fixed their hurdle rate according to the cost of borrowing in local currency plus a risk premium. Hurdle rates determined by the borrowing rate vary considerably from year to year and country to country depending on the rate of inflation, but are in general distinctly lower than those determined as a weighted average cost of capital.

Table 9.1 shows common hurdle rates and payback requirements according to Swedish studies during the last 35 years. The stability in the values is remarkable. The Table gives no support for the conclusion that hurdle rates were lower in the expansive 50s and 60s than today, rather the other way round. The average hurdle rate was in 1990 closer to 15 per cent than to Lundberg's (1961) 20 per cent, partly due to the practice of letting the cost of borrowing determine the hurdle rate. The rate of return of 30 to 40 per cent for rationalizing investments which Lundberg (1961) observed does not appear improbable even today, but many multinationals do not seem to demand 15 to 20 per cent for such strategic investments as major investment programmes.

Consideration of the effects of inflation and taxes on the hurdle rate strengthens the impression of stability. In the 50s and 60s cash flows were expressed in real terms and discounted with a nominal rate of interest. The

140

practice is the same today, although major investments later on are probably evaluated with regard to price level changes and taxes, which would mean that the discount rate is in fact lower. The rate of inflation was higher in the 70s, but this does not seem to have affected the average hurdle rate.

Table 9.1
Requirements on investments in Swedish industry

Year	Study	Payback	Hurdle rate	Inflation	Method
1957	(a)	1-5 years	20 %	4 %	PS and I
1964	(b)	-	15-20	3	M and I
1976	(c)	1-5	15-20	12	PS
1977	(d)	-	16-20	12	M
1973-83	(e)	-	17.2	6-14	PS major projects
1982	(f)	1-3	-	9	I major investor
1985	(g)	1½-3	18.5	8	PS companies
1986	(h)	2.7-3.1	19.5-20.4	8	PS companies
1990	(i)	1½-3	16.5	6	M

Notes: The data refer to the following studies: (a) Lundberg (1961), (b) Renck (1966), (c) Andersson, Gerbo and Krasse (1977), (d) Tell (1978), (e) Segelod (1986), 17.2% for 41 major projects; 15.7% for the 27 projects >100 MSEK (today approximately >£20 million.), (f) Gandemo (1983), (g) Andersson (1988), (h) Yard (1987), and (i) 29 manuals from 1990-91. The consumer price index of the year before the data were collected has been used as proxy of inflation. I stands for interviews, PS for postal survey and M according to investment manuals.

However, we should also remember that these are average values, and that the discount rate or cut-off rate differs greatly from group to group. Let us exemplify with the two extremes. One multinational basing its hurdle rate on the cost of local borrowing plus a risk premium of 2 per cent has since the first interviews in 1990 decided to subtract the rate of inflation when evaluating cash flows of certain major strategic investments if the cash flow is expressed in real terms. This means that their hurdle rate becomes very low for major strategic investments in countries like Germany and Japan which have low inflation and interest rates. The other corporation is also a multinational. In 1990 it had refrained from issuing a cut-off rate for the group, but the cut-off rate was previously 35 per cent. However, this rate was never used primarily for evaluating strategic investments, but for rationing capital to non-strategic investments. Thus although these two groups may seem to use very different hurdle rates the requirements imposed on, for instance, reinvestments and major strategic investments need not be much different.

Payback periods Given the economic life we can estimate the IRR which corresponds to a certain PBP (see Figure 9.1). Assuming an economic life of three years a payback of two years equals an IRR of about 20 per cent. If the economic life is expected to be ten years instead then the IRR approaches 50 per cent.

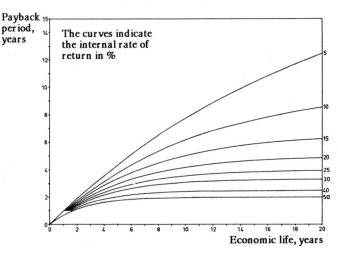

Figure 9.1   The connection between PBP and IRR

It can be observed that studies from the 50s and 60s tend to give a greater range for the PBP. One explanation thereof may be that some corporations then used the PBP as the sole criterion for both small reinvestments and strategic expansion investments. Today the required PBP for minor and medium sized investments varies between 1½ and 3 years. Strategic important investments may be allowed to have a much longer PBP. It should also be noticed that groups and companies in financial distress might sharpen their payback requirement. Gandemo (1983) and Arwidi and Yard (1985; 1986) recorded PBPs of 1 to 1½ years in such companies.

Three factors in particular have been pointed out in manuals and interviews as determinants of the PBP; country, strategy and the aforesaid factor economic life. It is common to demand shorter PBPs for investments in politically unstable countries. The longest PBP is accepted for investments in Japan, North America and Western Europe. However, if a subsidiary wishes to invest in a country affected by civil war or severe political instability then the company must present a very good reason. Major strategic investments, on the other hand, can sometimes be approved despite a much longer expected PBP. Seven to eight years were mentioned in several interviews. However, the requirement is claimed to be treated with flexibility in most groups, and especially in the strategic planning groups and those which put less emphasis on financial criteria; If the PBP is long then the other arguments have to be stronger instead.

Hurdle rates in the U.K. and U.S. There are a number of studies of hurdle rates in U.K. (Scapens and Sale, 1981; Pike and Wolfe, 1988) and U.S. (Gitman and Forrester, 1977; Schall, Sundem and Geijsbeck, 1978; Scapens and Sale, 1981; Gitman and Mercurio, 1982) corporations, which show that the hurdle rate varies considerably; between 5 to 40 per cent with an average of 15 to 24 per cent for U.K. companies and 12 to 17 per cent for U.S companies, a difference which seems reasonable considering that the inflation rate was often higher in Britain for the years in question. The only later U.S. study based on investment manuals (Mukherjee, 1988. p. 31) gives the figure 10 per cent to 25 per cent "when a single hurdle rate is given", which can be interpreted as suggesting that project-specific rates are somewhat higher.

Financial theory recommends investors to require a higher return from riskier projects. Some companies do this either through using project-specific hurdle rates, or different hurdle rates for different classes of investments or for different divisions. Critics (e.g. Pearson, 1987; McCullum, 1987; Reimann, 1990; Lefley, 1994) have maintained that this practice leads to unrealistically high hurdle rates, and have instead recommended the so-called certainty equivalent approach (Robicheck and Myers, 1965; 1966; Sick, 1986). In the latter case the riskfree cashflow is discounted by a riskfree rate of return.

Several studies show that U.K. (Pike and Wolfe, 1988) and U.S. (Gitman and Forrester, 1977; Oblak and Helm, 1980; Rosenblatt, 1980; Gitman and Mercurio, 1982; Kim, Crick and Farragher, 1984; Stanley and Block, 1984), and also Australian (Freeman and Hobbes, 1991) and New Zealand (Patterson, 1989) firms use risk-adjusted hurdle rates. However, as the survey questions are differently phrased it is impossible to tell how frequent this practice has become and for what kind of investments it is used. The percentage using such measures differs from one survey to another, from 15 per cent to 90 per cent according to a survey of surveys by Scott and Petty (1984). However, it is also interesting to see that about one third of the companies in these surveys claim not to adjust either their hurdle rate, or their payback requirement, to cater for risk. Thus, even if a third or more of all Anglo-Saxon groups use project-specific hurdle rates there are also many groups which do not do so.

Turning to Swedish practice we find that Swedish groups rarely adjust their hurdle rates for risk. Disregarding the facts that the multinationals differentiate their rates with regard to country, and that some groups use very high hurdle rates to evaluate changes in inventories as a part of their just-in-time policy, only two of the manuals state that the rate should be adjusted to the risk of the investment project. One of these uses a risk premium of 3 per cent for real-estate and one of 5 per cent for production equipment. The other uses no fixed rates for mandatory investments, 20 per cent for expansion, and 15 per cent for other investments. If project-specific rates are used in Swedish groups they seem to enter the decision process first in the assessment stage and be subjectively based. Thus, managers might accept a lower IRR for an investment intended to rationalize production, than for a pure reinvestment: and still lower IRR from expansion investments, and especially long-term strategic investments in new markets. Then there are of course the mandatory investments in improved environmental standards, many types of intangible investments, and sometimes also reinvestments, which are approved without making an DCF analysis.

Far from all major U.S. groups used risk adjusted hurdle rates. Ross (1986) investigated 400 projects in fifteen large U.S. firms and found that they typically had different requirements for replacement and expansion investments, or mandatory and discretionary investments as he terms these categories. Furthermore that the decision process for these firms differed with regard to project size, and whether or not they used the hurdle rate to ration capital at lower levels of the groups, as did our Swedish group with a very high cut-off rate. Four firms used a hurdle rate close to the firm's actual cost of capital of about 15 per cent for all discretionary investments which did not need approval from the CEO and the board. Six other firms used high hurdle rates for small projects (35 to 60 per cent), lower for medium-sized projects (25 to 40 per cent), and hurdle rates close to their actual cost of capital (15 to 25 per cent) for projects decided by the CEO and board. Ross (1986) termed the first group of companies "flexible-budgeting firms" and the other group "capital-rationing firms". The high rates found in some of the groups were explained by the use of a hurdle rate to rank investments and ration capital.

In a similar study of Swedish companies Yard (1987) found that the payback criterion predominated in companies which were either less or more profitable than the average. In the first category emphasis was placed on the PBP to strengthen the company's financial position and in the latter to create financial flexibility for an uncertain future. The negative effects of using short PBPs in profitable groups were reduced by applying other criteria to strategic investments.

The interviews only cover corporate level but it is clear that many of the groups ration capital to small and medium-sized investments mostly by requiring PBPs of 1½ to 3 years, equalling a hurdle rate of 10 per cent to 50 per cent if the economic life is assumed to be 4 years. Major investments which need group level approval, on the other hand, are evaluated with a DCF technique, longer PBPs accepted, hurdle rates lower, and most important, interpreted with considerable flexibility and of less relevance to the decision to invest; if investments are considered as necessary for strategic reasons they might be implemented even if the IRR and PBP are far below the official requirement. In particular the groups which in Chapter

8 were classified as strategic planners applied their requirement levels very flexibly, in these specific groups with regard to both major and minor investments.

The interpretation of hurdle rates We began this section by referring to an early Swedish study (Lundberg, 1961) and we end by quoting an early American study.

> The payoff period insisted upon ranges widely for the firms studied - from six months to ten years, with a cluster around one to three years on minor projects and five to seven years major projects. (Heller, 1951, p. 101)

More than 40 years have elapsed since Heller wrote these words and much has happened since then, but payback requirements have remained fairly stable. One to three years for minor investments is still valid for Swedish corporations, and five to seven years is a common limit for major and strategic investments.

It is also difficult to see that the average hurdle rate has been increased. The average hurdle rate seems more to be determined by the principle of fixing the hurdle rate - weighted average cost of capital or cost of local borrowing or the cost of financing a specific project - and the rate of inflation of the country in question. Low inflation could thus be one important factor helping German and Japanese firms to make more long-term investments.

Perhaps it could be alleged that the payback requirement for medium-sized investments has been sharpened, but the hurdle rate for major strategic investments has rather been decreased. Perhaps an effect of an heavier stress on strategic control by major corporations of today, which are reluctant to divide their resources among too many areas.

All groups make a very clear distinction in their procedures between, at the one extreme, small replacement investments, and at the other, major strategic investments. The interviewees emphasized that top management is very aware of the necessity of investing with a long-term perspective. While there is no objection in principle to these investments, it is impossible to have such an investment approved without evidence that it satisfies the criteria which management imposes. Upper management therefore must often override formal evaluation criteria to have such strategic investments carried out. Let us exemplify with a few quotations from some of the best known multinationals in the sample:

> We do not look at investments as academic as one could believe. It is much a matter of feeling, if it sounds reasonable. I think that is sound. It is difficult to prognosticate. There are so many factors. This then makes it important that one can justify long-term investments in for instance increased flexibility and new markets in another way, because the important thing is to identify the revenue and cost components. Which technique one uses is irrelevant. If it seems sensible then we

will invest anyhow. There are many investments with both seven and eight years PBP that have been approved.

We do not know whether the PBP or our cut-off rate is the limiting factor, but there is a deep understanding that we have to make long-term investments and then PBPs and IRRs are accepted that are completely outside all limits we have approved. The [top] management is aware of the kind of investment they want and then it does not matter what the PBP is. It does not make any difference. The right investment will be approved anyhow, but obviously those who let themselves be hypnotized by the PBP and IRR will of course never even think of long-term investments.

We have rather many requests where the yield is not especially good, but if it is strategically motivated then we will do it anyhow. ... A new plant can never be justified using a DCF model. That is more of a strategic investment, and therefore of course also the requirement for replacement investment is correspondingly higher to compensate for the less profitable investments.

Certain strategic investments have to be done, and then a short or long PBP becomes unimportant.

Small, non-strategic investments have to fulfil the requirements, at the same time as important strategic investments are given special treatment and approved on soft data although falling far short of these same requirements; a few examples have in fact even been given of strategic investments with an expected negative NPV which have been approved. Nevertheless top management was convinced that the investment was justified. To have them approved they have had to interfere in the capital budgeting process, or create a common understanding about how such strategic investments are to be handled.

A few of the groups have recently introduced some kind of annual strategic process in which strategic investments are decided. Decisions on strategic matters and investments have then been separated from the annual budgetary control process and completed beforehand. One experience of this new kind of process has been that it has reduced the importance of the traditional capital budgeting criteria in favour of soft data and strategic issues.

Since we introduced this strategic process the discount rate is no longer a crucial issue.

Investment decisions are once again based on more "subjective judgements" to use Heller's (1951) term.

146

Investments creating and exploiting investments

Before carrying the analysis any further, it is necessary to distinguish between investments creating and exploiting business opportunities, here exemplified by basic and contingent investments. This is a fundamental distinction applicable to many investment issues, and is in no way new. Early writers like Dean (1951a; b), Istvan (1961a) and Lundberg (1961) make it although they, as Istvan (1961a), may use the terms minor and major investments instead. Let us start by illustrating this distinction with an example from Segelod (1986) and the chemical industry.

> Market studies indicated that a chemical corporation could sell another 20,000 metric tons of one of its products. The company therefore built a new unit designed to produce 20,000 tons at normal operation. However, to make better use of scale economies they also designed the plant for a later extension to 30,000 tons. By so doing it would be cheaper to increase the capacity when and if the market demanded another 10,000 tons. The plant was taken into operation, extended to 30,000 tons and later tuned up to 48,000 tons after a large number of small investments "to remove bottle-necks", thit was the capacity of the plant when due to the high cost of production it was replaced by a new one.

Our company could of course have built a 30,000 tons plant at the outset. That would have needed a smaller total capital outlay, but also the capital cost of 10,000 unproductive tons; moreover there may also have been a higher technical risk or take longer period before the plant achieved normal production. The decision to build a 20,000 ton plant prepared for 30,000 tons is the basic investment with regard to the plant.

The contingent expansion investments will in general give more new capacity per invested £, than the basic investment. The life of the basic or creating investment is equivalent to the economic life of the plant, while many of the contingent or exploiting investments intended to replace worn-out parts of the plant, increase production or change the product mix will have a much shorter economic life and be repeated several times during the life of the plant. The basic investment is often seen as a ticket of admission which allows the company to operate in the industry and exploit the profitable contingent investments which the basic investment creates.

One reason why the project planners did not save money by utilizing the development potential of the plant and basic investment better already from the outset, was their wish to achieve planned product quality and capacity as fast as possible. It might be cheaper to optimize the plant harder at the drawing-board stage but this would also be associated with greater technical risks. New plants are based on experiences of how previous plants have performed and much of the work of optimization is done when the plant is in operation and has begun to pay for itself. This continuous optimization can in some technologies yield amazing results, as illustrated by our next example from Segelod (1995).

> Nonwoven is a process for producing a thin plastic fabric with many small holes which repel moisture at the same time as it lets the air through. The material is used for, *inter alia* , diapers and in the medical sector and produced in machines which superficially resemble a paper-making machine. Five years after Holmens Bruk AB had taken their machine into operation they could rejoice at the fact that the machine originally planned for 6,000-6,500 metric tons now produced 9,000 tons, due to a number of small contingent investments, successful tuning-in and improvements. Still, this was not the whole story. During these five years the producers had gradually learned to produce a thinner material, a development prompted partly by the consumers who preferred diapers with a thinner outer layer, partly by the higher price for thinner products. If output is measured by square meter the production increase becomes still more impressive, and this successful optimization was essential for the high profitability of this machine. If it had produced 6,500 tons of the product anticipated at the time of the decision to invest it would not have been a profitable investment five years later.

This distinction between basic and contingent investments, or between investments which make future profitable investments possible and investments that exploit such creating investments, applies in many areas and to many different types of investment. It can be a new paper-making machine, a new manufacturing plant or product line, an entry into a new market, the development of a new technology, a new family of aircraft models, or a new generation of products based on a common technology or design, etc. These basic investments take a long time to prepare and implement, have a long life if they are successful, and are capital-intensive. For the individual company ten years might pass between such decisions, and inbetween there are many contingent investments of various sizes intended to increase capacity, product quality, productivity, adjust the product mix to changes in the market, develop new products and markets based on the original concept which the basic investment represent.

The first generation of a new product group is by itself often unprofitable. Only through the extra return received from additional products which can utilize the technology of the initial project is the innovation made profitable. Major steps in technology such as completely new aircraft models or products using a new type of technology are often not profitable by themselves. The company making these advances must be able to use the technology developed in new models, which also means that successful models tend to stay in production for very long periods. However, it is of course not the same model which is built in the first as in the tenth year, as product development work is constantly in progress.

Appraisals of different types of investments

Investment criteria for basic investments Major investments are in general evaluated with the help of a DCF technique. The technique is in itself simple but presupposes that the appraiser can arrive at a reasonably good estimate of all future payments and receipts caused by the investment during its economic life, and that these payments are discounted with a discount rate not too far from the theoretical ideal. We have already referred to the great differences in the hurdle rates used by different investors, and now return to the problem of determining the relevant cash flow of the basic investment.

The appraiser has a tendency not to include in the appraisal the payments of consequences of the investment that he or she is uncertain will ever be realized. Since this conservatism biases the appraisal against uncertain options, it can be claimed that most investment appraisals are only partial. Thus the profitability of the basic investment tends to be

- under-estimated as the economic life of the investment is set at five to twenty years when in reality the investment project often has a far longer economic life and sometimes a PBP not much shorter than this planning horizon.
- under-estimated as the calculator disregards the profit received from future and profitable, albeit uncertain contingent investments increasing the capacity, productivity or product quality of the basic investment.
- over-estimated as the calculator disregards expenditures for future and uncertain investments necessary to adjust the basic investment to the changing market conditions.

The fact that the appraisers tend not to allow for all future payments and receipts caused by the investment contravenes the assumptions associated with the DCF technique but does not mean that these future options are not considered. Decision makers are usually aware of some of them, they are discussed and can also be described in the appraisal. However, an attempt is made to motivate the investment without including these uncertain options in the financial calculation. These permutations are instead made in the assessment process.

Instead of making a correct DCF evaluation including the estimated values of all future options, major strategic investments are assessed on a mixture of hard and soft data. The financial evaluation is sometimes performed to see whether the company has the financial resources to implement the investment successfully, rather than as an attempt to arrive at its actual IRR, and this can partly explain why the time horizon of the appraisal is sometimes not much longer than its realistic PBP. One part of this financial evaluation - when the investment is large compared with the company - examines how the balance sheet and income statement of the company are affected by the investment under different assumptions about the future and the financial options. The decision to invest is not based on an investment request promising a high IRR, but such an evaluation has to be presented in justification to have the investment approved. As uncertain future options are excluded the financial evaluation becomes an evaluation of financial risk. Let us exemplify with an investment in a new plant to increase capacity, an investment approaching three billion SEK. This is a major, a very long-term, and an important strategic investment for the company and group in question.

Let us take the expansion investment we were looking at last year. That is an investment in the size of three billion SEK. We do not reckon with that kind of investment, because it is impossible. It is a matter of structure. If we are to remain in this product area, then we have to make it. Then can we make it from a financial point of view. We think so. Then we will have to look at the future of the product area. Which growth do we have. Can we still dominate the market.

Based on this we will then make an assumption about the future, in this case the next eight years. What we actually do then is to try to construct an income statement and a balance sheet for the years ahead. Which borrowing requirements will we have? What will the cash flow look like? We do not look especially much at the return of the investment in that situation. It is more to estimate the funds-flow, what our rate of return earning capacity will look like. We will never manage a decent rate of return during such an effort, but the net yield has to be positive in a relatively short time and the borrowing requirements have to be within reasonable limits.

Then I as an economist have to make some form of investment appraisal out of this, and then we have an IRR requirement of X per cent, or what it might be. The decision makers are not interested in that kind of analysis. The board members are more interested in the funds-flow, to see that we can do it. The capital budgeting technique used in the request is rather irrelevant to the decision maker, but it is important that we can show the decision maker that we have gone through that process, also to convince our own conscience that this is an economically sound investment.

However, the question of this investment type SEK three billion is more a matter of a belief in the product and investment as such. The deciding factor is not whether the IRR is 25 or 30 per cent. However, if we are talking about smaller investments, say for instance an investment in an existing machine or plant of SEK 50 to 100 million to increase capacity, then the IRR becomes much more important and the PBP too, to count on that, but not with large structural investments.

Investment criteria for contingent investments There are many different types of contingent investments, and the distinction between replacement investment and regular maintenance and repair is sometimes vague. There are replacement, rationalizing, expansion, adjustment investments, that is, various types of contingent investments to adjust the production apparatus to changing prices of input, demands from the authorities and changes in the price and demand for the products produced. The feature which unites them is that they all exploit business opportunities created by earlier basic investments.

Replacement investments are sometimes not evaluated at all, sometimes with the PBP. If a part of a production system breaks down, either it can be replaced or production must cease altogether. It is as if a railway bridge were to collapse. Either it is rebuilt, or the whole railway line is closed down. If the production is profitable then there is no need to make an economic appraisal to confirm that the defective part has to be replaced; it is possible to evaluate different technical solutions which might also improve the production process. Other types of contingent investments are evaluated with the PBP criterion or a DCF technique.

Those who request a contingent investment must be able to prove that the capital expenditures can be recouped within two to three years, sometimes less. Assuming an economic life of five years this is equivalent to a rate of return of 20 to 40 per cent; at ten years 30 to 50 per cent. How can any contingent investment, apart from clear cut reinvestments in profitable production systems, be so very profitable? The explanation is to be sought in the fact that contingent investments contribute to better utilization of previous investments so that their profitability is improved. The contingent investments can be credited with these improvements without having to pay the initial outlay of these investments. The profitability of a contingent investment depends on its ability not only to exploit future business opportunity, but also to exploit earlier investments (Lundberg, 1961). The costs of the basic investment are not included in the appraisal and the investment is therefore a marginal analysis (Lundberg, 1961; Coulthurst, 1986). Basic investments cannot in the same degree utilize existing production apparatus. They have to pay their own cost.

Investment criteria and systems of classification The theory of investment tells us to calculate all investments in a similar manner so that they can be compared and ranked. That is, however, not the way resources are allocated to different types of investments. Investments are instead classified and different criteria applied to different classes (Barna, 1962; Cannon, 1966; Rosenblatt, 1980; Gitman and Mercurio, 1982; Ross, 1986). Critics (e.g. Baldwin, 1991; Clark and Baldwin, 1992; Porter, 1992a; b) have maintained that this practice causes mis-allocation, and recommended companies to "treat all forms of investment in a unified manner" (Porter, 1992b, p. 82). On the basis of investment manuals and interviews we can, broadly speaking, identify three different types of profitability criteria used in Swedish industry:

151

- The PBP criterion is used for all investments below a certain limit of initial outlay, for choices between design options, more often for contingent investments which are reinvestments rather than expansion investments, and as a supplement to a DCF criterion also for major investments.
- Different DCF criteria are used for major investments and expansion investments, the annuity and MAPI criteria for contingent investments pertinent to replacement.
- Different types of non-monetary criteria are used for obviously profitable reinvestments, investments necessary due to safety and environmental standards, sometimes to motivate important strategic investments and chiefly for the large group of intangible investments.

Concentrating on the use of the simple PBP criterion and the DCF criterion as the primary criterion the manuals reveal three different principles for choosing between these two types of criteria. They recommend either

- PBP for minor investments and a DCF criterion for major investments, or
- PBP for reinvestments or preserving investments and a DCF criterion for expansion investments, or
- the use of both the PBP and a DCF criterion.

The expenditure limit for when a DCF criterion is to be used varies between 0.1 and 5 MSEK. The group having the 5 MSEK limit is a multinational engineering group, which uses the DCF model only for certain investments that need group level approval. Another multinational machine engineering group which lacks fixed limits of authorization might in practice have an equally high limit. However, as both these groups also allow lower levels to develop supplementary instructions, it is possible that the DCF model is used on lower levels in some parts of the groups.

Some groups have supplemented this simple rule with a passage stipulating that also expansion investments above a certain limit must be evaluated using a DCF model. The reason is of course that also the revenue side has to be evaluated. This means that the reinvestment can be based on hard financial data from past production, while decisions on expansion investments must also consider the softer data of the market appraisal.

All forest groups and also two other groups instruct their compiler of investment requests always to calculate both the PBP and a DCF criterion. The reason may be that these groups have relatively large individual investment projects, compared with the other groups, which are planned and implemented through the framework of a project organization. Such investment projects can include many smaller projects and design choices, for which the payback criterion is usually used. However, these choices do not result in independent investment requests as they are made by the project management.

152

One distinction which appears in all the manuals is that between, on the one hand, investments that seek to maintain the existing direction and level of production, and, on the other, investments that aim to expand och change the course of existing production. Simpler terms found in many manuals for these two kinds of investments are reinvestment and expansion investments. The dividing line between these purposes is often difficult to draw and many groups also have several classes for investments which in varying degrees can be classified as exceeding the existing scope of production.

Several researchers (Dearden, 1968; 1969; Hayes and Garvin, 1982) have expressed fears lest the use of profit centre criteria introduce a bias against expansion investments, since upholding investments do not increase the capital stock to the same extent. The interviewees were well aware of this criticism and some remarked that they sometimes have to curtail the volume of reinvestment. Other researchers (Lundberg, 1961; Barna, 1962; Wright, 1964) suspected a bias against expansion investments, as decisions on upholding investments can be based to a greater extent on hard, more reliable data derived from the accounting system.

Criteria for design decisions Business economists often forget that PBP and DCF criteria are also used to evaluate design options, and not only to assess investment requests. An example serves to clarify. When a hydro-electric power station is designed the value of the water consumed in the plant is discounted for different design alternatives. In one case the design engineer used a 12 per cent discount rate for valuing the design alternatives, and the company a 4 per cent rate to evaluate the design alternative chosen for the investment request. The business economist who was in charge of capital budgeting procedures was unaware of the rent used by the design engineer, and the design engineer used the rent recommended by his former professor.

Large investments can usually be split up into smaller investments and design options. The designer can thus, at least in theory, choose between a low investment outlay, and low costs for operation and maintenance. In principle it should be possible to use the same principles of evaluation and criteria for these decisions as for the decision to invest. However, this is seldom the case (Ford, 1977; Segelod, 1986; 1992a; Dixon and Duffey, 1990).

There are few articles in the economic journals on how design alternatives are evaluated, but a study of eight major investments and capital investments in ten municipalities (Segelod, 1986) showed that the PBP totally predominated and that the requirements were two to three years. One of the new plants had been optimized using a payback criterion of five years, and in another project management had tried to use a life cycle costing (LCC) approach when evaluating tenders. The chief design engineer asserted that the five year plant had lower operational and maintenance costs and a longer repair-free life than any other plant in that industry. In the case where the design decisions were made by a consultant or engineering company none seemed to know which criteria had been applied, save that they were guided by safety and industry standards and the practice within the industry.

LCC is a technique to optimize the return on the design of an investment over its economic life. The technique was developed for military procurement, and on the civilian side has been used in the design of trains and certain other vehicles. Attempts have also been made to apply the technique to industrial plants but the diffusion process has been slow. Consumer products are rarely designed to give the lowest discounted cost over the economic life (Lund, 1978; Lund and Denney, 1978), and it has proved difficult to sell LCC designed products to buyers who lack advanced technical knowledge of the product.

Only two manuals treat the design aspect. Both state that the investment must be designed to yield the highest NPV etc. during its expected economic life. It is not allowed to choose a design alternative which gives a shorter PBP in order to gain swift approval of the initial outlay and investment.

> It is presumed that the design of the investment will be optimized with regard to the normal economic life of the type of investment in question. Thus, it is not allowed to choose design options that will shorten the PBP of the investment at the expense of its long-term profitability.

Investment criteria for reinvestment decisions Explaining the character of reinvestments we also touch upon the related issue of when a creating investment should be replaced by a more modern one. Boiteux (cited in Massé, 1962) once described this problem by referring to the choice between investing in an existing railway line, or replacing it by a road transport system. A railway line or service can have a very long technical life if it is given regular maintenance. If the costs of maintaining the line for the next few years are compared with the investment needed to replace it by a system of road transports, it will perhaps never be profitable to do so, and Massé therefore recommends us to draw up a long-term schedule for the replacement and maintain the system accordingly.

The problem is that contingent investments in the railway system become profitable as they can be credited with the increase in profit generated from past investments. Furthermore, that the change-over to a system of road transports is not credited with the superior flexibility of such a system, being able to offer transports from door to door and from and to any destination whither goods and passengers might wish to go. A proper replacement appraisal should in principle compare the total cost of running the railway system during a certain period, with the cost of running a road transport system, including the value of the flexibility offered by such a system. Observe that we are here talking about principles. Road and rail transports have of course other pros and cons which are not included in this example.

The replacement question has attracted renewed interest in connection with the growing importance of investments in flexible manufacturing systems (FMS). Recalling Chapter 2 we remember that computerized machines and equipment accounted for 31 per cent of fixed investments in Swedish industry in 1993, and 43 per cent of fixed investments in the engineering industry. Many companies have found it difficult to justify investments in FMSs with their traditional formula for appraising replacement investments. Many of the advantage of such flexible production equipment lies in the many options that it offers, and the value of these optional uses of the investment are both difficult to evaluate and excluded from the traditional appraisal. This has led to extensive empirical (see e.g. Currie, 1992; Wilner, Koch and Klammer, 1992) and theoretical research (see e.g. Finnie, 1988; Aggarwal, 1991; Wilkes and Samuels, 1991; Ramasesh and Jayakumar, 1993) on the evaluation of such investments. For a review of literature see Proctor and Canada (1992) and Son (1992).

Critics have carried this criticism still further and condemned traditional replacement appraisals as being biased against technical renewal (Hodder, 1986; Baldwin, 1991; Baldwin and Clark, 1992; 1994). They tend to underestimate the true development potential of a new technology and the market shares which can be gained by the first company to introduce a new technology. It is easier to gain market shares in the growth stage of a new technology, especially if a company is aggressive and uses forward pricing, as many Japanese producers have done.

It may seem only disadvantageous to be the technological leader and to discount incomes from anticipated future increases in sales by forward pricing, but experience has shown that this can be a less hazardous course in the long run. Furthermore, a firm which has once come to the fore as a technological leader with and a superior market position is better placed to hold its own position through the next product or technology change and to defend its market against new entrants. Analyses which take their point of departure in the existing situation tend to disregard these dynamic effects. Baldwin (1991) writes that

> [t]he inherent conflict between commitments to innovate and systems of capital budgeting in most apparent when a company considers replacing an existing product or process. Whether the decision is to introduce a product or invest in new equipment, financial analysis almost always favours postponement of the investment. (Baldwin, 1991, p. 39)

The same problem recurs viz the choice between creating and exploiting investments. The company must weigh the pros and cons of exchanging a secure profit from exploiting traditional products and technology, for the technical and market risks associated with a new product and technology and the creation of the future growth opportunities inherent in the being first to take such a step. This vital timing is a choice between short-term and long-term profitability and growth, and it is essential to find a balance which will not jeopardize the long-term harmonious development of the company.

155

The varied profitability of R & D Some R & D has a very long, and some product developments an amazingly short, PBP. As with investments in production equipment the PBP differs considerably with the character of the investment.

The pharmaceutical industry, for instance, has a large number of long term R & D projects. Joglekar and Patterson (1986) sought to estimate the profitability of such research. On the basis of historical data they tried to forecast the future cash flow of new chemical entities, which began to be developed in 1976 and were introduced on the market twelve years later in 1988. They demonstrated that, on average, it takes nine years from market introduction to the break-even point, and twelve years to give the same yield as corporate bonds. It should be profitable therefore to invest in R & D in the pharmaceutical sector, but it must then be borne in mind that these are averages. Half of the pharmaceutical drugs introduced will never recoup their costs of development, according to Joglekar and Patterson, and only a third give as good a return after twelve years as a risk-free investment in corporate bonds. The profit comes from a small number of highly profitable drugs.

If the firm finds that it has developed one of these highly profitable products then it will also worth its while to invest in the necessary production equipment. No economic calculation is needed to establish this fact. Nor is there any point in looking back and discontinuing a drug which will probably not recoup its total R & D costs. The question is whether a production could return a surplus or not.

Whether or not radical R & D is profitable also depends on the extent to which the firm pursuing the research can make use of the new knowledge which emerges thereby. There is often a considerable spill-over effect in research. New knowledge is often easily disseminated within an industry so that other companies can also benefit from the results produced by other firms. Research can therefore be profitable for the development of the society as a whole, at the same time as it is unprofitable for the company actually financing the same research, and this is one argument for state support of basic research. Several researchers (Griliches, 1979; Jaffe, 1986; Bernstein and Nadiri, 1989) have tried to estimate this spillover effect and arrived at amazingly large figures. Bernstein and Nadiri (1989), for instance, conclude that

> [t]he existence of R & D spillovers implies that the social and private rates of return to R & D capital differ. We estimated that the social return exceeded the private return in each industry. However, there was significant variations across industries in the differential between the returns. For chemicals and instruments, the social return exceeded the private return by 67 and 90%, respectively. Machinery exhibited the smallest differential which amounted to 30%, and the petroleum industry exhibited the greatest differential as the social rate exceeded the private rate be 123%. (Bernstein and Nadiri 1989, p. 264)

Leaving the long-term research, the development of new competencies and product platforms, and turning our attention to the development of new products the PBP can in fact be extremely short if the technical development is very fast. Mobile telephones are a good example. The technical development is very fast and new models are today introduced once a year. If a new model has not paid for itself within three months it will probably never do so.

There are very many normative articles suggesting criteria for R & D projects (e.g. Cochran *et al.*, 1971; Baker and Freeland, 1975; Sounder, 1978; Becker, 1980; Jackson, 1983; Saunder and Mandakovic, 1986), but very few recent surveys of their use. Cook and Rizzuto (1989) who surveyed major R & D firms in the U.S. is an exception. Their study showed that basic research was assessed in a similar way to other strategic investments and not subjected to formal economic analysis. Product development projects, on the other hand, were often evaluated with the same DCF and PBP criteria as used for fixed investments. We can here recall that eight of the manuals stipulated that also product development projects were to be calculated according to the manual, and in most of these cases also that the same form should be used as for fixed investments. Some writers have seen the use of such criteria for new product developments as a sign of short-termness. However, considering the short life cycles of products on fast developing high-tech markets, as illustrated by the mobile telephone example, their use becomes much more understandable.

The profitability of ventures in new areas Another type of long term investments are ventures in new areas. It takes time, and it is very costly, to develop new business areas by internal development (See Normann, 1977; Biggadike, 1979a; 1979b; Weiss, 1981; Segelod, 1995a). A study by Biggadike (1979), using PIMS data collected from firms which had entered new product-markets by internal development found that it took eight years for the median entrant before the cash flow of the venture became positive, and twelve years before the median venture generated cash flow ratios similar to those of the mature businesses. Depressing figures, yet we must remember that these are survivors. Many entrants had wound up their ventures long before they had reached break even. However, we should also remember that exactly as for Joglekar and Patterson's (1986) drug projects some of the ventures were highly successful. Eighteen per cent of the ventures were producing a positive cash flow already after two years, whereof the most successful had already achieved a pretax return on investment of 80 per cent. Exactly as for pharmaceutical research there are ventures in new areas which are extremely profitable, with a considerable spillover effect to other firms which can profit from the new business opportunities created by such a venture.

Pharmaceutical research and ventures in new areas are only examples of projects which create new business opportunities. There are also infrastructure investments, e.g. canals, railways (Sayer, 1952), roads, airports, which have opened up new areas for exploitation. However, new technologies, services and business concepts are often similar. They create new opportunities and have a spillover effect. Moreover it often happens that radical innovations are connected with one or several entrepreneurs, need capital infusion and have to be reorganized several times.

Investments rich and poor in options We commenced our detour into creating and exploiting investments by referring to a plant built by a chemical corporation. The plant was built to produce 20,000 tons and prepared for an extension to 30,000 tons if and when the market could absorb another 10,000 tons. The investment request showed that a plant producing 20,000 tons could be made profitable. The cashflow evaluation did not include the cashflow from a possible future expansion to 30,000 tons, but this option was described in the investment request. The management knew that such an extension was feasible and perhaps also that the development potential of the plant was even higher, and this knowledge was of course one factor influencing their assessment of the investment. The expansion can be termed an option and the NPV of the investment appraisal the static NPV as it does not consider the dynamic effects of the investment (see e.g. Kester, 1984; 1986; Trigeorgis and Mason, 1987; Persson, 1990; Sharp, 1991; Dixit and Pindyck, 1994):

Expanded NPV = static NPV + option premium

According to option theory a profitable investment can have a negative static NPV if this is weighed up by the value of the options which it engenders. An option is not an obligation, but a possibility to take advantage of an investment opportunity in a certain future which would not have been available had not the earlier investment been implemented. It has a duration, which makes the timing of investments important, and its value increases with uncertainty; without uncertainty there are no options, which, for instance, can explain why firms in high uncertainty may prefer to hold options which they later strike in times of low uncertainty. Reorganization and major changes in strategies are usually explored and adopted when the future of the present strategy seems bleak, and exploited when all goes well. The option model can also explain why top managers sometimes approve strategic investments which are expected to have PBPs and IRRs far removed from what is officially approved; "Certain strategic investments have to be done, and then a short or long PBP becomes unimportant", as stated in one of the quotations. It can be assumed that top management add up the options attached to a strategic investments and therefore find the expanded NPV of the investment positive.

The decision to expand operations to 30,000 tons by investing in a real asset can be termed a real option. Management was aware of this possibility and decided to strike this option when there was a market for such a output.

The management could probably also foresee a still higher capacity in the future. Experience from other plants had shown that it often proved possible to extract an even higher production from the initial basic investment, but these options were hidden in the future, dependent on the result of earlier investments and partly also on technological development, viz., learning in one way or another. Persson (1990) calls these concealed options pre-options and Bowman and Hurry (1993) shadow options. Experienced decision-makers are aware that such hidden options exist, but they cannot know exactly what they imply. First they have to be recognized and formulated as real options and this is a continuous process of learning. As managers learn more about the plant and how preconditions change they become aware of new real options and investment opportunities.

The option approach allows us to see investments as a chain of hidden or shadow options becoming real options which eventually materialize through investments. It enables us to understand how uncertainty is gradually resolved and new profitable investment opportunities arise, are explored and exploited. As a description it gives a far more realistic picture of investment activities than the traditional static investment model, as can be seen by comparing the traditional model with the examples given earlier in this chapter.

Investments are sequential in character. New investments are made possible by earlier investments and learning. Companies rarely make a total calculus for a major creating investment, instead they tend to take it step by step. The cash flow estimation is based on the first part of the expected economic life of the investment and often intended to prove that the company can implement the investment financially. Then, when this step has been secured and the company has a positive cashflow they start making investment requests for contingent investments which can enhance the profitability of earlier investments; indeed as illustrated by the Fiberweb example, the successful identification and implementation of such real options is often a precondition for making the initial creating investment profitable at all. This sequential character is perhaps even more evident in major R & D projects, which are often decided step by step as more and more is learned about the product under development.

It is difficult to assign the correct value to an option. Assuming that the stock market can rightly assess the value of the bundle of options held by certain major U.S. corporations Kester (1984; 1986) estimated the value of their total options to 25 to 75 per cent of the market value of the same corporations. It is easier to state that certain types of investments offer fewer options than other types of investments (see Table 9.2). Long-term investments, for instance, have on average a higher option premium than short-term investments as the option value increases with duration. The option premium of intangible investments like product or market development, on the other hand, is often higher than that of more easily quantifiable investments like buildings and machines, as their implementation is a process of learning and many of their options therefore are hidden in the future. This is not to say that intangible investments are more profitable, only that their assessment rests more on soft data and that less reliance can be attached to the traditional DCF model. Consequently, we can also observe that the DCF model is more frequently used in connection with investments with a relatively small option premium.

Options can be divided into different categories. Sharp (1991), for instance, distinguishes between incremental and flexibility options. Incremental options are connected to a specific investment opportunity, while an investment in a flexibility option is of a more general nature creating resources and the ability to strike incremental options in a later period. Relating this to investments in competence we can, for instance, differentiate the new competence which ensues from the completion of specific projects paid for by customers, from the general investments in developing new competencies applicable to different customers and assignments.

Table 9.2
Investments and the option premium

Option premium small	*Option premium large*
Contingent investments	Basic investments
Short-term investments	Long-term investments
Traditional machines	Flexible manufacturing systems
Tangible investments	Intangible investments
Investments in existing area	Investments in new area
Product developments	Product platform developments

Incremental options, on the other hand, exist as call and put options. A call option can be an option to expand operation, and a put option an option to abandon a project or reduce production.

The drawbacks of the option approach to investments in real assets consist in difficulties of valuing real options and the complex computations needed to use option formulas. However, great expectations have long been associated with the technique; "Five years from now option models for capital investments will be standard" (Ballen, 1989, p. 61), prophesied a McKinsey employee in an interview. The complex computations can be handled when simple user-friendly computer programmes are generally available for this purpose, but the problem of quantifying soft data persists of course and is not solved by the technique as such.

The advantage of the approach lies in its ability precisely to describe actual investment behaviour. It shows that the value of an investment is the sum of its NPV and options, and gives us a rationale for considering options when evaluating and assessing investments. Companies of course discovered this long ago. As said in Chapter 7, eight of the manuals urged the user to evaluate additional investments, sixteen to evaluate flexibility in one form or another and almost all contained some phrase telling the requester to describe how the investment relates to other investments, the company and its environment. All these measures help to identifying and visualize options and this is perhaps where the option approach can make its most important contribution. Once the options are visible it is easier for decision-makers to form an opinion about the expanded NPV and this alone should reduce uncertainty and make it easier to evaluate high-risk investments.

Does the DCF technique cause short-term practice

Returning to our initial question whether hurdle rates are too high or the use of the DCF technique has caused companies to behave in a more short-term manner, as some writers claim, we must conclude that the evidence is inconclusive. There is no support for the notion that requirement levels in Swedish-based groups are higher today than in the 50s and 60s when economic growth was rapid, and there is no conclusive evidence that U.K. and U.S. companies have developed much differently apart from the observation that some, but far from all, firms have introduced risk-adjusted hurdle rates. On the contrary, the hurdle rate and PBP requirements have remained amazingly impervious to changes in growth and inflation.

We distinguished between creating and exploiting investments and showed that this distinction applies to many different types of investment. Exploiting investments becomes profitable partly because they can utilize earlier creating investments without contributing to their capital outlay, and creating investments are often unprofitable if they are not followed by additional exploiting investments. These two kind of investments are calculated in different ways. As illustrated by a quotation regarding a basic investment the cash flow evaluation was not done to determine whether or not the project had a positive NPV, and should therefore be implemented, but, *inter alia* , to convince those involved that the company and the group had the financial capacity to complete the project, which was essential if the company wanted to remain a dominant actor on the market. Exploiting investments, on the other hand, can become very profitable. PBPs of two to three years and IRR of 30 per cent to 60 per cent do not seem improbable, and it is therefore important to know in which situation a certain hurdle rate or payback requirement is used. Depending on the character of the investment, the way it is calculated, and the structure of the resource allocation system, the requirement level and the flexibility with which it is applied might differ significantly without this implying that the level itself affects the trade-off between long- and short-term investments.

It is true that U.K., U.S. and Swedish industries have been losing market shares to regions with faster growth rates. There has also been too little organic growth by ventures in new areas, and perhaps too much acquisition growth on mature markets. The agents of the economies could not keep pace by renewal of their product portfolios.

It is also true that the cost of capital has been lower in Germany and Japan. This ought to have affected the volume of investment, but there is no clear connection between the actual cost of capital and the discount or cut-off rates. These rates differ enormously, from 5 to 10 per cent, based on estimations of the social time preference or social opportunity cost for public sector projects according to a survey of practice in ten countries (Rapp and Selmer, 1979) to 10 to 30 per cent, even 5 to 40 per cent, for private sector projects. Anecdotal evidence suggests that German and Japanese companies use lower rates but it should then be remembered that since these rates are average values there are also some Swedish, U.K. and U.S. groups which use rates as low as those of many German and Japanese groups. It is difficult fully to understand why rates can differ so much and why some firms have for years been using lower or higher rates than their competitors. One important factor influencing the hurdle rate is of course the principle for its determination, and another concerns the types of investments for which the hurdle rate is used. Without knowledge of the role of the hurdle rate only assumptions can be made regarding its influence on the trade-off between long- and short-term investments.

Many U.K. and U.S. researchers have expressed fears of unduly high hurdle rates due to the usage of divisional and project-specific hurdle rates. This practice that seems to be rare in Swedish groups. If such an adjustment occurs it is instead made at the assessment stage. However, the practice does not seem to be as widespread as many writers appear to believe. Surveys have given very different results but several studies have shown that perhaps only a third of all major U.K. and U.S. corporations do so, and also that another third do not adjust their calculus for risk at all.

One must remember that it is important that the hurdle rate be on the right level, at least in theory. If it is too high then priority will be given to short-term investments with high cost of operation and repair, and vice versa. The hurdle rate must be on the right level to allow payments and receipts to be balanced in the near and distant future. Groups using the lower hurdle rate will, in theory, choose more long-term and capital-intensive investments. It can be shown that they will build up more capacity than their competitors and invest more in long-term projects like developing new technologies, products and competencies. In the long run this should give them a larger market share and more high-tech products than their competitors.

The practice of adding a risk premium to the discount rate is controversial. It implies that the level of risk is directly propotional to the time value of money. A more realistic assumption would be to separate time and risk by adjusting the components of the cash flow for risk and discount this cash flow with a risk free rate of discount. Robichek and Myers (1965; 1966) recommended this so-called certainty equivalent method and thereby started a continuing debate on whether cash flows or discount rates, as in, for instance, the CAPM, should be adjusted for risk when evaluating investments within the firm. In the U.S. 5 to 25 per cent (Gitman and Forrester, 1977; Oblak and Helm, 1980; Gitman and Mercurio, 1982; Kim, Crick and Farragher, 1984) claim to use this method, although it is very difficult to interpret such survey results. However, the method might in practice be widely used unbeknown to managers, as appraisers tend to include only payments and receipts with consequences of which they are reasonably certain. The consequences of uncertain options are not included in the cash flow projection but described in the investment request and communication on the investment.

The debate on the role of the DCF technique and hurdle rates in the decline of the Western economies rests in part on a prescriptive model of capital budgeting decisions. It is assumed that managers do evaluate the NPV of their investment ideas and implement those which promise a positive result. This is, as we have seen, far too simplistic a model of the role of such techniques. In fact, it is not difficult to find examples of investment decisions which were reached before a DCF evaluation was made (Petty, Scott and Bird, 1975). Examples showing that investments are sometimes not calculated until the investment budget has to be curtailed were given in the interviews and we can also recall the earlier quotation regarding a major investment.

The Boiteux example served to illustrate the problem of deciding when to stop exploiting an existing system and replace it with a new one. Such decisions have to be based on a total evaluation of the old and the new system, or creating investments. There is an obvious risk that renewal will be postponed if such a separation is not done and too high a priority is given to the IRR of the alternatives.

Another problem is the increasing volume and importance of intangible investments seen in many lines of industry. However, the distinction between creating and exploiting investments applies also to these types of investment, although we then talk about new product platforms and products, or general and specific investments in markets, training and new competencies, etc. The volume of intangible investments is in many industries today significantly higher than in tangible investments. The cash flow of these investments is in general not projected, nor are, for instance, creating investments of these different types ranked against each other and against fixed investments and decided within the framework of a unitary process for all investment decisions. Our knowledge of how intangible investments are administered is poor, partly because such decisions are not perceived as investment decisions although they involve long-term commitments. However, these decisions often seem to be taken in different parts of the organization, and there is also a tendency to centralize more important types of investments. The latter point can be exemplified by service groups which have decided centrally to develop a new type of software or taken on a non-profitable tender for a partly new type of project to enhance their competencies within that area.

This fragmentation of investment decisions has led some researchers to reject the traditional bottom-up type of resource allocation systems found in most Swedish, U.K. and U.S. divisionalized groups and to recommend more top-down planning; another reason for this was the observation that many German and Japanese groups have more top-down involvement in their resource allocation processes.

There very few comparable surveys (Kim and Song, 1990; Yoshikawa, Mitchell and Moyes, 1994) of Japanese practice published in Anglo-Saxon journals, and fragmentary evidence from studies and interviews in a limited number of Japanese companies (Tsurumi and Tsurumi, 1985; Hodder, 1986; Hiromoto, 1988; Yoshikawa, Innes and Mitchell, 1989; Currie, 1991a; b; c; 1992; Jones, Currie and Dugdale, 1993). It is difficult to generalise from these case studies of large unknown Japanese corporations, but a few remarks can of course be made.

Japanese companies seem to rely less on written routines and more on verbal communication transmitted by a large group of liaison managers or staff people. Project evaluation techniques, for instance, are simple. Only a few companies use DCF techniques. ARR and PBP with a requirement of two to three years predominate. More effort is devoted to discussing the assumption and creating consensus for the decision.

The accounting system is more future oriented and loosely connected to external reporting. Capital budgets are integrated and include both depreciated expenditures and expenses pertinent to the investment project. Investments are related to a long-term strategy and assessed by a wide array of financial and non-financial performance measures. The top management team contains a high proportion of engineers and engages actively in the setting of priorities which gives the resource allocation system a top-down character. Acquisitions and mergers have been rare. Growth has been organic and Japanese groups also share many of the characteristics typical of strategic planning groups and Western corporations which have grown through internal development, e.g. engineers in the top management team, large technical staff units, and flexible performance measures.

A few Swedish groups have moved in this direction by introducing an annual strategic process. This and the growing importance of intangible investments have been claimed to reduce the importance of the hurdle rate and DCF evaluation. Some groups have taken a step in the same direction by issuing directions that major investments and investment programmes have to be approved before appropriation can be sought for sub-investments of such a programme.

Another measure has been to change the definition of an investment and state that also certain types of intangible investments important for the group should be handled according to the same routine as for fixed investments. Perhaps some groups also place more emphasis on executive meetings and other fora for contacts which can improve both vertical and horizontal coordination of different types of investments.

The level of the hurdle rate is only a part of a complex system of project planning and implementation, review and learning, approval and coordination, which casts doubt on the belief that the hurdle rates which we observe cause companies to behave in a more short-term manner than we think they should. First, we need to know more about how different measures of control are perceived by lower levels, and how different types of tangible and intangible investments are handled and coordinated. A few empirical studies (Östman, 1977; Barton *et al.*, 1992) indicate that too heavy an emphasis on ROI types of measures might cause lower levels to behave in a more short-term manner than intended. The interviewees seemed aware of this risk and some said that they have sometimes had to encourage lower levels to choose more long-term investments.

Furthermore, we can only understand the structure of the resource allocation system by connecting it to connect this to the organizational structure of the group and its system of ideas, and as several researchers have done during the last decade, also to the function of the capital market. It would lead far beyond the scope of this book to explore the importance of these factors for the trade-offs which firms make between the long- and short-term, so must be content merely to indicate the factors that may affect this trade-off.

Organizational structure Berg (1973) compared four internal developers and five acquisition diversifiers. He found that the corporate-level staff was much larger in the four internal developers. They had, on average, three times as many people at their corporate level. Most corporate-level staff in acquiring companies were finance people, while the largest group in internal developer worked in R & D although several other categories were also represented. These structural differences between groups growing through acquisition and internal development were confirmed and elaborated by Pitts (1974; 1976), Song (1982), Yip (1982), Goold and Campbell (1987), Hoskinsson and Hitt (1988) and Michel and Hambrick (1992). Pitts (1974; 1976), for instance, showed that managerial transfers - managers shifting positions between the companies in the group - were more common in internal diversifiers, and that performance measurements for divisional general managers were more subjective. Internal developers tend to attack growth markets, often by introducing some kind of innovation (Yip, 1982). Firms growing through acquisitions, on the other hand, tend to operate on and enter mature markets, and rely more on financial measures of control than internal developers. The latter use a wider array of measures and interpret them with greater flexibility (Goold and Campbell, 1987a; Hoskisson and Hitt, 1988; Michel and Hambrick, 1992).

Corporate system of ideas Internal development has been the wholly predominant growth strategy of Japanese groups (e.g. Ohmae, 1982; Abbegglen and Stalk, 1985; Watanabe, 1987). They have chosen the strenuous path of developing new business areas by using and training their own employees and competencies, and by waiting the ten or more years such ventures need to pay for themselves, and have a structure adjusted to this type of growth. Watanabe (1987) explains the preference for internal development by a strong corporate culture in which the development of new businesses is an integral part. Successes within new areas kindle enthusiasm and support the corporate culture.

Comparative studies of organizations (e.g. Hofstede, 1980) have shown a correlation between hierarchy and detailed control among Western firms. However, firms in South-East Asia are also claimed to combine clear hierarchies with a more vague management by objective style of control and, for instance, Karlsson and Åhlström (1994) hold that Western firms must also adopt such a structure to be able to harvest the full benefits from lean production. Thus, there is a connection between structure, whereof the resource allocation system is one important part, and corporate culture.

The capital market It is commonly believed that the stock market likes long-term investments, but only when the time of harvest is at hand. The value of a firm showing low profits due to long-term investments can be depressed, meanwhile. However, simply because it takes so long to reap the benefit of such investments it is also a difficult hypothesis to prove.

It has been shown that share prices often rise in the days after an announcement of a long-term investment (McConnell and Muscarella, 1985; Woolridge and Snow, 1990; Miles, 1993); also that the stock market reacts positively to announcements of increased R & D expenditures, as long as they come from companies which it thinks should spend large amounts of money on research (Chan, Kensinger and Martin, 1992).

However, long-term investments are just long-term and the average holding period has declined in recent decades; Why wait for ten years if the money in the meantime can give a better yield elsewhere. German and Japanese listed companies are in this respect in a better position as they are often controlled by stable owners who are well informed about their company and have a long-term commitment to the firms that they control (Kester, 1992); in the Japanese case by reciprocal ownership structures and in the German through banks and other owners with access to insider information. The latter makes it easier to communicate information about long-term investments to the owners and give owners both the information and ability to influence the management of the company. Much has been done in the U.S., U.K. and later on also in Sweden to hinder insider dealings and give all owners equal access to information. Nevertheless these measures have probably also made owners less stable so that, for instance, Jacobs (1991) and Porter (1992a; b) have urged U.S. companies to seek

166

long-term owners with whom they can develop long-term relationships and to whom they can give a direct voice in governance.

What causes some companies to choose more short-term investments than other companies is a complex matter. The fundamental issue is of course whether companies can, or the extent to which they can, choose their growth strategy, and thereby their organizational structure and resource allocation system, or whether their situation forces them to persue a certain strategy if they want to survive; the unanswered question of strategic versus environmental choice.

10 Resource allocation systems in change

The evolution of the capital budgeting manual

The pioneers Before discussing trends in the design of resource allocation systems and speculating on their future development, it may be helpful to set them and the techniques analysed in this book in an historical perspective. It may, for instance, prove useful to bear in mind that firms have always invested, but only during the last thirty to forty years have DCF calculations been used with some regularity to evaluate investment requests.

Faulhaber and Baumol (1988, p. 583) tell us that Italian merchants in the 14th century "often provided a discount (sconto) to a foreign customer who paid his bill before its due date, and the discount was calculated on the basis of the present value of the face amount of the bill at the future due date". However, a long time would elapse before German forest economists developed the technique of discounting to capital investments (see e.g. Faustmannn, 1849).

Later on these ideas were activated or reinvented and developed by three different groups of professionals, namely accountants, economists and engineers, creating three different traditions of research on capital investments. The engineering economists were probably the first on the scene. Lesser (1969) described the development of their tradition in the U.S. and mentioned in particular the early works on investments in the railway industry by Wellington (1887) and Fish (1915). The use of DCF techniques when planning the railway between the iron ore mines in the far north of Sweden and the Norwegian cost, laid in 1900s, is an early Swedish example of the pioneering role of engineering economists in applying the DCF analysis to capital investments.

Railway investments were very capital-intensive and the industry became the single most important investor in fixed assets in the 19th century. However, as railway fixed assets have a very long life if they receive proper maintenance some companies refrained from charging depreciation in their income statement, causing them to overstate their profit and pay excessive dividends. This brought on a need to regulate the calculation of depreciations (Most, 1977), and compelled accountants to study how fixed assets should be depreciated; some of the pioneers were Schmalenbach (1908; 1919) and Schmidt (1922).

At the same time economists had started to apply the DCF technique to capital markets and showed how they could thereby relate investments to savings and the value of the firm. Fisher (1907) advocated the use of the NPV criterion to assess investments, and von Böhm-Bawerk (1889) and Keynes (1936) the IRR. Economists also wrote textbooks (e.g. Schneider, 1944; Dean, 1951a; b; Massé, 1959) showing how the DCF principle could be applied to the appraisal and ranking of investments.

From market establishment to penetration When Heller (1951) studied investment decisions he recorded the use of limits of authorization, systems of classification and the incipient use of the PBP and ARR criteria. However, most managers still relied on their subjective judgements and hesitated to introduce these "fancy formulas".

> Some type of formal cost-savings or payoff calculation is increasingly used by the Twin Cities firms. ...
>
> Yet some managements resist these 'fancy formulas' as a basis for their decisions, giving such reasons as: 'We rely on the judgment of the operating people,' or 'There are so many intangibles that the computation is misleading,' or 'We don't have enough funds to do more than replace the machines that are obviously ready for the scrap heap.' (Heller, 1951, p. 100-1)

Do the arguments sound familiar? Replace payoff with DCF and the same reactions could have been recorded a decade later when such criteria had begun to win general acceptance in the business world.

U.K. (Carter and Williams, 1958; Ashton, 1962), U.S. (Canada and Miller, 1985; Dulman, 1989) and Swedish (Renck, 1966) companies started to adopt these new techniques in the 50s, and also introduced capital budgeting manuals. Istvan (1961a, p. 3) writes that the technique of "scientific evaluation of capital expenditures has been developed only during the past five to ten years", and Renck (1966) assumed that the companies which he studied had developed their manuals during the late 50s and early 60s; he saw the many descriptions of their company procedures given by industrial representatives in the journals (Eriksson, 1959; Rydin, 1961; Bohlin, 1962; Eriksson, 1963; Wärnberg, 1963; Lindholm, 1965) as a sign thereof.

The adaptation process of these new investment evaluation techniques can best be studied with the help of U.S. data. Figure 10.1 is based on 15 surveys of Fortune 500 corporations. As the samples differ the growth and decline curves have been smoothed out. There is no question that the use of DCF criteria has increased, while that of the ARR and PBP criteria as primary measure has declined during the last thirty years. Furthermore, that early adapters of the DCF technique preferred the IRR, while late comers chose the NPV. Data from Australia (e.g. Freeman and Hobbes, 1991), Canada (e.g. Blazouke, Carlin and Kim 1988; Roubi, Barth and Faseruk, 1991), New Zealand (e.g. Patterson, 1989), Sweden (Renck, 1966; Tell, 1978), and the U.K. (e.g. Pike and Wolfe, 1988) are less comprehensive but in no way contradict these general development tendencies.

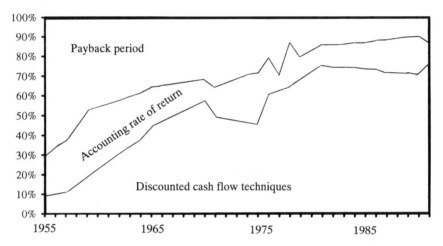

Figure 10.1 The dissemination of the DCF technique in the U.S.

The character of a process of adaptation and learning is distinct, despite a few contradictory results (e.g. Jones (1986) concerning the U.K.) and the fact that it is of course ill-advised to compare different samples (Rappaport, 1979; Aggarwal, 1980; Pike, 1984). The process started in the U.S.. British and Swedish companies eventually followed suit, and fragmentary evidence suggests that the growth curve perhaps became steeper for the small and homogeneous Swedish business society once the penetration process had started (compare Table 6.1, 6.2, and Figure 10.1).

The last thirty years

Renck's (1966) and Tell's (1978) studies of capital budgeting manuals give us a good ground to study how the investment manual has evolved during the last thirty years, and especially the economic calculations of the investment request. However, the investment manual is only one part of the resource allocation system and we know far less about the other means of control and administrative routines used by large companies in the 60s and 70s. Istvan's (1961a) and Renck's (1966) interviews give us some insight into the system as a whole in the late 50s and early 60s, and Eliasson (1976) presents the planning system used in the early 70s, but by and large we have relatively few grounds for comparison when studying how the resource allocation system in its entirety has evolved.

However, we can assume that changes in the resource allocation system reflect changes in the composition of investments and organizational structures as such. Many of the changes which we can observe in the investment manual and the resource allocation system can be explained by a continuous process of decentralization, others by the increasing importance of intangible investments; we shall in this section describe some of these changes.

The investment request Comparing early and recent capital budgeting manuals we can see that they have gradually cut down on educational material and adapted more standardized principles of calculation. The trend has been towards simple evaluation techniques and today it is generally assumed that the appraisor knows how to calculate the PBP or IRR.

Almost all companies have abandoned the accounting-based definition of an investment, which means that they today also include certain expense kind of expenditures associated with the investment project in the initial outlay. This also presupposes that the capital budget is supplemented with an expense budget. Some groups have urged their companies also to make investment requests for certain intangible types of investment, but the extent to which such investments also give rise to requests is unknown. The number of investment classes has increased and so probably also the number of decision routines.

Different businesses and investments may need different types of routine. There is a choice between creating an investment manual applicable to all investments and businesses of a group, or using different manuals for different investments and businesses. The study has given examples of both alternatives. Five of the groups had abandoned the group manual and allowed lower levels to determine their own administrative routines. Other had couched their manuals in more general terms and allowed lower levels to issue supplementary routines. As a result many manuals have become less specific on, for instance, how the cash flow should be determined.

Turning to the choice of investment criteria the most striking result can be claimed to be the small changes which have taken place during the last three decades. Companies do not change criteria from one year to another.

This point can be illustrated by the seven relatively unstructured groups which are present in all three studies. One of these groups uses the same criterion today, as they did in 1977 and 1964. Four of the groups introduced a new criterion between 1964 and 1977 and two between 1977 and 1990: four of the six have abandoned discounted PBP and introduced a DCF criterion. The others have changed from one DCF criterion to another. If these groups are representative for companies in general then the introduction of a new criterion is a rare event, and the existence of different kinds of criterion a rather stable phenomenon. A further indication thereof is a multinational which introduced the IRR some fifteen years ago. The change never really disseminated down to all companies, and requests continued to be submitted with the old criterion, the discounted PBP, which contributed to the decision two years later to withdraw the new criterion. There may be more than one reason for retaining old routines as long as they are not obviously inappropriate.

The determination of hurdle rates seem to have undergone a change in that the more multinational groups have introduced hurdle rates differentiated with regard to the country of the investment based on the cost of borrowing in local currency, which in general should lead to lower hurdle rates. However, Swedish groups do not in general seem to use project-specific hurdle rates, as some Anglo-Saxon groups do, but to demand shorter or longer PBP to cater for project risk.

Comparing manuals conveys the impression that companies consider the effects of inflation and taxes less often today than in the 70s. The explanation seems to be the decentralization of appraisals. In general the first appraisal is made disregarding inflation and taxes. Then if it is later deemed necessary to consider these issues then such an evaluation is made in cooperation with a staff unit.

Renck (1978) could conclude that more stress had been placed on risk evaluation techniques during the 70s than during the 60s. We infer that the trend has been reversed to some extent. The manuals of today place less emphasis on formal risk analysis, but more on evaluating the flexibility of major investments. Groups today rely more on their ability to adapt to changes in their environment than on their ability to predict such changes. Renck also found that some companies had begun to use computer programmes to ease the calculations, and that more stress had been placed on post-completion reviews. The extent to which these trends have continued is difficult to assess from the horizon of corporate level as post-completion reviews are decentralized and the computer department has been superseded by personal computers.

Towards more intangible investments Fixed investment accounts for a diminishing proportion of the total volume of investment. Indeed many companies today have much larger investments in markets, product development and employee training and development than in buildings and machinery, and the amount of production equipment which is computer controlled has also increased. In particular the engineering industry has today a great mixture of tangible and intangible investments; this has led to instructions to treat certain important types of intangible investments according to the same administrative routines as apply to tangible investments. Some groups have referred decisions on investments in, primarily, information technology to a higher level by demanding that a staff unit be contacted before such an investment is decided, while others have issued supplementary instructions for certain intangible investments.

However, when the intangible investments predominate the importance of the investment manual seems to decline as this instrument is most suitable for fixed investments. If market and product development investments are pre-eminent then management tends to refer these decisions upwards and allow them to precede decisions on fixed assets; hence major market and product development investments tend to drive investments in fixed assets.

Increased decentralisation There is no systematic study of when Swedish groups changed to a divisionalized structure, but only a cursory knowledge of Swedish industry is needed to understand that many of the corporations in the 1964 study must have had a functional structure; moreover we may surmise that also some of Istvan's (1961a) major U.S. corporations had such a structure. However, during the following decade most of them would adapt a divisionalized structure, or be bought up and become a part of a divisionalized group. This process of decentralization continued during the 80s also in those groups which then had already developed a divisionalized structure. They have continued to decentralize former corporate staff units, or abolished them to the extent that most groups have few technical staff left at corporate level.

This decentralization has of course had a profound influence on the resource allocation procedures of major Swedish corporations. We can perceive the increased decentralization of investment issues during the 80s in the higher limits of authorization especially for divisions. However, we can also observe that the possible loss of control caused by this decentralization was counteracted by several measures to strengthen higher levels' control of investment requests.

The investment manual can be said to make decentralization possible by stipulating how top management would have lower managers appraise and handle investments. It helps top management to retain control over certain assumptions made in investment requests. Further decentralization has strengthened this need for control. We can see this in the fact that many multinationals have only decentralized the simplest evaluations and do not allow their appraisers to make assumptions on the future rate of inflation and taxes. Finance is centralized and the financial options are often evaluated by a staff unit. Control has also been strengthened by more clearly specifying who is responsible for what in the investment process, and by improving pre-approval review procedures. Comparison of earlier studies of pre-approval review procedures (Istvan, 1961a; Eliasson, 1977) with those

173

observed in this study demonstrates that pre-approval procedures have been improved. Especially the multinational engineering groups today have a well constructed system of pre-approval review or hierarchical control, while, for instance, the forest groups seem to rely more on project management procedures to achieve such feedback.

We can also observe the consequences of this process of decentralization in the shift in purpose assigned to the investment manual. The manual was introduced to create unitary principles of evaluation so that investment requests could be compared, and as companies lacking a manual seem to have looser routines, we can assume that they also served this purpose. However, corporate managers today are just as likely to emphasize the role of the manual in helping higher levels to exert financial and strategic control. The divisional structure assigns different roles to the business, division and corporate levels as researched by Bower (1970).

The corporate level emphasis on financial control is reflected in the centralization of financial decisions. Individual companies cannot borrow or choose special finance for an investment without approval from the head office.

The emphasis on strategic control is reflected in the focus on pre-approval review and the effort to identify strategic investments and subject them to closer scrutiny by means of differentiated limits of authorization. We can also observe that four of the groups have introduced some kind of annual investment or strategic process, and that six require their companies to have their investment programmes and major investments approved before requests for individual investments can be processed. As there are no records of such procedures, or of differentiated expenditure limits, in earlier studies we infer that these measures to strengthen strategic control were in most cases introduced during the 80s, an assumption which is also supported by some of the interviews.

We can also observe a shift in focus, from evaluating and ranking individual investments, towards evaluating and assessing investment programmes and their financial effects on the investing company as exemplified by strategic processes, instructions to evaluate investment programmes and their financial impact on the company, instructions to evaluate additional investments, and the flexibility of major investments. One explanation of this shift could be that companies experience their environment as less stable than in the 60s and 70s and therefore find it necessary to hold more flexibility options. The decentralization can by itself be a sign thereof at the same time as it may also necessitate such routines to enable coordination of individual investments.

Towards an international standard One observation was that the development favoured simple, well-known methods. Renck (1966), for instance, recorded two different formulas for calculating the annuity index, four for the profitability index and eight for the simple and discounted PBP. In addition a few companies used the ARR and the modified internal rate of return. Today only some of the manuals contain a formula telling the user how to calculate the criteria used by the group, and these use the simple standard variants taught by textbooks.

The tendency has been towards simple methods which everybody knows and can use, especially in the multinationals. It is true to say that smaller groups use less advanced procedures and criteria than larger groups, but also that the more multinational groups use simpler evaluation techniques than the less multinational groups. The formal pre-approval review procedures are far more complex than in the small national groups, but the evaluation techniques recommended by the manuals are not necessarily more complicated. If more advanced evaluations are needed, for instance, taxes and financial options must be considered, then a staff unit is consulted. Decentralization presupposes simple routines which everybody can understand, especially in heterogeneous multinationals. This demand for a common group language delimits the possibilities of introducing highly sophisticated techniques, or as respondents in two of the most multinational groups expressed it.

> We have a problem, you see, but I suppose it is also a strength. We are so many producing units. You have a hundred different companies making all kinds of investments. There competency in economic matters differs very much. The manual has to be kept relatively simple. Some will say; 'This can't be correct.' One has to disregard that because it is extra study for many investors. When it comes to the really big investments then we come in and look at them right from the start. If they are building a new plant, then we look at a lot of parameters.

> Simplicity and understanding for the method. I think that's the requirement. People have to understand it. It must not be too complicated.

Turning to the question of why a certain criterion was chosen we must remember that a manual is somebody's child. Somebody initiated the development of a new routine, the manager in charge of the manual or somebody else. To help them they often had their previous knowledge and experience of investment procedures and one or several manuals from other Swedish, European or U.S. companies from which they borrowed ideas thought suitable for their own company.

> We have simply looked at other [company's] instructions. They should be internationally useful. We will find these wherever we travel in Europe, or the U.S.. Everybody understands what we mean. They are easy to understand, of course. It is a simple way of proving an investment.

Investment practice seems to be more standardized in companies using an investment manual. Written routines standardize behaviour. Such is of course one of the purposes of written routines, but at the same time may also help to preserve routines which may need to be changed. We have observed how project evaluation techniques are a relatively stable phenomenon. An evaluation technique or manual which works is seldom replaced by a completely new routine as long as the old one seems to serve its purpose, and companies think more than once before introducing a more advanced evaluation technique or criterion. The existing written routines, as well as the need for evaluation techniques which can be understood and used by all proposers in multinational groups, might therefore counteract the introduction of new, more advanced routines.

Possible future lines of development

The study has identified certain connections between, on the one hand, the design of the resource allocation system and its formal routines, and on the other, the character of the investments which the system must handle and the competitive situation of the group. It is in no way a distinct, unambiguous connection. The investment manual and the instructions contained therein are only one instrument in a complex system, in which the same end result can probably be achieved by several combinations of instruments. There also seems to be an inertia embedded in routines, especially when they have been put on paper. Companies seldom seem to adapt completely new routines as long the old ones perform satisfactorily, and somebody must take the initiative to develop a new routine. The history of the company and the experience of the managers responsible for the formal routines is no doubt an important factor influencing the choice of the capital budgeting routines.

When the DCF technique and capital budgeting manuals were introduced in the 50s and 60s Swedish industry experienced strong growth. All new capacity tended sooner or later to be absorbed. This made forecasts easier. It was more a matter of when than whether the new capacity was needed. The 70s brought zero growth and portfolio management. It became important to hold a portfolio of businesses in different stages of their life cycle. Then followed the 80s with increased market orientation, restructuring and concentration to core areas, and large acquisitions of foreign competitors. Some groups grew rapidly by buying new markets and businesses. The drawbacks soon became evident. Organic growth and productivity increases declined. Ventures in new areas through internal development were wound up or sold off and became a rarity. However, the recession forced companies once again to concentrate on internal efficiency, and there are signs that these issues will remain in focus throughout the 90s and that we shall see more organic growth.

Standardization and differentiation The development has, as earlier reported, gone towards simpler, more standardized project evaluation techniques. Decentralized and multinational groups in particular need simple techniques with which managers in different companies and cultural areas are familiar.

At the same time as these routines are standardized we can also discern a line of development towards more diverse resource allocation systems. There is no ideal system suitable for all types of businesses and we may assume that resource allocation systems will be more and more designed to fit the business which each is expected to serve. Several of the groups have used slightly different administrative routines in their different parts. It is difficult to say whether this is a growing phenomenon, but it might very well be. Increased competition and faster changes make it necessary to focus harder on developing the competencies possessed by the company and this could necessitate a more careful adjustment of routines to the problems which they are supposed to solve.

Companies in the engineering industry have experienced a dramatic shift in the composition of their investments, from fixed investments to intangible investments and computer-controlled machines. The intangible investments have surpassed the tangible in volume and given major engineering groups a great mixture of large and small tangible and intangible investments. The result can be discerned in instructions to treat intangible investments as tangible and in more complex routines for pre-approval review; perhaps we shall see still more drastic changes during the next ten years.

The changes have been smaller in, for instance, the forest industry, where tangible investments still are predominate even though their machines too are computer controlled. Nor is there any indication that the composition of investments will drastically change; thus it would not be surprising to find ten years from now that their routines remain almost the same. The service groups, on the other hand, did not have investment manuals. One reason for this may be that the Swedish service groups are relatively small and nationally based; perhaps we shall see some new types of routines intended to formalize the treatment of intangible investments.

Tangible and intangible investments Tangible investments as a proportion of the total volume of investment have and are increasing and the distinction between tangible and intangible investments is blurred as, for instance, many machines are now computer-controlled. However, the effects of intangible investments are difficult to quantify. This has obliged decision-makers to rely more on soft data for investment decisions, and made learning more important than the ability to predict and plan production. The growing importance of intangibles reflects a long-term change from pure industrial mass production towards more knowledge-intensive products, from classical industrial products like textiles and shoes, steel and ships, towards the service industry and specialized, knowledge-intensive industrial products.

Traditional project evaluation techniques based on quantification and discounting of expected payments and receipts proved inadequate to handle these more intangible investments. This has led to fears lest the use of such evaluation techniques would focus attention on tangible investments and lest non-quantifiable effects on tangible investments be ignored.

Major engineering groups in particular have tried to resolve this problem by issuing instructions that intangible investments be treated like tangible ones and their effects if possible also be quantified, but it is questionable to what extent such investment requests are actually made. Groups with very large intangible investments have in general centralized the valuation of their principal types thereof by treating them in a planning process or an investment committee. This has reduced the importance attached to traditional evaluation techniques.

There is an obvious risk that certain important types of intangible investments involving long-term irreversible commitments are not really recognized as such and referred to the right level for approval. Strategic control presuppose an ability to identify those events which will have the greatest impact on the long-term direction of the businesses of a group and these may not be investments in real assets but in product development, market investments, investments in human resources, and structural changes and innovations.

There is a need to develop administrative routines better to structure the effects of intangible investment, and such routines will presumably be introduced. However, as it is difficult to quantify such effects it might be necessary to rely on cultural rather than bureaucratic control (see e.g. Ouchi, 1977; 1979; Baliga and Jeager, 1984; Eisenhardt, 1985); to develop a shared understanding of company goals and decisions on different types of resource commitments, rather than on investment manuals and written routines. This presupposes extensive vertical and horizontal verbal communication, and according to some researchers (e.g. Parthasarthy and Sethi, 1992; Karlsson and Åhlström, 1994), also new organizational structures and management styles. Perhaps the development within information technology can help to create such fora for communication on investment issues.

Decentralization and centralization The last few decades have been characterized by decentralization. We can speculate whether this trend will continue or if we shall see more involvement from the top in the resource allocation process at least in some industries. Eastman Kodak, for instance, is said to be abandoning project-by-project analysis in favour of analyses of strategies and how these can be pursued (Przybylowicz and Faulkner, 1993; Remer, Stopdyk and van Driel, 1993). A similar development can be observed in those Swedish groups which have introduced an annual strategic planning process and perhaps more companies will soon follow in their footsteps.

Bottom-up approaches are suitable when the individual business unit is the proper unit of analysis, but when resources in different business units have to be coordinated and adjusted to an overall strategy then there must also be some form of top-down planning. These groups have obviously found it necessary to introduce a stronger element of top-down planning in their resource allocation systems. A similar endeavour can be discerned in those mostly major engineering groups which have introduced special instructions for investment programmes.

The ideological foundation of this development has already been given by the resource-based view of the firm (for a review of literature see e.g. Mahoney and Pandian, 1992) and the increasing interest in organizational learning (for a review of literature see e.g. Hedberg, 1981; Levitt and March, 1988; Huber, 1991; Dodgson, 1993) and the continuous development of companies' core competencies (see e.g. Prahalad and Hamel, 1990; Prahalad, 1993). This not wholly new paradigm moves the focus of analysis away from the present situation of independent business units to the future situation and development of the groups' competencies. It becomes less important to achieve a large market share to reduce unit price and more important to be able to develop and learn new competencies faster than the competitors. Companies cannot be best at everything. They have to concentrate their resources on that which they can do better than their competitors and have particularly during the last decade we could witness a growing emphasis on strategic control and use of outsourcing. It has become important to control key technologies and achieve a leading position, which makes outsourcing (Bettis, Bradley and Hamel, 1992; Quinn and Hilmer, 1994), the deployment and development of competencies vital strategic issues.

The role of information technology It came as a surprise that major groups did not make more use of information technology. A few groups, all with young managers in charge of investment procedures, had developed electronic forms and programmes to help investment appraisers to calculate taxes and financial options, but on the whole, there were few more head offices offering such services in 1990 than in 1978. Spreadsheet programmes were probably used to evaluate investments in some companies but then on local initiatives. Investment requests and attached documentation were still sent by post or fax and filed by the head office.

There has long been talk of the paperless electronic office which is supposed to come into existence. The forest industry has been worried about a declining demand for paper, and ten years ago almost all telecommunication and computer corporations unsuccessfully merged in order to offer a complete product line for such an office, which has not yet been realized. The vision still exists but it will obviously be a long time before forms and communication are superseded by electronic mail and videophones.

It is probably safe to say that managers, both those appropriating for capital expenditures and those approving such expenditures, will during the 90s learn to communicate more through their computers, but it is very difficult to predict how this will influence the resource allocation system. It can be assumed that information technology will render some routines redundant and also promote the development of completely new routines, but the form these will take is hidden in the future as the introduction of this new technology is a process of learning. Information technology remains a great unknown in every attempt to forecast the details of future resource allocation systems which may bring wholly new types of capital budgeting routines already during the next decade.

Appendix A:
Research methodology

Renck's (1966) and Tell's (1978) analyses of capital budgeting manuals proved that such analyses can give a good picture of the capital budgeting techniques and procedures used in major corporations, especially if, as in Renck's (1966) case, they are combined with interviews with the managers responsible for investment procedures. The analysis of a company's written routines provided a fitting point of departure for later interviews in the same company. It also gave more detailed and more reliable answers than a traditional postal questionnaire would yield. Reliable insofar as the answer given was not dependent on the interpretation of the question and practice of the person filling in the survey form and the answer could be verified by reference to the written routines.

In an international perspective Renck's (1966) and Tell's (1978) studies seem well nigh unique. There is, however, one study by Istvan (1959; 1961a; b) which is worthy of mention. He examined the written routines of forty-eight large U.S. corporations and interviewed 147 financial executives, but his study has never been followed up, at least as far as the author knows; this of course is regrettable as it must still be considered to be among the best published studies of capital budgeting practice, although it describes the practice of major U.S. groups more than thirty-five years ago. A later study by Mukherjee (1988) should also be mentioned. He asked Fortune 500 corporations to send him a copy of their capital budgeting manual. However, the response rate was very low; only 12 per cent of the corporations supplied a complete manual, and the descriptions given thereof in Mukherjee's (1988) article are superficial. This state of affairs gave rise to the idea of a third study of investment procedures of major Swedish groups based on investment manuals and interviews with financial executives on group level; an awareness of the uniqueness and success of Renck's (1966) and Tell's (1978) studies and the fact that yet another thirteen years would have passed in 1990.

However, it was clear that such a study must also take into consideration the changes which industrial production and Swedish industry had undergone during the last thirty years. Thirty years is a long period. Many previously exporting companies with basically a functional structure have gradually been transformed into multinational groups with a divisionalized structure, and in consequence technical staff units and many kinds of decisions have been decentralized. A gradual shift has also appeared from, on the one hand, low knowledge-, labour-intensive products like shoes and clothing, and, on the other, capital-intensive products, like steel and textiles, towards capital-, knowledge-intensive products like pharmaceuticals, telecommunications systems, consultancy and other knowledge-intensive service industries. This transformation has caused a shift in the volume of investments from traditional fixed investments in property and machines, towards intangible investments like R & D, markets, computer software and the development of employee knowledge and skills, and also towards computer-controlled machines which can perform multiple tasks.

With these changes in mind it was adjudged essential not only to follow-up Renck's (1966) and Tell's (1978) studies but also to examine the consequences of these changes in the composition of investments and organizational structure for the investment practice of major Swedish corporations. This made it necessary to study not only capital budgeting manuals, but also practice with regard to expense kinds of investment and other means of controlling the direction of investments than the investment manual. This extension made it interesting also to include other corporations in the study than those which use an investment manual, and necessary to supplement the analysis of investment manuals with interviews with the managers responsible for investment procedures on corporate level. Thus the purpose of the study could be formulated as

1. to describe and analyse the capital budgeting manuals of major Swedish corporations in such a way that comparisons could be made with the earlier studies by Renck (1966) and Tell (1978),
2. to use these written routines as a point of departure and enlarge Renck's (1966) and Tell's (1978) area of study by also mapping how investment requests are handled in major corporations and the means of control used by corporate management to direct the investment of their group in groups with and without a capital budgeting manual.

The purpose of this enlargement was not to make a full investigation of these new issues but merely to survey the area and provide a basis for future studies of means of control and intangible investments.

The design of the study was of course strongly influenced by the intention to follow up two earlier studies. The first of these studies had covered

182

twenty-eight larger Swedish corporations, whereof twenty-two were listed on the Stockholm Stock Exchange. The selection technique was pragmatic, governed by the requirement that the corporation have a capital budgeting manual and be willing to participate in the study. Thirteen years later only twenty of these original corporations remained independent, and Tell (1978) therefore added ten new large Swedish corporations selected on the same pragmatic principles. These selection principles can of course be criticised but an evaluation of the samples indicates that they include many of the largest Swedish corporations at the time of these studies.

Furthermore it also soon became clear that only thirteen of Renck's (1966) and eighteen of Tell's (1978) corporations were still independent organizations, although in some of the cases more in name than in structure. The rest had been bought up or merged. The figures illustrate the comprehensive restructuring which Swedish industry has undergone during the last few decades. Another obstacle was the transformation of the composition of Swedish industry which has made Renck's (1966) sample less and less representative for the largest Swedish corporations as new industries have replaced the old. Because of these changes, it was considered better to study a cross-section sample of large Swedish groups quoted on the Stockholm Stock Exchange in 1990, than to concentrate on the original groups.

Therefore, with the knowledge generated by earlier studies about which groups could be expected to use a capital budgeting manual a request for a copy was sent to all fifty-four groups classified by the Swedish business magazine *Veckans Affärer* as engineering industry (including the electro-engineering and metal industry), chemical industry (including the pharma-ceutical industry), forest industry and the category remaining companies (companies which could not be categorised as building and real estate, trading and retailing, shipping, investment, or bank groups according to *Veckans Affärers'* list of corporations, viz. conglomerates, power industry, service industry, etc.) (see Sample I in Table A.1). The sample excluded the companies in the above mentioned lines of business which are entered on the over-the-counter list.

Table A.1
Groups studied

Sample I

Engineering groups, including electro-engineering and metal groups: Alfa-Laval International AB, ASEA AB, Atlas-Copco AB, Avesta AB, Componenta AB, Eldon AB, AB Electrolux, Telefonaktiebolaget LM Ericsson, ESAB AB, Garphyttan AB, Nobel Industrier Sverige AB, Pharos AB, Saab-Scania-Gruppen AB, Sandvik AB, SECO Tools AB, SKF AB, SSAB Svenskt Stål AB, Thorsman & Co AB, AB Volvo, Åkermans Verkstads AB.

Chemical groups, including pharmaceutical groups: AGA AB, AB Astra, Forsheda AB, Perstorp AB.

Forest groups: Korsnäs AB, Mo och Domsjö AB (MoDo), Munksjö AB, NCB AB, Svenska Cellulosa AB (SCA), Stora Kopparbergs Bergslags AB (STORA).

Remaining groups: Anticimex AB, Bilspedition AB, Borås Wäfveri AB, Cederroth International AB, Esselte AB, Euroc AB, FFNS Gruppen AB, Gambro AB, Gullspångs Kraftaktiebolag, Industri-Matematik AB, Inter Innovation AB, AB Jacobson & Widmark (J & W), Kramo AB, Tidnings AB Marieberg, Närkes Elektriska AB (NEA), Orrefors AB, Procordia AB, Programator AB, Sydsvenska Dagbladet AB, Swegon AB, Sydkraft AB, Trelleborg AB, VM-Data Nordic AB, AB Ångpanneföreningen (ÅF).

Sample II

Building and real estate groups: Paul Anderson Industrier AB, Arcona Fastighetsutveckling AB, BGB i Stockholm AB, BPA AB, Consta AB, Fabege AB, HILAB AB, Fastighets AB Hufvudstaden, JM Byggnads och Fastighetsbolag, Klövern Förvaltnings AB, L E Lundbergsföretagen AB, Nordstjernan AB, Piren AB, Pronator AB, Regnbågen AB, SIAB AB, Skanska AB.

Trade and retailing groups: Axel Johnson Trade AB, Bergman & Beving AB, Catena AB, H & M Hennes & Mauritz AB, AB Nordiska Kompaniet, Sandblom & Stohne AB, Skoogs Företagsgrupp AB.

Shipping groups: Argonaut AB, Rederiaktiebolaget Gotland, Nordström & Thulin AB, Stena Line AB.

Development groups: Almedahl-Fagerhult AB, Aritmos AB, Eken Industri & Handel AB, Finnveden Invest AB, Hexagon AB, Skrinet AB, Skåne-Gripen AB.

Bank groups: GOTA Bank AB, JP Bank, Nordbanken, Skandinaviska Enskilda Banken, Svenska Handelsbanken, Östgöta Enskilda Bank.

Otc engineering groups: Acora AB, Allgon AB, Alma Industri & Handel AB, Frico International AB, ITAB Industri AB, Lindab AB, Metallhyttan AB, Norden AB, Scandiafelt AB, SMZ-Industrier AB, Swepart Mecan AB, Tivox AB, VBG Produkter AB, Zetterbergs Industri AB.

Otc computer software groups: Cyncrona AB, Datema AB, Edata Scandinavia AB, ENEA Data AB, Finansrutin Data AB, International Business Systems (IBS) AB, Källdata AB, Memory Data AB, Modulföretagen DATA AB, Måldata AB, Pulsen i Borås AB, WSA AB.

Otc Remaining groups: Berg, BNL Information AB, Bongs Fabriker AB, BRIO AB, Depenova AB, Elanders Kommunikation AB, Ernströmgruppen AB, Fjällräven AB, Förvaltnings AB Hasselfors, Jeppson PAC AB, KABE AB, Emil Lundgrens Elektriska AB, Nolator

AB, Polarator AB, Rottneros Bruk AB, Spendrups Bryggeri AB, Strålfors AB, Sv Energinät, Utvecklings AB Sydostinvest, Thomée-Hörle AB, Tryckindustri AB, Vestmanlands Läns Tidning.

The request was addressed to the chief financial executive of the group, and in accordance with the practice developed by Renck (1966) and Tell (1978) participating companies were promised anonymity, viz., their identity would not be revealed when reference was made to different manuals and administrative routines. Those chief financial executives who did not answer the second letter were contacted by telephone whereby the response rate could be increased threefold. The facts that most executives knew Renck's (1966) dissertation and that the participants were promised anonymity in accordance with the two earlier studies, probably contributed to the high response rate and willingness to participate.

Thirty-nine of the fifty-four groups used a group manual, although three were under development and still not approved. Another five had abandoned the group manual and allowed the divisions to develop their own manuals. Three of these groups supplied the manuals of their core business. Altogether, twenty-nine manuals were received. Despite the restructuring of Swedish industry the manuals have a division among lines of business similar to those of the earlier studies (see Table A.2).

Table A.2
Manuals divided among lines of business

Line of industry	1964	1977	1990	Non-responses	
Engineering	8	9	11	3	(2)
Electro-engineering	3	2	2	0	(0)
Mines and metal	7	6	3	0	(0)
Chemical and pharmaceutical	2	2	3	1	(1)
Forest	3	3	5	1	(1)
Remaining groups	5	8	5	5	(3)
Total	28	30	29	10	(7)

Notes: Ten groups did not wish to participate in the study. However, only seven of these had an approved manual at the time of the request.

This means that the study is based on 74 per cent of the groups which used a manual; 81 per cent if we only consider those groups which had an approved manual at the time of the request. The principal reason for the refusal by some groups to participate in the study seems to have been that the financial executive of the group was unwilling to supply an outsider with

185

this internal document. However, all the large Swedish multinational groups which had an approved manual agreed to participate.

The analysis of manuals was followed up by interviews in nineteen of the fifty-four groups, whereof fourteen used a manual. These groups were selected by random numbers from the list of the fifty-four groups, stratified with regard to their market value. The interviews were conducted with the chief financial executive of the group, the corporate controller, or other person responsible for the capital budgeting routines of the group (see Sample I in Table A.3). All but two groups agreed to give interviews and these were replaced by similar groups. In 1993 short follow up interviews were held with the same people who had been interviewed previously to investigate the development during the recession 1990-93.

In order to set the manual in a wider context additional interviews were conducted on corporate level with financial executives of fifteen groups in lines of business which normally lack capital budgeting manuals. This series gave interviews in one building, one real estate, two bank, two shipping, two trade and retailing, one investment, two soft ware and consulting, two smaller engineering and two other smaller groups, whereof the last five mentioned were entered on the over-the-counter list (see Sample II in Table A.1 and Table A.3). The building group and two of the groups on the otc-list had a capital budgeting manual.

Table A.3
Interviews

	Sample I	*Sample II*	*Total*
Chief financial executives	8	12	20
Corporate controllers	7	1	8
Managers responsible for capital budgeting routines	6	0	6
Other managers	7	6	13
Total	28	19	47
Number of groups	19	15	34

The interviews were guided by an interview protocol sent to the respondents in advance. The interview protocol consisted of five pages of open-ended questions. It went into considerable detail as many of the interviews would be made by students participating in a course on capital budgeting as a part of their examination thesis. All the interviews were taped and transcribed. In all, forty-six employees in thirty-four groups were interviewed, and material, interviews and manuals, from forty-nine groups were analysed.

Appendix B:
An investment manual

This is a fictitious investment manual which has borrowed inspiration from especially the multinational engineering groups. It is important to notice that it does not claim to represent an ideal which should be followed. Its purpose is only to convey one possible structure and content of such a manual. Capital budgeting procedures vary from group to group. There are similarities between groups in similar industries but there are also differences and manuals can be very different.

The investment manuals of today are often an integral part of the financial and accounting manual of the group. They are updated in preparation for the annual budgetary control process, and their contents can be split up into the following headings:

(a)   Validity
(b)   Purpose
(c)   Applicability
(d)   Authorities
(e)   Procedures
(f)   Responsibilities
(g)   Profitability requirements
(h)   The investment request form
(i)   The templet for board decision
(j)   The capital expenditure plan

(a)   Validity

This instruction is to be followed by all companies within the MNC Group. Business Areas, Divisions and Local companies may issue complementary instructions as long as the requirements stipulated in this manual are fulfilled.

Any inquiries about this instruction should be made to the Controller Group Staff.

(b)   Purpose

Any decision on a cash expenditure expected to yield a future return is an investment decision. Such decisions affect the future fixed and intangible assets of the Group. The key factors in assessing investments are profitability and strategic considerations, and decisions on investments are therefore centralized even in an otherwise decentralized Group.

It is of the utmost importance to the Group that all investments are correctly scrutinized, planned and implemented so that their profitability and strategic importance can be assessed and achieved. It is also of utmost importance that this instruction is followed to ensure the uniform treatment of all investments within the Group which is necessary to make such an assessment possible.

(c)   Applicability

Traditionally, the term investment has been associated with fixed assets such as land, buildings, machinery and equipment which from an accounting point of view are balanced. It is, however, important that also investment decisions on product development, markets, computer software and other expense type of investments which have an immediate effect on the Income Statement are treated as far as possible in a uniform manner.

This instruction is valid for investments in land and buildings, production machinery and systems, storage and transportation equipment, computer hardware and software, systems and telecommunication equipment, market investments, patents and leasing.

The purchase of fixed assets for a specific sales contract is not considered as an investment if the purchase is made on behalf of, and will later become the property of the customer.

Regular repair, maintenance and rearrangements of machinery and equipment are not to be considered as investments.

Leased equipment is considered as an investment if the contract period exceeds one year. Alternative purchase price or capitalization costs may be used as an investment amount. A lease contract may not be signed without the approval of the Group Treasury Department, ordinary car and computer leases are exempted.

Acquisition of companies and shares follows special procedures, see the Acquisition Manual. The general rule is that all decisions regarding acquisitions are made by the Board of Directors of MNC AB.

Research and development follows special procedures, see Research and Development Manual.

Post-calculation is mandatory for all investments above SEK 1,000,000 and shall be made within two years after completion of the investment. The follow-up is made by the company or unit responsible for the investment and reported to the units which have approved the investment.

(d) Authorities

All requests must be approved and signed by the managers authorized to give such approval. The type of investment and size of the total expenditure will determine who must approve.

Limits for the CEO are set by the MNC Board of Directors. The present limit is SEK 10 million. Capital expenditures below 10 million are to be summarized and then reported to the Board of Directors.

In case of emergency the CEO is allowed to make decisions on amounts exceeding SEK 10 million, acquisitions and divestures after obtaining informal approval from the Board of Directors.

Limits for Business area and Divisional managers are set by the CEO. Limits may vary due to differences in the size of Business Areas and Divisions and the type of investment.

The Board of Directors and the CEO decides on all acquisitions and divestures of companies, and ventures which can alter the strategy agreed on for a company.

(e) Procedures

Each Investment Request should be summarized and presented on the standard Investment Request form. Group Board decisions are structured according to the Templet for Board Decision. Investments below SEK 10 million are summarized and reported to the Head Office.

The Investment Request form. All, or at least almost all, manuals give their users some help on how the forms should be filled-in and a few also contain examples of completed forms and the calculation of the PBP, IRR, etc.

The Templet for Board Decision. At least ten of the groups had supplemented their manuals with a one to three pages long document describing how an investment request presented to the Board - in a few of the groups all requests presented to a Company Board - should be structured.

The Capital Expenditure Plan. Investments below the limit of authorization are summarized and reported to the Head Office and the Board. Some groups include a structure for how such reports should be presented and some have forms for these presentations which are then also more detailed.

Pre-approval review. The MNC Group has a number of staff units which can assist on investment issues. They have an overview of past and planned investments of the Group and guarantee that knowledge and experience are diffused within the group. It is important that these units be approached at an early stage to ensure that their recommendations and views can be considered in investment planning, decisions and implementations.

All investments which require group level authorization should be reviewed by Group Staff. It is recommended that the Group Staff become involved in the projects as soon as possible to ensure that experience from similar projects within the group is utilized.

Land and buildings. When investing and divesting land and buildings the Group's Real-estate Company should always be consulted.

Computer and communication systems. There is a strong need for coordination within the Group regarding investments in computer and communication systems. Division staff must therefore be consulted before requests to invest in new such equipment are submitted.

Project finance and leasing. The responsibility for financing policy lies at corporate level. When considering leasing or project-specific finance the Group's Treasury Department should always be consulted to secure the best financing.

Local pre-approval review is made according to local instructions.

Signature. To ensure that all parties feel a personal responsibility for the decision the project leader and head/chairman of all units approving the decision should sign the approval.

Procurement. No orders are to be signed before grants have been approved.

Investment programmes. Investment programmes, major projects and strategic ventures must not be divided up so that requests are submitted for sub-project by sub-project. First an Investment Request and plan for the whole venture must be approved. Then, when the plan has been approved, approval for the independent sub-projects can be applied for.

During the implementation of major ventures, the underlying assumptions may change considerably. Therefore, the information should always be as up-to-date as possible and comments explaining the change in the assumptions should be given.

Project planning. Investment requests should be made for all project planning studies for major ventures or studies exceeding SEK 300,000 and approved by divisional management.

190

Cost overruns. If actual capital expenditures are expected to exceed the amount initially approved by more than 10 per cent, an additional approval must be obtained by the same units as approved the initial Investment Request. The additional request shall state the reasons for, and the effect on profitability of, the overrun.

Buy or make. Investments in production equipment should be concentrated to manufacture and components which for strategic reasons, when the company's own knowledge is essential, have to be kept in-house. It is recommended that products and parts of low volume value be manufactured by companies specializing in this kind of production.

Project design. Investment projects should be designed to optimize the yield of the investment during its expected economic life. Thus, capital expenditure and payback period must not be reduced by choosing technical solutions which will shorten the technical life or give unreasonably high costs of repair and maintenance.

Language. All Investment Requests sent to the head office should be written in English.

(f)   Responsibilities

Some of the manuals are very detailed when specifying who is responsible for what in the capital budgeting process and may devote several pages to this. The instructions may specify the responsibility of the proposer, controller, and manager of the investing company, the project manager appointed to plan and implement the project, divisional managers and staff units on different levels involved in the pre-approval and follow-up processes.

(g)   Profitability requirements

The hurdle rate is based on the current interest rate for a five year local currency loan plus a risk premium, and set in the annual budgetary control process.

(h)   The investment request form

INVESTMENT REQUEST

Project Number	Project Name	Currency	Investment Category
Company/Business Unit	Company Number	Type of IRE ☐ Regular IRE ☐ Initiative ☐ Reapproval	☐ Rationalization ☐ Replacement ☐ Capacity Expansion ☐ Quality Improvement ☐ Information Systems ☐ Other ....
Market Segment/Product Group			
Supplier		Project Manager	

Description:

Summary of Investment Calculation:

REQUEST AMOUNT	Expenditures	Expenses	Total	Profitability	Application	Follow-up
Company Budget for Investment Requests				Total Investment		
Whereof Approved				Payback Period		
This Request				Internal Rate of Return		
Estimated time for the Investment to be completed			Economic Life	Capacity Utilization per year		

Financing:

Proposed/Approved by:

	Date	Signature
Managing Director		
Local Board		
Division Board		
Business Area Board		
The MNC AB Board		

(i)   The templet for board decision

The MNC board of directors 199x-xx-xx

Company name: ...

(a)   The request: It is requested that the Board appropriate x million US$ to invest in ...

(b)   A general background and reason for the investment

(c)   A description and analysis of the investment (markets, products, lay-out, capacity, strategy, etc.)

(d)   A budget for the investment with a specification of the capital expenditures

(e)   A profitability analysis (cash flow, payback, DCF)

(f)   A plan for the finance of the investment

(g)   A timetable for the project

(h)   An assessment of project risks and flexibility

(j)   The capital expenditure plan

Unit	Investments	Capital expend.	Ex- penses	Total (KSEK)
Argentine	T production line	2.9	0.5	3.4
	Packaging machine	1.2		1.2
	Other investments	1.6	0.1	1.7
	Total	5.7	0.6	6.3
Belgium	Warehouse	7.3		7.3
	Computer equipment	1.2	1.7	2.9
	Fork trucks	1.9		1.9
	Other investments	1.9	0.2	2.1
	Total	12.3	1.9	14.2
England	T production line	8.8	1.0	9.8
	U production line	4.5	0.4	4.9
	laboratory equipment	4.4	0.3	4.7
	CAD/CAM system	0.7	2.3	3.0
	Computer equipment	1.2	1.4	2.6
	Cars	2.1		2.1
	The SESAM project	0.3	1.2	1.5
	Cutting equipment	0.8		0.8
	Other investments	4.3	0.7	5.0
	Total	27.1	7.3	34.4

and so forth

Bibliography

Aaker, D.A. and Mascarenhas, B. (1984) "The need for strategic flexibility", *Journal of Business Strategy*, 5(2): 74-82.

Abdelsamad, M. (1973) *A Guide to Capital Expenditure Analysis*, New York: Amacom.

Abegglen, J.C. and Stalk, G. (1985) *Kaisha, the Japanese Corporation*, New York: Basic Books.

Ackerman, R.W. (1970) "Influence of integration and diversity on the investment process", *Administrative Science Quarterly*, 15: 341-51.

Aggarwal, R. (1980) "Corporate use of sophisticated capital budgeting techniques: A strategic perspective and a critique of survey results", *Interfaces*, 10(2) 31-4.

Aggarwal, R. (1991) "Justifying investments in flexible manufacturing technology: Adding strategic analysis to capital budgeting under uncertainty", *Managerial Finance*, 17(2-3): 77-88.

Agrawal, A. and Mandelker, G.N. (1987) "Managerial incentives and corporate investment and financing decisions", *Journal of Finance*, XLII(4): 823-37.

Aharoni, Y. (1966) *The Foreign Investment Decision Process*, Cambridge, MA: Harvard University Press.

Allaire, Y. and Firsirotu, M. (1985) "How to implement radical strategies in large organizations", *Sloan Management Review*, 26(3): 19-34.

Allaire, Y. and Firsirotu, M. (1989) "Coping with strategic uncertainty", *Sloan Management Review*, 30(3): 7-16.

Amey, L.R. (1972) "Interdependencies in capital budgeting: A survey", *Journal of Business Finance*, (3): 70-86.

Andersson, B., (1988) *Kapitalkostnader och avkastningskrav*, Stockholm: Statens Energiverk.

196

Andersson, B. (1994) *Investeringar och energianvändning: Studier av industriföretagens initiering och bedömning av energiinvesteringar,* Göteborg: BAS.

Andersson, E., Gerbo, S.-E. and Krasse, B. (1977) "Investeringsbedömning i börsnoterade företag", *Affärsekonomi,* (3): 24-5.

Andreou, S.A. (1991) "Capital resource allocation for strategic quality management", *International Journal of Technology Management,* 6(3/4): 425-6.

Andrews. G.S. and Firer, C. (1987) "Why different divisions require different hurdle rates?", *Long Range Planning,* 20(5): 62-8.

Ang, J.S., Chua, J.H. and Sellers, R. (1979) "Generating cash flow estimates: An actual study using the delphi technique", *Financial Management,* (Spring): 64-7.

Arditti, F.D. and Levy, H. (1977) "The weighted average cost of capital as a cutoff rate: A critical analysis of the classical textbook weighted average", *Financial Management,* (Fall): 24-34.

Armstrong, J.S. (1982) "The value of formal planning for strategic decisions: Review of empirical research", *Strategic Management Journal,* 3(3): 197-211.

Armstrong, J.S. (1984) "Forecasting by extrapolation: Conclusions from 25 years of research", *Interfaces,* 14(6): 52-66.

Arwidi, O. and Samuelson, L.A. (1993) "The development of budgetary control in Sweden - A research note", *Management Accounting Research,* 4: 93-107.

Arwidi, O. and Yard, S. (1985) "Investment planning in some Swedish companies - Criteria and uses", *Scandinavian Journal of Management Studies,* (May): 271-96.

Arwidi, O. and Yard, S. (1986) *Kriterier för investeringsbedömning,* Lund: Doxa.

Ashton, A.S. (1962) "Investment planning in private enterprise", *Lloyds Bank Review,* 66(October): 23-9.

Baker, J.C. (1987) "The cost of capital of multinational companies: Facts and fallacies", *Mangerial Finance,* 13(1): 12-7.

Baker, N.R. and Freeland, J. (1975) "Recent advances in R & D benefit measurement and project selection methods", *Management Science,* 21(10): 1164-75.

Balakrishnan, R. (1991) "Information acquisition and resource allocation decisions", *Accounting Review,* 66(1): 120-39.

Baldwin, C.Y. (1991) "How capital budgeting deters innovation - and what to do about it", *Research-Technology Management,* 34(6): 39-45.

Baldwin, C.Y. and Clark, K.B. (1992) "Capabilities and capital investment: New perspective on capital budgeting", *Journal of Applied Corporate Finance,* 5(2): 67-82.

Baldwin, C.Y. and Clark, K.B. (1994) "Capital-budgeting systems and capabilities investments in U.S. companies after the Second World War", *Business History Review*, 68(1): 73-109.

Baldwin, R.H. (1959) "How to assess investment proposals", *Harvard Business Review*, 37(3): 98-104.

Balinga, B.R. and Jaeger, A.M. (1984) "Multinational corporations: Control systems and delegation issues", *Journal of International Business Studies*, (Fall): 25-40.

Ballen, K. (1989) "The new look of capital spending", *Fortune*, 119(6): 59-62.

Banerjee, A.V. (1992) "A simple model of herd behavior", *Quarterly Journal of Economics*, CVII(3): 797-817.

Barius, B., 1987, *Investeringar och marknadskonsekvenser*, Stockholm: Företagsekonomiska institutionen, Stockholms Universitet.

Barius, B. (1992) "Market appraisals before investment decisions - on possibilities of appraising future market consequences of investments", in Hägg, I. and Segelod, E. (eds.) *Issues in Empirical Investment Research*, Amsterdam: North-Holland: 107-26.

Barna, T. (1962) "Investment and growth policies in British industrial firms", *N.I.E.S.R. Occasional Paper XX*: 30-3.

Bartlett, C.A. and Ghoshal, S. (1987) "Managing across borders: New organizational responses", *Sloan Management Review*, 29(1): 43-53.

Bartlett, C.A. and Goshal, S. (1989) *Managing Across Borders: The Transnational Solution*, London: Hutchinson Business Books.

Barton, H., Brown, D., Cound, J., Marsh, P. and Willey, K. (1992) "Does top management add value to investment decisions?", *Long Range Planning*, 25(5): 43-58.

Barwise, P., Marsh, P., Thomas, K. and Wensley, R. (1986) "Research on strategic investment decisions", in McGee, J. and Thomas, H. (eds.) *Strategic Management Research*, Chichester: Wiley: 23-52.

Barwise, P. Marsh, P.R. and Wensley, R. (1989) "Must finance and strategy clash?" *Harvard Business Review*, 67(5): 85-90.

Baumgartner, H. and Irvine, V. (1977) "A survey of capital budgeting techniques used in Canadian companies", *Cost and Management*, (1): 51-4.

Bavishi, V.B. (1981) "Capital budgeting practices at multinationals", *Management Accounting* (New York), (August): 32-5.

Becker, R.H. (1980) "Project selection checklists for research, product development, process development", *Research Management*, 23(September): 34-6.

Berg, N. (1973) Corporate role in diversified companies", in Taylor, B. and MacMillan, K. (eds.) *Business Policy: Teaching and Research*, New York: Wiley: 298-347.

Bergendahl, G. (1980) Brister i offentliga myndigheters kalkylmetodik vid samhällsinvesteringar, Göteborg: Göteborgs Universitet, Företagsekonomiska institutionen.

Bergholm, F. and Jagrén, L. (1986) "Mjukvaruinvesteringarnas storlek och betydelse", *Ekonomisk Debatt*, 14(4): 297-304.

Bernhard, R.H. (1989) "Base selection for modified rates of return and its irrelevance for optimal project choice", *Engineering Economist*, 35(1): 55-65.

Bernstein, J.I. and Nadiri, M.S. (1989) "Reseach and development and intra-industry spillovers: An empirical application of dynamic duality", *Review of Economic Studies*, 56: 249-69.

Berry, A.J. (1984) "The control of capital investment", *Journal of Management Studies*, 21(1): 61-81.

Bettis, R.A., Bradley, S.P. and Hamel, G. (1992) "Outsourcing and industrial decline", *Academy of Management Executive*, 6(1): 7-22.

Bhattacharya, K. (1983) "Balance sheet optics - the shareholders" friend", *Accountancy*, (November): 137-8.

Biggadike, R. (1979a) *Entry, Strategy, and Performance*, Cambridge, MA: Harvard University Press.

Biggadike, R. (1979b) "The risky business of diversification", *Harvard Business Review*, 57(3): 103-11.

Blazouske, J.D., Carlin, I. and Kim, S.H. (1988) "Current capital budgeting practices in Canada", *CMA Magazine*, 62(2): 51-4.

Bofors årsredovisning (1978) "Om investeringar": 36-41.

Bohlin, E. (1995) *Economics and Management of Investments: An International Investigation of New Technology Decision-Making in Telecommunications*, Göteborg: Chalmers University of Technology.

Bohlin, S. (1962) "Investeringar - beslut och uppföljning", *Iba praktikskrift*, (1).

von Böhm-Bawerk, E.V. (1889) *Positive Theorie des Kapitales*, Jena: Fischer.

Boiteux, M. (1950) "Réflexions sur la concurrence du rail et de la route, le déclassement des linges non rentables et le dédicit du chemin de fer", the National Federation of Highway Transport.

Bower, J.L. (1970) *Managing the Resource Allocation Process*, Division of Research, Graduate School of Business Administration, Boston: Harvard University.

Bower, J.L. (1972) *Managing the Resource Allocation Process*, Homewood, Ill: Richard D. Irwin.

Bower, J.L. (1974) "Planning and control: Bottom-up or top-down, *Journal of General Management*, 1: 20-31.

Bower, J.L. (1985) "Capital budgeting as a general management problem", in Rhodes, E. and Wield, D. (eds.) *Implementing New Technologies*, Basil Blackwell, Oxford: 249-63.

Bowman, E.H. and Hurry, D. (1993) "Strategy through the option lens: An integrated view of resource investments and the incremental-choice process", *Academy of Management Review*, 18(4): 760-82.

Bradley, T.G. and Branch, B. (1987) "'Allocating' capital more effectively", *Sloan Management Review*, 29(1): 21-31.

Bromiley, P. (1986) "Corporate planning and capital investment", *Journal of Economic Behavior and Organization*, 7: 147-70.

Brigham, E.F. (1975) "Hurdle rates for screening capital expenditure proposals", *Financial Management*, 4(3): 17-26.

Burchell, S., Clubb, C., Hopwood, A., Hughes, J. and Nahapiet, J. (1980) "The role of accounting in organizations and society", *Accounting, Organization and Society*, 5(1): 5-27.

Burgelman, R.A. (1983a) "A process model of internal corporate venturing in the diversified major firm", *Administrative Science Quarterly*, 28: 223-44.

Burgelman, R.A. (1983b) "Corporate entrepreneurship and strategic management: Insights from a process study", *Management Science*, 29: 1349-64.

Burgelman, R.A. (1984) "Managing the internal corporate venturing process", *Sloan Management Review*, 25(Winter): 33-48.

Business Week (1993) "The technology payoff: A sweeping reorganization of work itself is boosting productivity", (June 14): 36-43.

Business Week (1993) "More for less? The goal: Cut R&D costs without cutting R&D", (June 28): 50-7.

Butler, R., Davies, R., Pike, R. and Sharp, J. (1991) "Strategic investment decision-making: Complexities and processes", *Journal of Management Studies*, 28(4) 395-415.

Calderón-Rossell, J.R. (1992) "Is the ROI a good indicator of the IRR?", *Engineering Economist*, 37(4): 315-39.

Camillus, J.C. (1984) "Designing a capital budgeting system that works", *Long Range Planning*, 17(2): 103-10.

Campbell, A., Goold, M. and Alexander, M. (1995) "Corporate strategy: The quest for parenting advantage", *Harvard Business Review*, 73(2): 120-32.

Canada, J.R. (1986) "Annotated bibligraphy of computer integrated manufacturing systems", *Engineering Economist*, 31(2): 137-50.

Canada, J.R. and Miller, N.P. (1985) "Review of surveys on use of capital investment evaluation techniques", *Engineering Economist*, 30(2): 193-200.

Cannon, C.M. (1966) "The limited application of minimum profitability requirements to capital expenditure proposals", *Journal of Industrial Economics*, XV(1): 54-64.

Carr, C., Tomkins, C. and Bayliss, B. (1991) "Strategic controllership - A case study approach", *Management Accounting Research*, 2: 89-107.

Carr, C., Tomkins, C. and Bayliss, B. (1994a) "Financial or strategic controls? An Anglo-German case study", *European Management Journal*, 12(1): 102-13.

Carr, C., Tomkins, C. and Bayliss, B. (1994b) *Strategic Investment Decisions*, Aldershot: Avebury.

Carter, C.F. and Williams, B.R. (1958) *Investment in Innovation*, Oxford: Oxford University Press.

Carter, E.E. (1971a) "The behavioral theory of the firm and top-level corporate decisions", *Administrative Science Quarterly*, 16: 413-28.

Carter, E.E. (1971b) "Project evaluations and firm decisions", *Journal of Management Studies*, 8: 253-79.

Chan, S.H., Kensinger, J.W. and Martin, J.D. (1992) "The market rewards promising R&D - and punishes the rest", *Journal of Applied Corporate Finance*, 5(2): 59-66.

Chandler, Jr., A.D. (1962) *Strategy and Structure: Chapters in the History of the Industrial Enterprise*, Cambridge, MA; MIT Press.

Chandler, Jr., A.D. (1991) "The functions of the HQ unit in the multibusiness firm", *Strategic Management Journal*, 12: 31-50.

Claesson, K. and Hiller, P. (1982) *Investeringsprocessen i några svenska verkstadsföretag*, Stockholm: EFI.

Clancy, D.K., Collins, F. and Chatfield, R. (1982) "Capital budgeting: The behavioural factors", *Cost and Management*, 56(5): 28-32.

Clancy, D.K. and Finn, D.W. (1985) "Capital project life cycle: A reorientation of project selection", *Cost and Management*, 59(4): 6-10.

Coates, J., Davis, T. and Stacey, R. (1995) "Performance measurement systems, incentive reward schemes and short-termism in multinational companies: A note", *Management Accounting Research*, 6: 125-35.

Cochran, M.A., Pyle, E.B., Greene, L.C., Clymer, A.A, and Bender, D. (1971) "Investment model for R & D project evaluation and selection", *IEEE Transaction on Engineering Management*, EM-18, (3).

Collier, P. and Gregory, A. (1995) "Investment appraisal in service industries: A field study analysis of the U.K. hotels sector", *Management Accounting Research*, 6(1): 33-57.

Cook, T.J. and Rizzuto, R.J. (1989) "Capital budgeting practices for R&D: A survey and analysis of Business Week"s R&D scoreboard", *Engineering Economist*, 34(4): 291-303.

Copeland, T.E. and Weston, J.F. (1979) *Financial Theory and Corporate Policy*, Reeding: Addison-Wesley.

Cooper, D.J. (1975) "Rationality and investment appraisal", *Accounting and Business Research*, 5(19): 198-202.

Cooper, J.C. and Selto, F.H. (1991) "An experimental examination of the effects of SFAS no. 2 on R & D investment decisions", *Accounting, Organizations and Society*, 16(3): 227-42.

Cooper, W.D., Cornick, M.F. and Redmon, A. (1992) "Capital budgeting: A 1990 study of Fortune 500 company practice", *Journal of Applied Business Research*, 8(3): 20-3.

Coulthurst, N.J. (1986) "The application of the incremental principle in capital investment project evaluation", *Accounting and Business Research*, (Autumn): 359-64.

Cowling, K. (1990) "A new industrial strategy: Preparing Europe for the turn of the century", *International Journal of Industrial Organization*, 8(2): 165-83.

Cummings, S. (1995) "Centralization and decentralization: the never-ending story of separation and betrayal", *Scandinavian Journal of Management*, 11(2): 103-17.

Currie, W. (1991a) "Managing production technology in Japanese industry: An investigation into eight companies: Part 1", *Management Accounting* (London), 69(6): 28-9.

Currie, W. (1991b) "Managing production technology in Japanese industry: An investigation into eight companies: Part 2", *Management Accounting* (London), 69(7): 36-8.

Currie, W.L. (1992) *The Strategic Management of Advanced Manufacturing Technology*, CIMA: London.

Currie, W. (1993) "The strategic management of AMT in Japan, the USA, the UK and West Germany - Part 3: Developing AMT strategy for world class manufacturing", *Management Accounting* (London), 71(1): 56-8.

Cyert, R.M. and March, J.G. (1963) *A Behavioral Theory of the Firm*, Englewood Cliffs, NJ: Prentice-Hall.

Cyert, R.M., March, J.G. and Starbuck, W.H. (1961) "Two experiments on bias and conflict in organizational estimation", *Management Science*, 7(April): 254-64.

Danielsson, A. (1967) "A note on the allocation of capital in the firm", *Swedish Journal of Economics*, (1).

Davies, A. (1991) "Strategic planning for the board", *Long Range Planning*, 24(2): 94-100.

Davis, D. (1985) "New projects: Beware of false economies", *Harvard Business Review*, 63(2): 95-101.

Dean, J. (1951a) *Capital Budgeting*, New York: Columbia University Press.

Dean, J. (1951b) *Managerial Economics*, New York: Prentice-Hall.

Dearden, J. (1962) "Mirage of profit decentralization", *Harvard Business Review*, 40(6): 140-54.

Dearden, J. (1969) "The case against ROI control", *Harvard Business Review*, 47(3): 124-.

DeThomas, A.R. (1981) "Forecasting cash flows: The practical side of capital budgeting", *Managerial Planning*, (May/June): 38-47.

Detrie, J.-P. and Ramanantsoa, B. (1986) "Diversification - The key factors for success", *Long Range Planning*, 19(1): 31-7.

Diacogiannis, G.P. and Lai, R. (1989) "Survey on the investment and financing decisions of the companies in the USM", *Warwick Papers in Management No. 33*, Coventry: School of Industrial and Business Studies.

Dixit, A.K. and Pindyck, R.S. (1994) *Investment under Uncertainty*, Princeton, NY: Princeton University Press.

Dixon, J.R. and Duffey, M.R. (1990) "The neglect of engineering design", *California Management Review*, 32(2): 9-23.

Dodgson, M. (1993) "Organizational learning: A review of some literatures", *Organization Studies*, 14(3): 375-94.

Donaldson, G. and Lorsch, J. (1983) *Decision Making at the Top: Shaping of Strategic Direction*, New York: Basic Books.

Doz. Y.L. and Prahalad, C.K. (1981) "Headquarters influence and strategic control in MNCs", *Sloan Management Review*, 23(1): 15-29.

Doz, Y. and Prahalad, C.K. (1984) "Patterns of strategic control within multinaltional corporations", *Journal of International Business Studies*, (Fall): 55-72.

Downing, T. (1989) "Eight new ways to evaluate automation", *Mechanical Engineering*, 111(7): 82-6.

Dugdale, D. and Jones, C. (1991) "Discordant voices: accountants' view of investment appraisal", *Management Accounting* (London), 68(November): 54-6, 59.

Dugdale, D. and Jones, C. (1994) "Finance, strategy and trust in investment decision-making", *Management Accounting* (London), 72(April): 52-4, 56.

Dulman, S.P. (1989) "The development of discounted cash flow techniques in U.S. industry", *Business History Review*, 63(Autumn): 555-87.

Edgren, J., Rhenman, E. and Skärvad, P.-H. (1983) *Divisionalisering och därefter: Erfarenheter av decentraliserad organisation i sju svenska företag*, Stockholm: Management Media.

Ehrbar, A.F. (1979) "Unraveling the mysteries of corporate profits", *Fortune*, (August 27): 90-6.

Ehrhardt, M.C. and Reeve, J.M. (1991) "Creating value: The appropriate use of capital budgeting", *Mangerial Finance*, 17(5): 3-13.

Einhorn, H.J. and Hogarth, R.M. (1987) "Decision making: Going forward in reverse", *Harvard Business Review*, (1): 66-70.

Eisenhardt, K.M. (1985) "Control: Organizational and economic approaches", *Management Science*, 31(2): 134-149.

Eisenhardt, K.M. (1989) "Agency theory: An assessment and review", *Academy of Management Review*, 14(1): 57-74.

Eliasson, G., (1976) *Business Economic Planning*, New York: Wiley.

Engwall, M. (1995) *Jakten på det effektiva projektet*, Stockholm: Nerenius & Santérus förlag.

Eriksson, B. (1959) "Synpunkter på investeringskalkyler", *Teknisk Information*, (6).

Eriksson, Å. (1963) "Lönsamhetsbedömning vid kapitalkrävande rationaliseringar", *Industriell Teknik*, (19).

Fama, E. and Jensen, M. (1983) "Separation of ownership and control", *Journal of Law and Economics*, 26: 301-325.

203

Fama, E.F. and Jensen, M.C. (1985) "Organizational forms and investment decisions", *Journal of Financial Economics*, 14: 101-19.

Fama, E. and Miller, M. (1972) *The Theory of Finance*, New York: Holt, Rinehert & Winston.

Farragher, E.J. (1986) "Capital budgeting practice of non-industrial firms", *The Engineering Economist*, 31(4): 293- 302.

Faulhaber, G.R. and Baumol, W.J. (1988) "Economists as innovators: Practical products of theoretical research", *Journal of Economic Literature*, XXVI(June) 577-600.

Faustmann, M.(1849) "Berechnung des Werthes, welchen Waldboden, sowie noch nicht haubare Holzbestände für die Waldwirthschaft besitzen", *Allgemeine Forst- und Jagd-Zeitung*, (12 December): 441-55.

Feldman, M.S. and March, J.G. (1981) "Information in organizations as signal and symbol", *Administrative Science Quarterly*, 26(2): 171-186.

Ferreira, E.J. and Wiggins, C.D. (1987) "How large companies have adjusted their capital-budgeting decision for inflation", *Mid-South Business Journal*, 7(2): 3-8.

Findlay, M.C. and Williams, E.E. (1980) "A positive evaluation of the new finance", *Financial Management*, 9(Summer): 7-17.

Finnie, J. (1988) "The role of financial appraisal in decisions to acquire advanced manufacturing technology", *Accounting and Business Research*, 18(79): 133-9.

Fish, J.C.L. (1915) *Engineering Economics*, New York: McGraw-Hill.

Fisher, I. (1907) *The Rate of Interest*, New York: Macmillan.

Fisher, I. (1930) *The Theory of Interest*, New York: Macmillan.

Ford, H. (1977) "Innovation in a wast economy", *Omega*, 5(2): 121-132.

Forsgren, M. (1989) *Managing the Internationalization Process: The Swedish Case*, London: Routledge.

Franko, L.G. (1974) "The move toward a multidivisional structure in European organizations", *Administrative Science Quarterly*, (December): 493-505.

Freeman, C. (1974) *The Economics of Industrial Innovations*, London: Penguin Books.

Freeman, M. and Hobbes, G. (1991) "Capital budgeting: Theory versus practice", *Australian Accountant*, 61(8): 36-41.

Fremgen, J.M. (1973) "Capital budgeting practices: A survey", *Management Accounting*, 54(11): 19-25.

Frenckner, P. (1972) "Kriterier vid bedömning av investeringar: En översikt och några kommentarer", *The Finnish Journal of Business Economics*, (4): 339-351.

Gallagher, T.J. and Zumwalt, J.K. (1991) "Risk-adjusted discount rates revisited", *The Financial Review*, 26(1): 105-114.

Gallinger, G.W. (1980) "Capital expenditure administration", *Sloan Management Review*, 22(1): 13-21.

Gandemo, B., (1980) "The influence of increased environmental turbulence on corporate investment and financial planning", in Crum, R. and F. Derkinderen (eds.) *Capital Budgeting Under Conditions of Uncertainty*, The Hague: Martinus Nijhoff Publishing: 21-37.

Gandemo, B., 1982a, Företagens investeringsbeteende, *SIND 1982: 14*, Stockholm: Liber.

Gandemo, B., 1982b, Investeringar i företag: Analys och intervjuer, *SIND 1982: 17*, Stockholm: Liber.

Gandemo, B., 1983, Investeringar i företag, *SIND 1983: 5*, Stockholm: Liber.

Gandemo, B. (1992) "Capital investment behaviour - Results from some Swedish studies", in Hägg, I. and Segelod, E. (eds.) *Issues in Empirical Investment Research*, Amsterdam: North-Holland: 39-59.

Ghertman, M. (1988) "Foreign subsidiary and parents' roles during strategic investment and divestment decisions", *Journal of International Business Studies*, (Spring): 47-67.

Gimple, M.L. and Dakin, S.R. (1984) "Management and magic", *California Management Review*, XXVII(1): 125-36.

Gitman, L.J. and Forrester, J.R. (1977) "A survey of capital budgeting techniques used by major U.S. firms", *Financial Management*, VI(3): 66-71.

Gitman, L.J. and Mercurio, V.A. (1982) "Cost of capital techniques used by major U.S. Firms: Survey and analysis of Fortune"s 1000", *Financial Management*, 11(4): 21-9.

Gold, B. (1976) "The shaky foundations of capital budgeting", *California Management Review*, XIX(2): 51-60.

Gold, B. and Boyland, M.G. (1975) "Capital budgeting, industrial capacity, and import", *Quarterly Review of Economics and Business*, 15(3): 17-32.

Goold, M. and Campbell, A. (1987a) *Strategies and Styles: The Role of the Centre in Managing Diversified Corporations*, Oxford: Basil Blackwell.

Goold, M. and Campbell, A. (1987b) "Many best ways to make strategy", *Harvard Business Review*, 65(6): 70-6.

Goold, M. and Campbell, A. (1988) "Managing the diversified corporation: The tensions facing the chief executive", *Long Range Planning*, 21(4): 12-24.

Goold, M. and Quinn, J.J. (1990) "The paradox of strategic controls", *Strategic Management Journal*, 11(1) 43-57.

Goold, M. (1991) "Strategic control in the decentralized firm", *Sloan Management Review*, 32(2) 69-81.

Goold, M., Campbell, A. and Luchs, K. (1993) "Strategies and styles revisited: Strategic planning and financial control", *Long Range Planning*, 26(5): 49-60.

Goold, M., Campbell, A. and Luchs, K. (1993) "Strategies and styles revisited: 'Strategic control' - is it tenable?", *Long Range Planning*, 26(6): 54-61.

Göppl, H. and Hellwig, K. (1973) "'Vermögensrentabilität - ein einfaches dynamisches Investitionskalkül' - kritische Anmerkung zu einem gleichnamigen Aufsatz von M. Henke", *Zeitschrift für Betribswirtschaft*, 747-52.

Gordon, L.A. (1989) "Benefit-cost analysis and resource allocation decisions", *Accounting, Organizations and Society*, 14(3): 247-258.

Gordon, L.A., Pinches, G.E. and Stockton, F.T. (1988) "Sophisticated methods of capital budgeting: An economics of internal organization approach", *Managerial Finance*, 14(2-3): 36-41.

Gordon, L.A. and Smith, K.J. (1992) "Postauditing capital expenditures and firm performance: The role of asymmetric information", *Accounting, Organizations and Society*, 17(8): 741-57.

Gramlich, E.M. (1994) "Infrastructure investment: A review essay", *Journal of Economic Literature*, 32: 1176-96.

Grant, E.L. (1930) *Principles of engineering economy*, New York: The Ronald Press.

Greenley, G.E. (1994) "Strategic planning and company performance: An appraisal of the empirical evidence", *Scandinavian Journal of Management*, 10(4): 383-396.

Griliches, Z. (1979) "Issues in assessing the contribution of R & D to productivity growth", *The Bell Journal of Economics*, 10(1): 92-116.

Guilding, C. and Pike, R. (1990) "Intangible market assets: A managerial accounting perspective", *Accounting and Business Research*, 21(18):41-9.

Gulliver, F.R. (1987) "Post-project appraisal pay", *Harvard Business Review*, 65(2): 128-32.

Gup, B.E. and Norwood III, S. W. (1982) "Divisional Cost of Capital: A Practical Approach", *Financial Management*, (Spring): 20-4.

Gupta, S.K. and Rosenhead, J. (1968) "Robustness in sequential investment decisions", *Management Science*, 15(2): B-18-29.

Gurnani, C. (1984) "Capital budgeting: Theory and practice", *The Engineering Economist*, 30(1) 19-46.

Gutenberg, E. (1959) *Untersuchungen über die Investitionsentscheidungen industrieller Unternehmen*, Köln und Opladen.

Gutenberg, E. (1992) "Investment policy in industrial enterprises", *Management International Review*, 32(1): 17-28.

Häckner, E. (1988) "Strategic development and information use", *Scandinavian Journal of Management*, 4(1/2): 45-61.

Hägg, I. (1977) "Reviews of capital investments", *Research Report No 3*, Uppsala, Department of Business Studies, Uppsala Universitet.

Hägg, I. (1979) "Reviews of capital investments: Empirical studies", *The Finnish Journal of Business Studies*, (3): 211-25.

Hägg, I, (1979) Fundering kring investering, Uppsala: Department of Business Studies, Uppsala University.

Hägg, I. (1992) "On investments and accounting with a focus on immaterial investments", in Hägg, I. and Segelod, E. (eds.) *Issues in Empirical Investment Research*, Amsterdam: North-Holland: 201-8.

Hägg, I., Magnusson, Å. and Samuelson, L.A. (1988) "Research on budgetary control in the nordic countries - A survey", *Accounting, Organization and Society*, 13(5): 535-47.

Hägg, I. and Segelod, E. (1992) *Issues in Empirical Investment Research*, Amsterdam: North-Holland.

Haka, S.F. (1987) "Capital budgeting techniques and firm specific contingencies: A correlational analysis", *Accounting, Organizations and Society*, 12(1): 31-48.

Haka, S.F., Gordon, L.A. and Pinches, G.E. (1985) "Sophisticated capital budgeting selection techniques and firm performance", *The Accounting Review*, LX(4) 651-69.

Hall, P. (1980) *Great Planning Disasters*, London: Weidenfeld & Nicolson.

Hall, W.K. (1979) "Changing perspective on the capital investment process", *Long Range Planning*, 12(1): 37-40.

Harris, R.S., O'Brien, T.J. and Wakeman, D. (1989) "Divisional cost-of-capital estimation for multi-industry firms", *Financial Management*, (Spring): 74-84.

Harrison, E.F. (1991) "Strategic control at the CEO Level", *Long Range Planning*, 24(6): 78-87.

Hastie, K.L. (1974) "One businessman's view of capital budgeting", *Financial Management*, (Winter): 36-44.

Hayes, R.H. and Abernathy, W.J. (1980) "Managing our way to economic decline", *Harvard Business Review*, 58(4).

Hayes, R. H. and Garvin, D. A. (1982) "Managing as if tomorrow mattered", *Harvard Business Review*, 60(3): 70-9.

Hayes, R. H. (1985) "Strategic planning - forward in reverse?", *Harvard Business Review*, 63(6): 111-9.

Hayes, R.H. and Wheelwright, S.C. (1984) *Restoring Our Competitive Edge: Competing Through Manufacturing*, New York: Wiley.

Hayes, R.H., Wheelwright, S.C. and Clark, K.B. (1988) *Dynamic Manufacturing: Creating the Learning organization*, New York: The Free Press.

Haynes, W.W. and Solomon, M.B. (1962) "A misplaced emphasis in capital budgeting", *The Quarterly Review of Economic & Business*, 2(1): 39-46.

Hedberg, B.L.T. (1981) "How organizations learn and unlearn", in Nystrom, P.C. and Starbuck, W.H. (eds.) *Handbook of Organizational Design, Volume 1*, New York: Oxford University Press.

Hedberg, B. and Jönsson, S.A. (1977) "Strategy formulation as a discontinuous process", *International Studies of Management and Organisation*, 7(2): 88-102.

Heister, M. (1962) *Rentabilitätsanlayse von Investitionen*, Köln und Opladen.

Heller, W.W. (1951) "The anatomy of investment decisions", *Harvard Business Review*, XXIX(2): 95-103.

Henders, B. (1992) "Investment and position - An example from the UK newsprint/newspaper network", in Hägg, I. and Segelod, E. (eds.) *Issues in Empirical Investment Research*, Amsterdam: North-Holland: 225-44.

Hendricks, J.A. (1983) "Capital budgeting practice including adjustments: A survey", *Managerial Planning*, (1): 22-8.

Henke, M. (1973) "Vermögensrentabilität - ein einfaches dynamisches Investitionskalkül", *Zeitschrift für Betriebswirtschaft*, (3): 177-98.

Henke, M. (1974) "Vermögensrentabilität - ein einfaches dynamisches Investitionskakül, Zugleich Erwiderung auf einen Beitrag von Göppl, Hellwig in der ZfB", *Zeitschrift für Betribswirtschaft*, 593-602.

Hirshleifer, D. (1993) "Managerial reputation and corporate investment decisions", *Financial Management*, 22(2): 145-160.

Hirshman, A.O. (1967) *Development Projects Observed*", Washington D.C.

Ho, S.S.M. and Pike, R.H. (1992) "Adaption of probabilistic risk analysis in capital budgeting and corporate investment", *Journal of Business Finance & Accounting*, 19(3): 387-405.

Hodder, J.E. (1986) "Evaluation of manufacturing investments: A comparison of U.S. and Japanese practices", *Financial Management*, (Spring) 17-24.

Hodder, J.E. and Riggs, J.E. (1985) "Pitfalls in evaluating risky projects", *Harvard Business Review*, 63(1): 128-35.

Hoffman, P.J. and Blanchard, W.A. (1961) "A study of the effects of varying amounts of predictor information on judgment", Oregon Research Institute Research Bullitin.

Hogarth, R.M. (1981) "Beyond discrete biases: Functional and dysfunctional aspects of judgmental heuristics", *Psychological Bulletin*, 90(2): 197-217.

Holmstrom, B. and Ricart i Costa, J. (1986) "Managerial incentives and capital management", *Quarterly Journal of Economics*, 101(4): 835-60.

Honko, J. (1966) *On Investment Decisions in Finnish Industry.* Helsinki: The Helsinki Research Institute for Business Economics.

Honko, J. and Virtanen, K. (1975) *The Investment Process in Finnish Industrial Enterprises.* Helsinki: The Helsinki School of Economics, Acta Academiae Oeconomicae Helsingiensis, Series A:16.

Hopwood, A. (1974) *Accounting and Human Behaviour*, London: Haymarket.

Hoshi, T., Kashyap, A. and Scharfstein, D. (1991) "Corporate structure, liquidity, and investment: Evidence from Japanese industrial groups", *Quarterly Journal of Economics*, 106(1): 33-60.

Hoskisson, R.E. and Hitt, M.A. (1988) "Strategic control systems and relative R&D investment in large multiproduct firms", *Strategic Management Journal*, 9: 605-21.

Hoskisson, R.E. and Turk, T.A. (1990) "Corporate restructuring: Governance and control limits of the internal capital market", *Academy of Management Review*, 15(3): 459-77.

Hout, R., Porter, M.E. and Rudden, E. (1982) "How global companies win out", *Harvard Business Review*, (5): 98-108.

Huber, G.P. (1991) "Organizational learning: The contributing processes and the literature", *Organization Science*, 2(1): 88-115.

Hunsicker, J.Q. (1980) "The malaise of strategic planning", *Management Review*, (March): 9-14.

Istvan, D.F. (1959) The Capital-Expenditure Decision-Making Process in Forty-eight Large Corporations. Bloomington, Ind.: D.B.A. dissertation, Indiana University.

Istvan, D. F. (1961a) *Capital Expenditure Decisions: How hey are made in large corporations*. Bloomington, Ind.: Indiana Business Report, No. 33, Indiana University.

Istvan, D.F. (1961b) "The economic evaluation of capital expenditures", *The Journal of Business*, XXXIV(1): 45-51.

Jackson, B. (1983) "Decision methods for evaluating R & D projects", *Research Management*, 26(July-August): 16-22.

Jacobs, M.T. (1991) *Short-Term America: The Causes and Cures of Our Business Myopia*, Cambridge, MA.: Harvard Business School Press.

Jaffe, A. (1986) "Technological opportunity and spillovers of R & D", *American Economic Review*, 76(5): 984-1001.

Jansson, D. (1989) "The pragmatic uses of what is taken for granted: Project leaders' applications of investment calculations", *International Studies of Management & Organization*, 19(3): 49-63.

Jansson, D. (1992) *Spelet kring investeringskalkyler: Om den strategiska användningen av det för-givet-tagna*, Stockholm: Norstedts.

Jean, W.H. (1989) "Interest rate-independent present value rankings", *The Engineering Economist*, 34(2): 129-48.

Jemison, D.B. and Sitkin, S.B. (1986) "Corporate acquisitions: A process perspective", *Academy of Management Review*, 11(1): 145-63.

Joglekar, P. and Paterson, M.L. (1986) "A closer look at the returns and risks of pharmaceutical R & D", *Journal of Health Ecnomics*, 5: 153-77.

Johanson, J. and Mattsson, L.-G. (1985) "Marketing investments and market investments in industrial network", *International Journal of Research in Marketing*, 2: 185-195.

Johnson, H.T. and Kaplan,, R.S. (1987) *Relevance Lost: The Rise and Fall of Management Accounting*, Cambridge, MA: Harvard Business School Press.

Jones, C.J. (1986) "Financial planning and control practices in U.K. companies: A longitudinal study", *Journal of Business Finance & Accounting*, 113(2) 161-85.

Jones, T.C., Currie, W.L. and Dugdale, D. (1993) "Accounting and technology in Britain and Japan: Learning from field research", *Management Accounting Research*, 4: 109-37.

Jones, T.C. and Dugdale, D. (1994) "Academic and practitioner rationality: The case of investment appraisal", *Brittish Accounting Review*, 26(1): 3-25.

Junnelius, C. (1974) *Investeringsprocessens utformning vid olika organisationsstrukturtyper*, Helsingfors: Svenska Handelshögskolans skrift nr 22.

Kakati, M. and Dhar, U.R. (1991) "Investment justification in flexible manufacturing systems", *Engineering Costs & Production Economics*, 21(3): 203-9.

Karlsson, C. and Åhlström, P. (1994) "The difficult path to lean production development", *2nd Internationl Product Development Management Conference on New Approaches to Development and Engineering*, Gothenburg, Sweden: 410-23.

Kato, Y. (1986) "Management accounting practices in Japan's largest manufacturing firms (2)", *Sangyokeiri*, 46(4). (In Japanese)

Kee, R. and Bublitz, B. (1988) "The role of payback in the investment process", *Accounting and Business Research*, (18)70, 149-55.

Kester, W.C. (1984) "Today"s options for tomorrow"s growth", *Harvard Business Review*, 62(2): 153-60.

Kester, W. C. (1986) "An option approach to corporate finance", in Altman, E. I. (ed.) *Handbook of Corporate Finance*, New York: Wiley: 5.1-5.35.

Kester, W.C. and Taggart, R.A., Jr. (1989) "Capital allocation - Hurdle rates, budgets, or both?", *Sloan Management Review*, 30(3): 83-90.

Kester, W.C. (1992) "Governance contracting, and investment horizons: A look at Japan and Germany", *Journal of Applied Corporate Finance*, 5(2): 83-98.

Keynes, J.M. (1936) *The General Theory of Employment, Interest and Money*, London.

Kim, I. and Song, J. (1990) "US, Korea, and Japan: Accounting practices in three countries", *Management Accounting* (USA), 72(2): 26-30.

Kim, M.K. (1979,) "Inflationary effects in the capital investment process: An empirical examination", *Journal of Finance*, (September): 941-50.

Kim, S.H. (1982) "An empirical study on the relationship between capital budgeting practices and earnings performance", *The Engineering Economist*, 27(3), 185-96.

Kim, S.H., Crick, T. and Farragher, E.J. (1984) "Foreign capital budgeting practice ussed by the U.S. and non-U.S. multinational companies", *The Engineering Economist*, 29(3), 207-15.

Kim, S.H. and Farragher, E.J. (1982) "Current capital budgeting practices", *Management Accounting*, (June): 26-30.

King, P. (1974) "Strategic control of capital investment", *Journal of General Management*, 2(1) 17-28.

King, P. (1975) "Is the emphasis of capital budgeting theory misplaced?", *Journal of Business Finance & Accounting*, 2(1) 69-82.

Kirsch, R.J. and Sakthivel, S. (1993) "Capitalize or expense? Accountants need guidance on software developed for internal use", *Management Accounting* (New York), LXXIV(7): 38-43.

Klammer, T. (1972) "Empirical evidence of the adoption of sophisticated capital budgeting techniques", *Journal of Business*, 45(3) 387-97.

Klammer, T. and Walker, M.C. (1984) "The continuing increase in the use of sophisticated capital budgeting techniques", *California Management Review*, XXVII(1): 137-48.

Klammer, T.P. and Walker, M.C. (1987) "Capital budgeting questionnaire: A new perspective", *Quarterly Journal of Business & Economics*, 26(3): 87-95.

Kruschwitz, L. (1976) "Finanzmathematische Endwert- und Zinsfuss-modelle", *Zeitschrift für Betriebswirtschaft*, 245-62.

Lambrix, R.J. and Singhvi, S.S. (1984) "Preapproval audit of capital projects", *Harvard Business Review*, 62(2): 12-4.

Lander, G.H. and Bayou, M.E. (1992) "Does ROI apply to robotic factories?", *Management Accounting* (New York), 73(11): 49-53.

Langley, A. (1988) "The roles of formal strategic planning", *Long Range Planning*, 21(3), 40-50.

Langley, A. (1989) "In search of rationality: The purposes behind the use of formal analysis in organizations", *Administrative Science Quarterly*, 34: 598-631.

Langley, A. (1990) "Patterns in the use of formal analysis in strategic decisions", *Organization Studies*, 11(1): 17-45.

Langley, A. (1991) "Formal analysis and strategic decision making", *Omega*, 19(2/3): 79-99.

Lefley, F.(1994) "AMT project hurdle rates too high?", *Management Accounting*, 72(5): 37, 46.

Leighton, D.S.R. and Thain, D.H. (1990) "Capital spending: A director"s view", *Business Quarterly*, 54(3): 5-10.

Lerner, E.M. and Rappaport, A. (1968) "Limit DCF in capital budgeting", *Harvard Business Review*, 46(5): 133-9.

Lesser, A. (1969) "Engineering economy in the United States in retrospect - an analysis", *The Engineering Economist*, 14(2): 109-15.

Leuthold, S.C. (1981) "Interest rates, inflation and deflation", *Financial Analysis Journal*, (1): 28-41.

Levitt, B. and March, J.G. (1988) "Organizational learning", *Annual Review of Sociology*, 14: 319-40.

Likert, R. (1961) *New Patterns of Management*, New York: McGraw-Hill.

Lilleyman, P. (1984) "Capital budgeting: Current practices of Australian organisations", *Australian Accountant*, (March): 130-3.

Lillis, A.M. (1992) "Sources of influence on capital expenditure decisions: a contextual study of accounting performance measurement", *Management Accounting Research*, 3(3): 213-27.

Lin, S.A.Y. (1976) "The modified internal rate of return and investment criterion", *The Engineering Economist*, 21(4): 237-47.
211

Lindblom, C.E. (1959) "The science of muddling through", *Public Administration Review*, XIX(2): 79-88.

Lindgren, U. and Spångberg, K. (1981) "Corporate acquisitions and divestments: The strategic decision-making process", *International Studies of Management and Organization*, (Summer): 24-47.

Lindholm, R. (1965) "Beslutsunderlag - ett praktikfall", *Affärsekonomi*, (19).

Lintner, J. (1975) "Inflation and security returns", *Journal of Finance*, (May): 259-80.

Logue, D.E. and Tapley , T.C. (1985) "Performance monitoring and the timing of cash flows", 14(3): 34-9.

Longmore, D.R. (1989) "The persistence of the payback method: A time-adjusted decision rule perspective", *The Engineering Economist*, 34(3): 185-94.

Lorange, P. (1993) *Strategic Planning and Control: Issues in the Strategy Process*, Oxford: Blackwell.

Lüder, K. (1976) "Die Beurteilung von Einzelinvestitionen unter Berücksichtigung von Ertragsteurn", *Zeitschrift für Betriebswirtschaft*, (8): 539-70.

Lumijärvi, O.P. (1991a) "Gameplaying in capital budgeting", *Liiketaloudellinen Aikakauskirja*, 40(2): 194-200.

Lumijärvi, O.P. (1991b) "Selling of capital investments to top management", *Management Accounting Research*, 2: 171-88.

Lund, R.T. (1978) "Life-cycle costing: A business and societal instrument", *Management Review*, (April): 17-23.

Lund, R.T. and Denney, W.M. (1978) "Extending product life: Time to remanufacture?", *Management Review*, (March): 21-6.

Lundberg, E. (1961) *Produktivitet och räntabilitet*. Stockholm: SNS.

Lutz, F. and Lutz, V. (1951) *The Theory of Investment of the Firm*, Princeton.

Mahoney, J.T. and Pandian, J.R. (1992) "The resource-based view within the conversation of strategic management", *Strategic Management Journal*, 13: 363-80.

Makridakis, S. (1981) "If we cannot forecast how can we plan?", *Long Range Planning*, 14(3): 10-20.

Mao, J.C.T. (1970) "Survey of capital budgeting: Theory and practice", *The Journal of Finance*, 25(2): 349-60.

MAPI (1950) *MAPI-Replacement Manual*, Chicago.

March, J.G. and Shapira, Z. (1987) "Managerial perspective on risk and risk taking", *Management Science*, 33(11): 1404-18.

Marsh, P., Barwise, P., Thomas, K. and Wensley, R. (1987) "Managing strategic investment decisions", Paper presented at the British Academy of Management Conference.

Marshuetz, R.J. (1985) "How American Can allocates capital", *Harvard Business Review*, 63(1): 82-91.

Mascarenhas, B. (1982) "Coping with uncertainty in international business", *Journal of International Business Studies*, (Fall): 87-98.

Massé, P (1959) *Le choix des investissements*, Paris: Dunod.

Massé, P. (1962) *Optimal Investment Decisions: Rules for Action and Criteria for Choice*, Englewood Cliffs, NJ: Prentice-Hall.

Mauriel, J.J. and Anthony, R.N. (1966) "Misevaluation of Investment Center Performance", *Harvard Business Review*, 44(2): 98-105.

Mayshar, J. (1977) "Should government subsidize risky private projects?", *American Economic Review*, 67(2): 20-8.

McCallum, J.S. (1987) "The net present value method: Part of our investment problem", *Business Quarterly*, 52(2): 7-9.

McCauley, P.B. (1980) "The quick asset effect: Missing key to the relation between inflation and the investment value of the firm", *Financial Analysts Journal*, (September-October): 57-66.

McConnell, J.J. and Muscarella, C.J. (1985) "Corporate capital expenditure decisions and the market value of the firm", *Journal of Financial Economics*, 14: 399-422.

McIntyre, A.D. and Coulthurst, N.J. (1986) *Capital Budgeting in Medium Sized Business*. London: CIMA.

McIntyre, A. and Coulthurst, N.J. (1987) "Planning and control of capital investment in medium-sized UK companies", *Management Accounting* (London), 65(3), 39-40.

McLaughlin, R. and Taggart Jr., R.A. (1992) "The opportunity cost of using excess capacity", *Financial Management*, (Summer): 12-23.

McMahon, R. (1981) "The determination and use of investment hurdle rates in capital budgeting: A survey of practice", *Accounting and Finance*, 15-35.

Meffert, H. (1969) "Zum Problem der betriebswirtschaftlichen Flexibilität", *Zeitschrift für Betriebswirtschaft*, 39: 779-800.

Meffert, H. (1985) "Grössere Flexibilität als Unternehmungskonzept", *Zeitschrift für betriebswirtschaftliche Forschung*, 37(2): 121-3.

Meyer, R.J. and Kuh, E. (1957) *The Investment Decision*, Cambridge, MA: Harvard University Press.

Michel, J.G. and Hambrick, D.C. (1992) "Diversification posture and top management team characteristics", *Academy of Management Journal*, 35(1): 9-37.

Miles, D. (1993) "Testing for short termism in the U.K. stock market", *The Economic Journal*, 103(421): 1379-96.

Miles, R.H. (1982) *Coffin Nails and Corporate Strategies*, Englewood Cliffs, NJ: Prentice-Hall.

Miller, E.M. (1987) "The competitive market assumption and capital budgeting criteria", *Financial Management*, 16(4): 22-28.

Miller, M.H. (1977) "Debt and taxes", *The Journal of Finance*, XXXII(2): 261-75.

Mills, R.W. and Herbert, P.J.A. (1987) *Corporate and Divisional Influence in Capital Budgeting*, London: CIMA.

Mills, R.W. (1988a) "Capital budgeting techniques in the UK and the USA", *Management Accounting* (London), 66(1): 26-7.

Mills, R.W. (1988b) "Capital budgeting - The state of art", *Long Range Planning*", 21(4), 76-81.

Mills, R.W. (1988c) "Measuring the use of capital budgeting techniques with the postal questionnaire: A UK perspective", *Interfaces*, 18(5), 81-7.

Mills, R.W. and Allison, J. (1988) "Post completion audit: Luxury or necessity?", *Management Accounting* (London), (July/August), 38-9.

Mills, R. and Kennedy, A. (1993a) "Experience in operating a post-audit system", *Management Acocunting* (London), 71(10): 26-28.

Mills, R. and Kennedy, A. (1993b) "Post completion audits and company style and strategy", *Management Accounting* (London), 71(11): 26-27, 30.

Mintzberg, H., Raisinghani, D. and Théorèt, A. (1976) "The structure of 'unstructured' decision processes", *Administrative Science Quarterly*, 21(2): 246-75.

Mintzberg, H. and Waters, J.A. (1985) "Of strategies, deliberate and emergent", *Strategic Management Journal*, 6(3): 257-72.

Mintzberg, H. (1987) "The strategy concept I: Five Ps for strategy", *California Management Review*, (Fall): 11-24.

Modigliani, F. and Cohn, R.A. (1979) "Inflation, rational valuation and the market", *Financial Analysts Journal*, (March-April): 24-44.

Moore, J.S. and Reichert, A.K. (1983) "An analysis of the financial management techniques currently employed by large U.S. corporations", *Journal of Business Finance & Accounting*, 10(2): 623-45.

Morgan, E.J. and Tang, Y.L. (1993) "Post-implementation reviews of investment: Evidence from a two-stage study", *International Journal of Production Economics*, 30-31(Special Issue): 477-88.

Morgan, G. (1988) "Accounting as reality construction: Towards a new empistemology for accounting practice", *Accounting Organizations and Society*, 13(5): 477-85.

Most, K.S. (1977) *Accounting Theory*, Columbus, Ohio: Grid.

Mukherjee, T.K. (1987) "Capital-budgeting survey: The past and the future", *Review of Business & Economic Research*, 22(2): 37-56.

Mukherjee, T.K. (1988) "The capital budgeting process of large U.S. firms; An analysis of capital budgeting manuals", *Managerial Finance*, 14(2/3), 28-35.

Mukherjee, T.K. (1991a) "A survey of corporate leasing analysis", *Financial Management*, 20(3): 96-107.

Mukherjee, T.K. (1991b) "Reducing the uncertainty-induced bias in capital budgeting decisions - A hurdle rate approach", *Journal of Business Finance & Accounting*, 18(5): 747-53.

Mukherjee, T.K. and Henderson, G.V. (1987) "The capital budgeting process: Theory and practice", *Interfaces*, 17(2), 78-90.

Myers, M.D., Gordon, L.A. and Hamer, M.M. (1991) "Postauditing capital assets and firm performance: An empirical investigation", *Managerial and Decision Economics*, 12(4): 317-27.

Myers, S.C. (1984) "Finance theory and financial strategy", *Interfaces*, 14(1): 126-37.

Narayanan, M.P. (1985) "Observability and the payback criterion", *Journal of Business*, 58(3): 309-23.

Neale, B. (1991) "A revolution in post-completion audit adoption", *Management Accounting* (London), 69(10): 44-6.

Neale, B. (1992) "Investment project management", *Credit Management*, (March): 32-4.

Neale, C.W. (1989) "Post auditing practices by UK firms: Aims, benefits and shortcomings", *British Accounting Review*, 21(4): 309-28.

Neale, C.W. (1991a) "The benefits derived from post-aditing investment projects", *Omega*, 19(2/3): 113-20.

Neale, C.W. (1991b) "Investment post-auditing practices: A comparison of manufacturing and service sector companies", *Service Industries Journal*, 11(1): 75-92.

Neale, B. (1993) "Linkages between investment post-auditing, capital expenditure and corporate strategy", *Management Accounting* (London), 71(2): 20-2.

Neale, C.W. (1994) "Investment post-auditing practices among British and Norwegian companies: a comparative study", *International Business Review*, 3(1): 31-46.

Neale, C.W. and Holmes, D.E.A. (1988) "Post completion audits: The costs and benefits", *Management Accounting* (London), (March): 27-30.

Neale, C.W. and Holmes, D.E.A. (1990) "Post-auditing capital projects", *Long Range Planning*, 23(4): 88-96.

Nees, D. and Danielle, B. (1978-79) "The divestment decision process in large and medium-sized diversified companies: A description model based on clincial studies", *International Studies of Management and Organization*, (Winter): 67-95.

Nees, D. (1981) "Increase your divestment effectiveness", *Strategic Management Journal*, (April-June): 119-30.

Nelson, C.R. (1976) "Inflation and capital budgeting", *Journal of Finance*, (June): 923-31.

Neuhauser, J.J. and Viscione, J.A. (1973) "How managers feel about advanced capital budgeting methods", *Management Review*, (November): 16-22.

Nilsson, P. (1988) *Produktionsinvesteringar och produktivitet: En problem-orienterad ansats*, Göteborg: Institutionen för industriell organisation, CTH.

Norgaard, C.T. (1979) "The post-completion audit of capital projects", *Cost and Management*, 53(1): 19-25.

Normann, R. (1971) "Organizational innovativness: Product variation and reorientation", *Administrative Science Quarterly*, 16(2): 203-15.

Normann, R. (1975) *Skapande företagsledning*, Stockholm: Aldus.

Normann, R. (1977) *Management for Growth*, Chichester: Wiley.

Northcote, E.F. (1975) "Improving plant investment decisions", *Management Accounting* (London), (December): 403-5.

Northcote, E.F. (1982) "Investment appraisal is mostly intuition", *Management Accounting* (London), (January): 20-1.

Northcott, D. (1991) "Rationality and decision-making in capital budgeting", *British Accounting Review*, 30(1): 219-33.

Oblak, D.J. and Helm, Jr., R.J. (1980) "Survey and analysis of capital budgeting methods used by multinationals", *Financial Management*, (Winter): 37-41.

Ohmae, K. (1982) Japan: From stereotypes to specifics", *The McKinsey Quarterly*, (Spring): 2-33.

Ohteki, K. (1991) "Strategic management in Japanese big enterprise", *Management Japan*, 24(1): 11-16.

Örtengren, J. (1992) "Capital formation in Swedish industry during the post-war period", in Hägg, I. and Segelod, E. (eds.) *Issues in Empirical Investment Research*, Amsterdam: North-Holland: 15-37.

Östman, L. (1977) *Styrning av redovisningsmått*, Stockholm: EFI.

Ouchi, W. (1977) "The relationship between organizational structure and organizational control", *Administrative Science Quarterly*, 22(March): 95-113.

Ouchi, W. (1979) "A conceptual framework for the design of organization control mechanisms", *Management Science*, 22(September): 833-48.

Ouchi, W. and Maguire, M. (1975) "Organizational control: Two functions", *Administrative Science Quarterly*, 20(December): 559-69.

Owen, G. and Harrison, T. (1995) "Why ICI chose to demerge", *Harvard Business Review*, 73(2): 133-42.

Papadakis, V.M. (1995) "The contribution of formal planning systems to strategic investment decisions", *British Journal of Management*, 6: 15-28.

Pascale, R. and Athos, A. (1981) *The Art of Japanese Management*, Harmondsworth: Penguin.

Parthasarthy, R. and Sethi, S.P. (1992) "The impact of flexible automation on business strategy and organizational structure", *Academy of Management Review*, 17(1): 86-111.

Patterson, C.S. (1989) "Investment decision criteria used by listed New Zealand companies", *Accounting and Finance*, 29(2): 73-89.

Paulo, S. (1991) "The weighted average cost of capital: Theory and South African empirical evidence", *Journal for Studies in Economics and Econometrics*, 15(2): 31-46.

Pearson, G.J. (1985) *The Strategic Discount: Ways to an Entrepreneurial Strategy*, Chichester: John Wiley.

Pearson, G. (1986) "The strategic discount - Protecting new business projects against DCF", *Long Range Planning*, 19(1): 18-24.

Pearson, G. (1987) "Why the Japanese Dominate", *Accountancy*, 99(1122): 84-5.

Penrose, E.T. (1959) *The Theory of the Growth of the Firm*, Oxford: Blackwell.

Persson, I. (1990) "Analysis of capital investment: A conceptual cash flow model", *Engineering Costs and Production Economics*, 20(1): 277-84.

Persson, I. (1992) "Investment process of companies - Effects and learning from government action in some companies", in Hägg, I. and Segelod, E. (eds.) *Issues in Empirical Investment Research*, Amsterdam: North-Holland: 61-79.

Petry, G.H. (1975) "Effective use of capital budgeting tools", *Business Horizons*, 18(5): 57-65.

Petty, J.W., Scott, D.F. and Bird, M.M. (1975) "The capital expenditure decision-making process of large corporations", *The Engineering Economist*, 20(3): 159-72.

Pike, R.H. (1982) *Capital Budgeting in the 1980s*, London: CIMA.

Pike, R.H. (1983) "A review of recent trends in formal capital budgeting processes", *Accounting and Business Research*, (Summer): 201-8.

Pike, R.H. (1984) "DCF trends and the problem of nonresponse bias", *Managerial Finance*, 10(3): 49-52.

Pike, R.H. (1985) "Owner-manager conflict and the role of the payback method", *Accounting and Business Research*, (Winter): 47-51.

Pike, R.H. (1988a) "An empirical study of the adoption of sophisticated capital budgeting practices and decision-making effectiveness", *Accounting & Business Research*, 18(72): 341-51.

Pike, R. (1988b) "The capital budgeting revolution", *Management Accounting* (London), (October): 28-30.

Pike, R. (1989) "Do sophisticated capital budgeting approaches improve investment decision-making effectiveness?", *The Enginering Economist*, 34(2): 149-61.

Pike, R.H. and Ho, S.S.M. (1991) "Risk analysis in capital budgeting: Barriers and benefits", *Omega*, 19(4): 235-45.

Pike, R. and Sharp, J. (1989) "Trends in the use of management science techniques in capital budgeting", *Managerial and Decision Economics*, 10(2): 135-40.

Pike, R. and Wolfe, M.B. (1988) *Capital Budgeting for the 1990's*, London: CIMA.

Pinches, G.E. (1982) "Myopia, capital budgeting and decision making", *Financial Management*, (Autumn): 6-19.

Piper, J.A. (1980) "Classifying capital projects for top management decision-making", *Long Range Planning*, 13(3): 45-56.

Pitts, R.A. (1974) "Incentive compensation and organization design", *Personnel Journal*, 53: 338-44.

Pitts, R.A. (1976) "Diversification strategies and organizational policies of large diversified firms", *Journal of Economics and Business* 28: 181-8.

Pitts, R.A. (1977) "Strategies and structures for diversification", *Academy of Management Journal*, 20: 197-208.

Pohlman, R.A., Santiago, E.S. and Markel, F.L. (1988) "Cash flow estimation practices of large firms", *Financial Management*, 7(2): 71-8.

Pope, R. (1986-87) "Current capital budgeting practices: A comparison of small and large firms", *Southwest Journal of Business & Economics*, 4(2): 16-24.

Porter, M.E. (1992a) "Capital choices: Changing the way America invests in industry", *Journal of Applied Corporate Finance*, 5(2): 4-16.

Porter, M.E. (1992b) "Capital disadvantage: America"s failing capital investment system", *Harvard Business Review*, 70(5): 65-82.

Posey, I.A., Roth, H.P. and Dittrich, N.E. (1985) "Post audit practices", *Cost and Management*, 59(3): 14-8.

Prahalad, C.K. (1993) "The role of core competencies in the corporation", *Research Technology Management*, 36(6): 40-7.

Prahalad, C.K. and Hamel, G. (1990) "The core competence of the corporation", *Harvard Business Review*, 68(3): 79-91.

Primrose, P.L. (1992) "Investment justification: Is anything really wrong with cost management?", *Journal of Cost Management*, 6(1): 48-57.

Proctor, M.D. and Canada, J.R. (1992) "Past and present methods of manufacturing investment evaluation: A review of the empirical and theoretical literature", *The Engineering Economist*, 38(1): 45-58.

Pruitt, S.W. and Gitman, L.J. (1987) "Capital Budgeting Forecast Biases: Evidence from the *Fortune* 500", *Financial Management*, (Spring): 46-51.

Pruitt, S.W. and Gitman, L.J. (1991) "The interactions between the investment, financing, and dividend decisions of major U.S. firms", *The Financial Review*, 26(3): 409-30.

Przybylowicz, E.P. and Faulkner, T.W. (1993) "Kodak applies strategic intent to the management of technology", *Research Technology Management*, 36(1): 31-8.

Quinn, J.B. and Hilmer F.G. (1994) "Strategic outsourcing", *Sloan Management Review*, 35(4): 43-55.

Ramasesh, R.V. and Jayakumar, M.D. (1993) "Economic justification of advanced manufacturing technology", *Omega*, 21(3): 289-306.

Ramsey, J.E. (1981) "Selecting R & D projects for development", *Long Range Planning*, 14(1): 83-91.

Rapoport, C. (1992) "How Barnevik makes ABB work", *Fortune*, 125(13): 24-7.

Rapp, B. and Selmer, J. (1979) "Den samhällsekonomiska diskonteringsräntan inom energiområdet", Stockholm: Företagsekonomiska institutionen, Stockholms Universitet.

Rappaport, A. (1979) "A critique of capital budgeting questionnaires", *Interfaces*, 9(3): 100-2.

Reichert, A.K., Moore, J.S. and Byler, E. (1988) "Financial analysis among large U.S. corporations: Recent trends and the impact of the personal computer", *Journal of Business Finance & Accounting*, 15(4): 469-85.

Reimann, B.C. (1990) "Why bother with risk adjusted hurdle rates?", *Long Range Planning*, 23(3): 57-65.

Remer, D.S., Stokdyk, S.B. and Van Driel, M. (1993) "Survey of project evaluation techniques currently used in industry", *International Journal of Production Economics*, 32(1): 103-15.

Renck, O. (1966) *Investeringsbedömning i några svenska företag*, Stockholm: Norstedts.

Rickardson, G.B. (1964) "The limits to a firm's rate of growth", *Oxford Economic Papers*, (1).

Robichek, A.A. and Myers, S.C. (1965) *Optimal Financial Decisions*, Englewood Cliffs, N J: Prentice-Hall.

Robichek, A. and Myers, S.C. (1966) "Conceptual problems in the use of risk-adjusted discount rates", *Management Science*, 21(December): 727-730.

Rockart, J.F. (1979) "Chief executives define their own data needs", *Harvard Business Review*, 58(2): 81-93.

Rockley, L.E. (1973) *Investment for Profitability: An Analysis of the Policies and Practicies of UK and International Companies*, London: Business Books.

Rosenblatt, M. (1980) "A survey and analysis of capital budgeting decision process in multidivision firms", *The Engineering Economist*, 25(4).

Rosenblatt, M.J. and Jucker, J.V. (1979) "Capital expenditure decision/making: Some tools and trends", *Interfaces*, 9(2): 63-9.

Ross, M. (1986) "Capital budgeting practices of twelve large manufacturers", *Financial Management*, (Winter): 15-22.

Roth, H.P. and Brown, R.M. (1982) "Post-Auditing Capital Investments Using IRR and NPV Models", *Management Accounting*, (February), 29-33.

Roubi, R.R., Barth, R.T. and Faseruk, A. (1991) "Capital budgeting use in Canada: Sophistication and risk attributes", *Journal of Applied Business Research*, 7(4): 83-9.

Rugman, A.M. and Verbeke, A. (1990) "Strategic capital budgeting decisions and the theory of internationalisation", *Mangerial Finance*, 16(2): 17-24.

Runyon, L.R. (1983) "Capital expenditure decision making in small firms", *Journal of Business Research*, 11(3): 389-97.

Rydin, B. (1961) "Ekonomiska synpunkter vid val av transportsystem", *Affärsekonomi*, (15).

Sager, T. (1992) "Why plan? A multi-rationality foundation for planning", *Scandinavian Housing & Planning Research*, 9: 129-47.

Sale, J.T. and Scapens, R.W. (1982) "The control of capital investment in divisionalized companies", *Management Accounting* (New York), 64(4): 24-9.

Sangeladji, M. A. (1979) "True rate of return for evaluating capital investments", *Management Accounting*, (February): 24-8.

Sangster, A. (1993) "Capital investment appraisal techniques: A survey of current usage", *Journal of Business Finance & Accounting*, 20(3): 307-32.

Sayer, J.E. (1952) "Entrepreneurial error and economic growth", *Explorations in Entrepreneurial History*, (2): 199-204.

Scapens, R.W. and Sale, J.T. (1981) "Performance measurement and formal capital expenditure controls in divisionalised companies", *Journal of Business Finance & Accounting*, 8(3): 389-419.

Scapens, R.W. and Sale, J.T. (1985) "An international study of accounting practices in divisionalized companies and their associations with organizational variables",*The Accounting Review*, LX(2): 231-47.

Scapens, R.W., Sale, J.T. and Tikkas, P.A. (1982) *Financial Control of Divisional Capital Investment*, London: CIMA.

Schall, L.D. and Sundem, G.L. (1980) "Capital budgeting methods and risk: A further analysis", *Financial Management*, (Spring): 7-11.

Schall, L.D., Sundem, G.L. and Geijsbeck, W.R. (1978) "Survey and analysis of capital budgeting methods", *Journal of Finance*, XXXIII(1): 281-7.

Scharfstein, D.S. and Stein, J.C. (1990) "Herd behavior and investment", *The American Economic Review*, 80(3): 465-79.

Schmalenbach, E., (1908) "Die Abschreibung", *Zeitschrift für handelswissenschaftliche Forschung*, 3: 81-8.

Schmalenbach, E. (1919) *Grundlagen Dynamischer Bilanzlehre*, Leipzig.

Schmidt, F. (1922) *Die Organische Tageswertbilanz*, Leipzig.

Schneider, E. (1944) *Investering og rente*, Köbenhavn.

Scholz, L. (1990) "Changing structure of investment in different industries", IVA and OECD conference on Technology and Investment in Stockholm 21-24 January 1990.

Scott, B.R. (1973) "The industrial state: old myths and new realities", *Harvard Business Review*, (2): 133-48.

Scott, D.F. and Petty, J.W. (1984) "Capital budgeting practices in large American firms: A retrospective analysis and analyses", *The Financial Review*, 19: 111-23.

Segelod, E. (1986) *Kalkylering och avvikelser*, Malmö: Liber.

Segelod, E. (1989) "Kapitalkostnad, kalkylränta, skatt och inflation", Department of Business Studies, *Working Paper 1989/8*, Uppsala: Department of Business Studies, Uppsala University.

Segelod, E. (1991a) "How to Avoid Cost Overruns", *Journal of General Management*, 16(4), 16-23.

Segelod, E. (1991b) *Capital Investment Appraisal: Towards a Contingency Theory*, Lund: Studentlitteratur.

Segelod, E. (1992a) "Project design in an important part of the capital budgeting decision", in Hägg, I. and Segelod, E. (eds.) *Issues in Empirical Investment Research*, Amsterdam: North-Holland: 159-71.

Segelod, E. (1992b) "Explanations of project deviations", in Hägg, I. and Segelod, E. (eds.) *Issues in Empirical Investment Research*, Amsterdam: North-Holland: 263-82.

Segelod, E. (1995a) *Renewal Through Internal Development*, Aldershot: Avebury.

Segelod, E. (1995b) "New Ventures - The Swedish experience", *Long Range Planning*, 28(4): 45-52.

Segelod, E. and Hägg, I. (1992) "Swedish empirical research on capital investments", in Hägg, I. and Segelod, E. (eds.) *Issues in Empirical Investment Research*, Amsterdam: North-Holland: 1-12.

Shapiro, A.C. (1988) "International capital budgeting", in Stern, J.M. and Chew, D.H. (eds.) *New Developments in International Finance*, Oxford: Basil Blackwell: 165-80.

Sharp, D.J. (1991) "Uncovering the hidden value in high-risk investments", *Sloan Management Review*, 32(4): 69-74.

Shields, M.D., Chow, C.W., Kato, Y. and Nakagawa, Y. (1991) "Management accounting practices in the U.S. and Japan: Comparative survey findings and research implications", *Journal of International Financial Management and Accounting*, 3(1): 61-77.

Shrivastava, P. (1983) "A typology of organizational learning systems", *Journal of Management Studies*, 20(1): 7-28.

Sick, G.A. (1986) "The certainty-equivalent approach to capital budgeting", *Finanical Management*, 15(4): 23-32.

Simons, R. (1994) "How new top managers use strategic systems as levers of strategic renewal", *Strategic Management Journal*, 15: 169-89.

Singer, A.E. (1991) "Meta-rationality and strategy",*Omega*, 19(2/3): 101-12.

Skeddle, R.W. (1973) "Major capital decisions and technological change", *Omega*, 1(5): 551-64.

Skinner, R.C. (1987) "Allocations and the validity of the incremental principle", *Accounting and Business Research*, 18(69): 75-8.

Skromme Baird, I. and Thomas, H. (1985) "Toward a contingency model of strategic risk taking", *Academy of Management Review*, 10(2): 230-43.

Solomon, E. (1956) "The arithmetics of capital budgeting decisions", *Journal of Business*, (2): 124-9.

Son, Y.K. (1992) "A comprehensive bibliography on justification of advanced manufacturing technologies", *The Engineering Economist*, 38(1): 59-71.

Song, J.H. (1982) "Diversification strategies and the experiences of top executives in large firms", *Strategic Management Journal* 3(4): 377-80.

Souder, W.E. (1978) "A system for using R&D project evaluation methods", *Research Management*, XXI(5): 29-37.

221

Souder, W.E. and Mandakovic, T. (1986) "R&D project selection models", *Research Management*, XXIX(4): 36-42.

Spångberg, K. (1982) *Strategi i diversifierade företag: Huvudkontorets roll*, Stockholm: EFI.

Stanley, M.T. and Block, S.B. (1984) "A survey of multinational capital budgeting", *The Financial Review*, 19(March): 36-54.

Stateman, M. and Tyebjee, T.T. (1985) "Optimistic capital budgeting forecasts: An experiment", *Financial Management*, (Autumn): 27-33.

Statistics Sweden (1986) Statistiska meddelanden, F 13 SM 8602.

Statistics Sweden (1987) Statistiska meddelanden, F 13 SM 8702.

Statistics Sweden (1988) Statistiska meddelanden, F 13 SM 8802.

Statistics Sweden (1989) Statistiska meddelanden, F 13 SM 8902.

Statistics Sweden (1990) Statistiska meddelanden, F 13 SM 9002.

Statistics Sweden (1991) Statistiska meddelanden, F 13 SM 9102.

Statistics Sweden (1992) Statistiska meddelanden, F 13 SM 9202.

Statistics Sweden (1993) Statistiska meddelanden, F 13 SM 9302.

Statistics Sweden (1994) Statistiska meddelanden, F 13 SM 9402.

Statistics Sweden (1995) Statistiska meddelanden, F 13 SM 9502.

Statman, M. (1982) "The persistence of the payback method: A principal-agent perspective", *The Engineering Economist*, 27(2), 95-100.

Steen, T.G. and Fjell, T. (1990) Post Competion Audits of Capital Projects, MBA Thesis, Oslo Business School.

Stonehill, A. and Nathanson, L. (1968) "Capital budgeting and the multinational corporation", *California Management Review*, X(4): 39-54.

Stonehill, A., Beekhuisen, T., Wright, R., Remmers, L., Toy, N., Pares, A., Shapiro, A., Egan, D. and Bates, T. (1975) "Financial goals and debt ratio determinants: A survey of practice in five countries", *Financial Management*, 4(3): 27-41.

Taggart, R.A., Jr. (1987) "Allocating capital among a firm"s divisions: Hurdle rates vs. budgets", *Journal of Financial Research*, 10(3): 177-89.

Taylor, W.B. (1981) "The use of life cycle costing in acquiring physical assets", *Long Range Planning*, (6): 32-43.

Taylor, W. (1991) "The logic of global business: An interview with ABB's Percy Barnevik", *Harvard Business Review*, 69(2): 91-105.

Teichroew, D., Robichek, A.A. and Montalbano, M. (1965a) "Mathematical analysis of rates of return under certainty", *Management Science*, 11(3): 395-403.

Teichroew, D., Robichek, A.A. and Montalbano, M. (1965b) "An analysis of criteria for investment an financing decision under certainty", *Management Science*, 12(3): 151-79.

Tell, B. (1978) *Investeringskalkylering i praktiken*, Lund: Studentlitteratur.

Terborgh, G. (1949) *Dynamic Equipment Policy*, New York.

Terborgh, G. (1958) *Business Investment Policy*, Washington.

Thakor, A.V. (1989) "Strategic issues in financial contracting: An overview", *Financial Management*, 18(2): 34-58.

Thakor, A.V. (1990) "Investment 'myopia' and the internal organization of capital allocation decisions", *Journal of Law, Economics and Organization*, (Spring): 129-154.

Thakor, A.V. (1993) "Corporate investments and finance", *Financial Management*, 22(2): 135-44.

Tideman, T.N. and Tucker, D.P. (1976) "The tax treatment of business profits under inflationary conditions", in Aaron, H.J. (ed.) *Inflation and the Income Tax*, Washington, D.C.: Brooking Institution.

Tomkins, C. (1991) *Corporate Resource Allocation: Financial, Strategic and Organizational Perspective*, Oxford: Basil Blackwell.

Trigeorgis, L. and Mason, S.P. (1987) "Valuing managerial flexibility", *Midland Corporate Finance Journal*, (Spring): 14-21.

Tsurumi, Y. and Tsurumi, H. (1985) "Value-added maximizing behavior of Japanese firms and roles of corporate investment and finance", *The Columbia Journal of World Business*, XX(1): 29-35.

Tyebjee, T.T. (1987) "Behavioral biases in new product forecasting", *International Journal of Forecasting*, 3: 393-404.

Vandell, R.F. and Stonich, P.J. (1973) "Capital budgeting: Theory or results?", *Finacial Executive*, (August): 46-56.

Vandermerwe, S. (1993) "A framework for constructing Euro-networks", *European Management Journal*, 11(1): 55-61.

Wagner, H.M. (1984) "Profit wonders, investment blunders", *Harvard Business Review*, 62(5): 121-35.

Walker, R.G. (1961) "The judgement factor in investment decisions", *Harvard Business Review*, 39(2): 93-9.

Wallace, W.J. and Thuesen, G.J. (1987) "Annotated bibliography of investing in flexible automation", *The Engineering Economist*, 32(3): 247-57.

Wallén, L. and Sjöblom, B. (1990) "Kompetenta medarbetare", *Ekonomi & Styrning*, (1), 15-8.

Vandell, R.F. and Stonich, P.J. (1973) "Capital budgeting: Theory or results?", *Financial Executive*, (August): 46-56.

Wärnberg, , K. (1963) "Modifierad pay-off-metod - en enklare beräknings-metod vid investeringsbedömning", *Affärsekonomi*, V(10).

Watanabe, T. (1987) *Demystifying Japanese Management*, Tokyo: Gakuseisha Publishing Co.

Weaver, J.B. (1974) "Organizing and maintaining a capital expenditure program", *The Engineering Economist*, 20(1), 1-35.

Weaver, S.C. (1989) "Capital budgeting", *Financial Management*, 18(1): 10-17.

Weaver, S.C. (1989) "Divisional hurdle rates and the cost of capital", *Financial Management*, 18(1): 18-25.

Weiss, L.A. (1981) "Start up businesses: A comparison of performance", *Sloan Management Review*, 23(Fall): 37-53.

Welam, U.P. (1992) "Svåra brister i FMS-kalkyler", *Ekonomi & Styrning*, (2): 22-8.

Wellington, A.M. (1887) *The economic theory of the location of railways*, New York: Wiley.

Weston, F. (1973) "Operation research techniques relevant to corporate planning function practices: An investigative look", *Academy of Management Journal*, (September): 507-10.

Whittington, R. (1989) *Corporate Strategies in Recession and Recovery: Social Structure and Strategic Choice*, London: Unwin Hyman.

Whittington, R. (1991) "Recession strategies and top management change", *Journal of General Management*, 16(3): 11-28.

Wildavsky, A. (1973) "If planning if everything, maybe it's nothing", *Policy Sciences*, 4: 127-53.

Wilkes, F.M. and Samuels, J.M. (1991) "Financial appraisal to support technological investment", *Long Range Planning*, 24(6): 60-6.

Williams, B.R. and Scott, W.P. (1965) *Investment Proposals and Decisions*. London.

Wilner, N.A., Koch, B.S. and Klammer, T.P. (1992) "Justification of high technology capital investment - An empirical study", *The Engineering Economist*, 37(4): 341-53.

Wilson, M. (1988) *Capital Budgeting for Foreign Direct Investment*. London: CIMA.

Wilson, M. (1990) "Empirical evidence of the use of a framwork of risk and return in capital budgeting for foreign direct investment", *Managerial Finance*, 16(2), 25-34.

Woods, M., Pokorny, M., Lintner, V. and Blinkhorn, M. (1985) "Appraising investment in new technology: The approach in practice", *Management Accounting*, (October): 42-3.

Woolridge, J.R. and Snow, C.C. (1990) "Stock market reaction to strategic investment decisions", *Strategic Management Journal*, 11: 353-63.

Wright, F.K. (1964) "Project evaluation and the managerial limit", *The Journal of Business*, XXXVII(2): 179-85.

Yard, S. (1987) *Kalkyllogik och kalkylkrav*, Lund: Lund University Press.

Yard, S. (1991) *Kalkyler för investeringar och verksamheter*, Lund: Studentlitteratur.

Yip, G.S. (1982a) *Barriers to Entry: A Corporate-Strategy Perspective*, Lexington, MA: Lexington Books.

Yip, G.S. (1982b) "Diversification entry: Internal development versus acquisition", *Strategic Management Journal*, 3: 331-45.

Yoshikawa, T., Innes, J. and Mitchell, F. (1989) "Japanese management accounting: a comparative survey", *Management Accounting*, 67(10): 20-3.

Yashikawa, T., Mitchell, F. and Moyes, J. (1994) *A Review of Japanese Management Accounting Literature and Bibliography*, London: CIMA.